MAPPING THE SECULAR MIND

MODERNITY'S QUEST FOR A GODLESS UTOPIA

MAPPING THE SECULAR MIND

MODERNITY'S QUEST FOR A GODLESS UTOPIA

HAGGAG ALI

THE INTERNATIONAL INSTITUTE OF ISLAMIC THOUGHT
LONDON • WASHINGTON

© The International Institute of Islamic Thought, 1434AH/2013CE

The International Institute of Islamic Thought
P.O. BOX 669, HERNDON, VA 20172, USA
www.iiit.org

LONDON OFFICE
P.O. BOX 126, RICHMOND, SURREY TW9 2UD, UK
www.iiituk.com

ISBN 978–1–56564–593–6 *Limp*
ISBN 978–1–56564–594–3 *Cased*

Typesetting and cover design by Sideek Ali
Printed in Malta by Gutenberg Press Ltd

CONTENTS

ACKNOWLEDGMENTS

THIS book has its inception early in 2006, when I started writing my doctoral dissertation at Cairo University and the Humboldt University of Berlin. The work was initially supported by DAAD (The German Academic Exchange Service), and then later developed during my postdoctoral fellowship at Wissenschaftskolleg zu Berlin within the research programme "Europe in the Middle East; the Middle East in Europe." In its final stage, this work was supported by KAAD (The Catholic Academic Exchange Service) and the Georges-Anawati Scholarship for Research Projects on the Dialogue between Islam and Christianity.

I owe gratitude to my Egyptian professors who supported me with all means: Abdul Aziz Hamouda, Mohamed Yahia and Heba Raouf Ezzat at Cairo University; Abdelwahab Elmessiri, Mona al-Wahsh and Jehan Farouq at Ain Shams University. Thanks are also due to Michi Knecht and Christoph Markschies at Humboldt University of Berlin. Last but not least, thanks go to Zygmunt Bauman at the University of Leeds, Oksana Bulgakowa at the Centre for Culture and Literature in Berlin, Cem Deveci at the Middle East Technical University in Ankara and Michael Hviid Jacobsen at the University of Aalborg.

FOREWORD

HAGGAG ALI'S *Mapping the Secular Mind: Modernity's Quest for a Godless Utopia* critically examines issues of reason, rationality, and secular materialism, to explore how these mental perceptions, or ways of mapping the world, have affected human interaction and sociological development. He does this by comparing and contrasting the ideas of Abdelwahab M. Elmessiri (1938–2008) and Zygmunt Bauman (1925), focusing on similarities and differences in their thinking, what influenced their perspectives (specifically Marxism), and the historical context of their life and work. Bauman for instance, an eminent Jewish scholar, has known war and exile and is strongly anti-Zionist. The dynamics are interesting.

In doing so, Ali is also able to introduce and study some of the most important epistemological metaphors used to describe, analyse and understand society and the human condition. For instance, the analogies of man and society as a machine (the clockwork universe) and of society as an organism were heavily criticised by Elmessiri.

Renowned for their work, both thinkers have been highly influential in their field. Zygmunt Bauman is retired Emeritus Professor at the University of Leeds and one of the world's foremost sociologists. A prolific author, his most famous and compelling publication is arguably *Modernity and the Holocaust* (1989), discussed by Ali at length. In the work Bauman makes the remarkable case that rather than being an example of accidental deviation from modern principles, including rationalism, the Holocaust, as well as the whole Nazi enterprise, were in fact consistent with the very essence of modernity and its worldview, Social Darwinism taken to its logical course. The reasons underpinning the rise of the fascist state are examined in order to warn humanity of the dangers of a modernity that furnishes the "necessary conditions" for its undertaking and for the neatly legitimised disappearance of unwanted people.

The late Egyptian scholar Abdelwahab M. Elmessiri, one of the foremost intellectuals of his age, was Professor Emeritus of English literature and critical theory at Ain Shams University, Cairo. Also a prolific writer he published many articles and books on various subjects including, Zionism, modernism, postmodernism, secularism, and materialist philosophy. Elmessiri was particularly interested in the issue of bias in the social sciences and how this influenced the way in which reality was perceived, deconstructed and reconstructed.

According to Ali, the various epistemological paradigms that form the foundations of Western thought, whilst challenging religion's function as the route to Ultimate Truth and targeting it as the source of human primitiveness, have in the postmodern era themselves failed to deliver. The many hands that made up Enlightenment philosophers (or *les philosophes* as they are referred to in French) had a grand plan: to fashion an earthly paradise of man's own making, doing away with ignorance, superstition and backwardness. This was to be achieved through the vehicles of science, rationalism, and reason, with Man at the helm – that is at the centre of all discourse and of all that matters, controlling and shaping his destiny, and modeling society under new norms of behaviour.

Some of this was fantasy. Postmodern society is in fact dysfunctional on many levels. It is also a far cry from the utilitarian utopia so enthusiastically envisaged by a philosophy that to this day views the mind as self-sufficient for human progress. Ali points to the delusions of such utopianist thinking.

Written in a clear and lucid style, the book will benefit both general and specialist readers, increasing their awareness of the question of cognitive mapping, and how human beings devise paradigms to form a mental picture of the world around them.

This study is being published to widen discourse, invite scholars to respond, and hopefully pave the way for further research. Readers may agree with some of the issues raised, and disagree with others, but it is hoped that for the most part both general and specialist readers will benefit from the perspective offered and the overall issues examined.

Where dates are cited according to the Islamic calendar (hijrah) they are labelled AH. Otherwise they follow the Gregorian calendar and labelled CE where necessary. Arabic words are italicized except for those which have entered common usage. Diacritical marks have been added only to those Arabic names not considered modern. English translations taken from Arabic references are those of the author.

The IIIT, established in 1981, has served as a major centre to facilitate serious scholarly efforts based on Islamic vision, values and principles. The Institute's programs of research, seminars and conferences during the last thirty years have resulted in the publication of more than four hundred titles in English and Arabic, many of which have been translated into other major languages.

We express our thanks and gratitude to the author for his cooperation throughout the various stages of production. We would also like to thank the editorial and production team at the IIIT London Office and all those who were directly or indirectly involved in the completion of this book including, Shiraz Khan, Maida Malik, Dr. Maryam Mahmood, and Salma Mirza. May God reward them for all their efforts.

IIIT LONDON OFFICE
Safar 1434 AH / January 2013 CE

I

Introduction: Cognitive Mapping and Metaphoricity

THE term "cognitive map" can be best introduced through an interesting anecdote that goes back to the sixteenth century. According to the well-known Islamic studies scholar and world historian Marshall Hodgson, the Italian missionary Matteo Ricci brought to China a European world map to show the Chinese the new discoveries in America. As he expected, the Chinese were very impressed by these discoveries, but he realized that they felt offended when they saw the map splitting the earth's surface down the pacific, thus making China appear off at the right-hand edge. What is at stake here is that the contours of this geographical map contradict the Chinese cognitive map and refute their perception of China as literally the "middle kingdom" i.e. the centre of the universe and thus the centre of the map. Though embarrassed and perplexed, Ricci managed to overcome this awkward situation by drawing another map, splitting the Atlantic instead, thus making China appear more central. The significance of this anecdote lies in the fact that human conceptual systems are significant and influential maps which are prior to the contours of natural, geographical and political maps. Drawing a map, geographical or cognitive, is thus a compromise of what mapmakers would like to include and what they want to exclude.[1]

The term "cognitive map" has a long history in many psychological studies that used it in the 1940s as a metaphorical reference to the accurate memory of space determination and the ability of constructing mental patterns that enhance the process of place expectation.[2] Cognitive maps, schemata, scripts and frames of reference have become the most dominant metaphors used to underline the epistemological and ontological systems people use to perceive, understand, code and decode complex problems and phenomena.

The importance of these metaphors in the postmodern world derives from the excessive celebration of a value-free, fragmentary and free-floating culture based on the disappearance of all centres, both divine and human: "the death of God," "the death of man," "the death of the author," "the deconstruction of the subject," "the dissolution of identity," "the displacement of the ego" and "the end of History." Within this context, cognitive mapping and remapping transcend spatial orientation and information processing to embrace all attempts at asserting the ontological and epistemological authority of history and legitimizing the human resistance to fragmentation and perpetual becoming. Thus, the metaphorical entailments of cognitive maps go beyond the mere idea of spatial layout, and they can be used to underline the mental maps that people use not only to map space but to perceive and deal with human reality, to code and decode complex texts and narratives.

As the secular mind has laid the foundations of modernity, that is our modern and post- modern world (including its problems), an attempt will be made to explain the term "modernity" and its semantic field before further analysis. By the early 1980s, the "modernism/ postmodernism" constellation in the arts and "modernity and post-modernity" in critical and social theory had become one of the most contested terrains in the intellectual life of western societies.[3] The term modernity is very controversial, and no definition can fully describe its dynamics, achievements and consequences. It was the French philosopher Jean Jacques Rousseau who first used the word *moderniste* in the ways used in the nineteenth and the twentieth centuries.[4] The word modernity, however, came into existence only in the late 1980s and Raymond Williams's revised edition of *Keywords* (1983) is cited by Tony Blackshaw as an evidence that there was hardly any recognition of the term modernity in specialized dictionaries and glossaries; the discourse on modernity started only with the emergence of theories of postmodernism, and it gave rise to the opposition between modernism and postmodernism on the one hand, and modernity and postmodernity on the other.[5] In other words, modernity is usually explained and defined in comparison with the term "postmodernity," which is also fiercely contested.

Perry Anderson points out that Jean-Francois Lyotard's *The Postmodern Condition: A Report on Knowledge* (1979) is believed to be the first book to approach postmodernity as a comprehensive change of human condition, particularly the rise of the post-industrial society theorized by Daniel Bell and Alain Touraine. The most defining feature of postmodernity is "the loss of credibility of meta-narratives," including classical socialism, Christian redemption, Enlightenment progress, Hegelian spirit and Romantic unity.[6] In other words, modernity can be defined as the celebration of secular meta-narratives, especially the Enlightenment progress.

1.1 THE PROJECT OF COGNITIVE MAPPING

The project of cognitive mapping was launched by American Marxist critic Fredric Jameson in the late 1980s as a socialist political strategy directed at creating a global class-consciousness that could resist late capitalism and the confusion it had created in our human condition. Jameson's major argument is that we are unable to map our position in the postmodern world in the same way the dwellers of the city fail to locate their position in the complex urban space. Thus one of the major characteristics of cognitive mapping is that it presupposes the existence of a condition of loss and confusion. The cartographers themselves are no exception; they are like nomads who attempt to overcome this confusion and re-examine the foundations of our position towards the grand issues of existence, our worldviews and their consequences.

Cognitive mapping is introduced as an outlet from a state of confusion and as a strategy aimed at creating representational patterns capable of promoting class-consciousness. The latter is seen as the ultimate goal of cognitive mapping, since it is expected to help people locate themselves in the urban totality dominated by the "cultural logic of late capitalism." This conception of cognitive mapping echoes the concept of *Totalitatsintention* (the drive towards totality) developed by the Marxist critic Georg Lukács in *History and Class Consciousness* to conceptualize the relationship between the dynamics of social relations and the resistance to reification and fragmentation resulting from the dominance of the capitalist paradigm in western modernity.7 Jameson states this fact in his book *Postmodernism, or, the Cultural Logic of Late Capitalism* (1991) and points out that cognitive mapping is a "code word for class consciousness" within the "new spatiality implicit in the postmodern."8

Jameson's cognitive mapping and utopia are seen as two major related concepts that have the potential to overcome the current failure of dialectical criticism, which is expected to map a totality i.e. a class conciousness. Cognitive mapping in this sense is closely related to the concepts of representation and figurability, which were the fundamental preoccupation of literary criticism of the early 1970s. What is remarkable about figuration is that the represented object transcends the particular and concrete in favour of an abstract idea that goes beyond the surface appearance of things. The representational object of cognitive mapping is also an abstract concept but it articulates a concrete totality that goes beyond empirical verification, and thus uncovers the mysterious forces that constitute our world and existence. Cognitive mapping is thus performed and created in discourses that introduce representational structures to make truth intact but without a direct access or reference to external reality. Like cognitive mapping, utopia is not seen as a realm of fantasy or a form of ideality but as a cognitive procedure that uncovers the dynamics of the present and the iron cages of "unfreedoms."9

Commenting on Jameson's use of the term cognitive mapping, Adam Roberts argues that it re-defines ideology as the representation of the subject's imaginary relationship to his "real" conditions of existence. It is an attempt to "fantasize" our condition in a wider framework of mythic narratives that have the potential to represent the "political unconscious" of social totality so as to grasp the change in our mode of being-in-the-world.[10]

1.2 ABDELWAHAB ELMESSIRI AND THE NEW ISLAMIC DISCOURSE

In the last few decades, Western critique of modernity has inspired Muslim intellectuals to develop new ideas, images, terms and concepts that state their positions towards the tendencies of secular modernity, its transformations and consequences. Modernity is usually equated with the lofty ideals of the Enlightenment, particularly the promise of nature, reason and progress to establish a rational and progressive system. This perspective changed to a large extent after the Second World War and the development of a very sophisticated western self-scrutiny discourse, heightened by the works of the Frankfurt school.

In his attempt to deconstruct the dominant perception of modernity, the Arab Egyptian Muslim intellectual Abdelwahab Elmessiri (1938–2008) benefited from this western critical legacy and traced the reversals of idealism and materialism, of transcendentalism and immanentism in western discourse. Elmessiri's opposition between immanence (the essence of the secular modern) and transcendence (usually interpreted as the Islamic worldview), has led many Arab scholars to identify him as one of the proponents of a new Islamic discourse. Elmessiri's awareness of the decline of the leftist movements and the rise of political Islam enabled him to envisage the possibility of a break with modernity. Elmessiri's critique of modernity can be seen as an attempt to Islamize modernity but ironically via western critique itself.

In his attempt to explore the features of the new Islamic discourse, Elmessiri provided the following diachronic classification: (1) the traditionalist Islamic discourse, which emerged as a direct and immediate reaction to the colonial invasion of the Muslim world and prevailed until the mid-1960s, and (2) the new Islamic discourse, which assumed a definite form in the mid-1960s. Both discourses, in Elmessiri's view, endeavour to provide an Islamic answer to the questions raised by modernization and colonization. There are, however, radical points of divergence between them due to the fact that the bearers of the new Islamic discourse could recognize the other face of modernity, one which is totally different from the glorious Western modernity known, experienced and studied by the first generation of the pioneers, including Shaykh Mohammad Abduh and Shaykh Rifaʿa al-Tahtawy.[11]

Though "late capitalism" constitutes one of the major drives behind the interest of Muslim intellectuals in cognitive mapping, it is not the only force that directs and shapes their critique of the secular modern. Unlike Jameson, Elmessiri launched the cognitive mapping of secular modernity not to legitimate Marxism and its perception of history but to present a critique that uncovers the forces and the implications of its emergence, its inherent worldview and consequences. He attempted to provide us with maps, codes and signs that may inform our choice by making us aware of the tendencies and the consequences of the modern secular worldview.

Elmessiri agrees with Jameson that capital has defied all cultural specificities and all forms of authenticity in favour of the dominance of only one value: the value of exchange. Elmessiri, however, deciphers the code of capitalism and replaces it with secularism. In his two-volume work *al-ʿAlmāniyyah al-Juzʿiyyah wa al-ʿAlmāniyyah al-Shāmilah* [Partial Secularism and Comprehensive Secularism], he puts it this way:

> [Jameson's] analysis of the general value of exchange that annuls [human and cultural] specificities is not about capital as an economic matter, but as a mechanism with an epistemological dimension (ultimate and total), leading to the deconstruction and destruction of all that is unique, special, authentic, sacred, mysterious and ambivalent.... Capital is thus a mechanism that throws man away from complex history and civilization into the simple and monistic world of nature; it is the mechanism of the dominance of the monistic and materialistic natural laws. Capital is thus the most important mechanism of the desanctification of man. But it is not the only mechanism; there are many others.[12]

Introduction: Cognitive Mapping and Metaphoricity

For almost four decades, Elmessiri was engaged in a philosophically oriented study of western modernity and its relationship with Nazism and Zionism. In his autobiography *Riḥlaty al-Fikriyyah: al-Bidhūr wa al-Judhūr wa al-Thimār* [My Intellectual Journey: The Seeds, The Roots, and The Harvest], Elmessiri underlines the influence of humanist Marxism on his thought, especially its integration of both theoretical foundations and the critique of man's historical and social condition. The Marxist critique of western modernity and its emphasis on *Gemeinschaft* (community) are believed to have saved Elmessiri from 'nihilism' and to have provided him with a 'solid critical foundation.'[13] Elmessiri puts it this way:

> Marxism reinforced some of my inherent positions such as the rejection of injustice and exploitation; the necessity of establishing justice on earth; the importance of transcending the existing reality and never surrendering to it; most importantly, Marxism provided me with a critical ground that enabled me to have a critical distance from my bourgeois milieu in Egypt and later from the American life during my stay in the United States.[14]

Elmessiri's intellectual background and his project of cognitive mapping, however, are wider than the ideals of Marxism and its ambitions. Born in a traditional and conservative milieu in the village of Damanhur in Egypt, Elmessiri was brought up in a community that celebrates the ideals of diversity, tolerance and family ties. At High school, almost at the age of twelve, Elmessiri joined the Muslim Brothers and participated in their religious activities for a period of two years. At the age of sixteen, he was obsessed with the common questions about the origin of evil in the world. This hermeneutics of suspicion failed to find convincing answers in his ideological and religious background, and it led him to embrace Marxism as a tool of philosophical understanding and as a means of fighting social injustice. In the mid-1950s, he became a member of the Communist Party and participated in its activities till 1959. Elmessiri, however, stresses that what he learned from Marxism melted entirely into his "humanistic Islamic vision."[15]

At Rutgurs University and in the post-1967 period, Elmessiri and his friend Kevin Reilly launched the Socialist Forum, and the first lecture he delivered was entitled "A Lecture by an Arab Socialist on the Arab-Israeli Conflict." Elmessiri used this forum as a platform to discuss this conflict regardless of the proposed and announced themes.[16] Elmessiri's critique of Zionism shows clearly in his early writings, including *Nihāyat al-Tarīkh: Muqaddimah li Dirāsat Binyat al-Fikr al-Ṣuhyūnī* [The End of History: An Introduction to the Study of the Structure of Zionist Thought, 1972], a 500 page work *Mawsūʿat al-Mafāhīm wa al-Muṣṭalaḥāt al-Ṣuhyūniyyah* [The Encyclopaedia of Zionist Concepts and Terminology, 1975], *Al-Firdaws al-Arḍī: Dirāsāt wa Intibaʿāt ʿan al-Haḍārah al-Amrīkiyyah al-Ḥadīthah* [The Earthly Paradise: Studies and Impressions about Modern American Civilization], 1979], and a two volume work entitled *Al-Iydyūlūjiyyah al-Ṣuhyūniyyah: Dirāsah Ḥālah fī ʿIlm Ijtimāʿ al-Maʿarifah* [Zionist Ideology: A Case Study in the Sociology of Knowledge, 1982-1983].

After getting his doctoral degree in comparative literature from Rutgers University in 1969, Elmessiri was introduced by Osama al-Baz, the political adviser of former Egyptian president Hosni Mubarak, to the most well-known Egyptian journalist and historian Mohamed Hassanein Heikal. The latter was then the editor-in-chief of the most popular Egyptian daily newspaper *Al-Ahram* and he encouraged Elmessiri to work at the Centre for Political and Strategic Studies as a specialist on Zionism. By the late 1970s, Elmessiri, however, could not even step in to the *Al-Ahram* offices because he publically opposed the Camp David Accords. Elmessiri decided to devote his intellectual endeavour to editing and complying the entries of *Mawsūʿat al-Yahūd wa al-Yahūdiyyah wa al-Ṣuhyūniyyah* [Encyclopedia of the Jews, Judaism and Zionism, henceforth *Mawsūʿat*], which was published by Dār al-Shurūq in Cairo in 1999, and then in 2001 in a CD by Bayt al-ʿArab li al-Tawthīq al-ʿAṣrī wa al-Naẓm. Elmessiri did not see his career as mere academic work but as a symbol of "man's battle against injustice, as this eternal struggle between an authentic human being (who tries to transcend the realm of the five senses) and the natural/materialistic man who is consumed by this realm."[17]

Elmessiri was aware that he had transcended the existing facts that had been pointing at the possibility of reaching peace in the Middle East; he kept viewing the events, contemplating them and writing the *Mawsūᶜat* over 25 years during which people were under the illusion that the Arab-Israeli conflict was approaching its end and perpetual peace would prevail.[18]

Elmessiri usually refers to his sojourn in the United States during two separate periods (1963-69/1975-79) as a very crucial moment that shaped his understanding of the transformation of western modernity as a "paradigmatic sequence" that starts with solid rational materialism and ends with liquid non-rational materialism.[19] Elmessiri's reference to the 1960s is very important because the very idea of modernization, according to Dean Tipps, was developed and promoted by American social scientists in the period after the Second World War, reaching its climax in the mid-1960s during which there was a widespread attitude of complacency towards American society and a remarkable expansion of American political, military and economic interests throughout the world.[20]

The 1970s, however, are crucial to an understanding of Elmessiri's critique of modernity because this period witnessed the rise of political Islam which managed, after the Arab defeat by Israel in 1967, to fill the vacuum left by the leftist movements, their rhetoric of technological progress as well as their idealistic discourse of Arab socialism, one that was (mis) used to justify the loss of political freedom in exchange for the rhetoric of national development and technological progress. The 1970s and the early 1980s, according to Sami Zubaida, can be seen as the charismatic period of political Islam which was embraced by many of the prominent Egyptian leftists, including Hassan Hanafi, Tariq al-Bishri and Adel Hussien, as a vehicle of popular contestation and national liberation.[21] This period had a great impact on Elmessiri whilst he was writing the *Mawsūᶜat*. Elmessiri states:

> [I]t was in the period of 1984 and 1985 that Islam was transformed before my eyes from a mere faith that I profess into a worldview from which one can generate highly explanatory paradigms and answers to the grand questions of existence.[22]

However, it was not until the 1990s that Elmessiri fully crystallized his two major interpretative paradigms, namely, immanentism and comprehensive secularism.[23]

In his book, *Al-Ṣuhyūniyyah wa al-Nāziyyah wa Nihāyat al-Tārīkh* [Zionism, Nazism and the End of History], Elmessiri expresses a deep sense of belonging to a new Arab and Islamic intellectual trend that started in the 1940s, reaching its climax in the last few decades. In Elmessiri's view, this trend was an attempt to contribute to human civilization, taking into account the cultural and historical specificity of the Arab and Islamic worldview. Among the prominent names that Elmessiri associates with this trend are Jamal Hemdan, Anwar Abdel Malek, Adel Hussein, Tareq al-Bishri, Jalal Amin, Asem al-Dusuqi, Qasim Abduh Qasim and Rafiq Habib.[24] In a private conversation with the author of this book, Elmessiri stressed that he abandoned the materialistic paradigm in favour of Islamic humanism because he came to realize that:

> Islam represents a worldview that rejects the materialistic Promethean and Faustian outlook. It calls for a balance between man and the universe rather than establishing paradise on earth or putting an end to history or harnessing man and nature in the service of the powerful.[25]

In his late life, Elmessiri was much involved in politics, and he had a great impact on the political scene. He was one of the founding members of the Islamically-oriented Al-Wasaṭ Party, which was founded in the 1990s by Abu al-Ela Madi as a centrist and moderate branch of the Muslim Brotherhood. It was Elmessiri who reformulated the principles of the Al-Wasaṭ Party and who wrote a twelve-page introduction to the party programme in August 2004. The party succeeded in mobilizing public opinion in favour of a moderate centrist view of Islam based on dialogue with the West, the principles of democracy and the support of the rights of women and non-Muslims.

Elmessiri was also the general co-ordinator of the Egyptian popular movement for change *Kifāyah* (Enough), which has been calling for peaceful change and democratic transformation in Egypt long before the fall of Hosni Mubarak's regime. Elmessiri died in 2008, that is, two and a half years before the January Egyptian Revolution. However, his discourse on secular modernity still has a major attraction not only in Egypt but also all over the Arab world, especially among religiously-oriented intellectuals, scholars and politicians, including even the prominent Coptic intellectual and politician Rafiq Habib who is currently the vice-president of the Muslim Brotherhood's political party *Al-Ḥuriyyah wa al-ʿAdālah* [Freedom and Justice]. A recent interactive online conference held by Elmessiri's disciples on 27 June 2011 entitled "Abdelwahab Elmessiri: The Present Absent in the Egyptian Revolution" underlined the significance of Elmessiri's discourse on the current debates on modernity, secularism, citizenship and the Arab-Israeli conflict in the Middle East.

In both western and Arab discourses, modernity is almost always related to the ideals of the Enlightenment, particularly the promise of Reason and science to promote our human and social existence. Elmessiri refers to this understanding of modernity as "partial secularism," which he describes as "moral secularism" or "humanistic secularism."[26] According to Elmessiri, the acceptance of this moderate secularism as an integral part of pluralism is embraced by the major Islamic trend, which is advocated by Fahmi Huwaidi, Yusuf al-Qaradawi, Mohammed Salim al-Awa, Abu al-Ela Madi, and Adel Husain (Egypt), Rachid Ghannouchi (Tunisia), Taha Jabir al-Alwani (Iraq), AbdulHamid AbuSulayman (Saudi Arabia), Azzam Tamimi (Palestine), Parviz Manzur (Pakistan), and Ahmet Davutoğlu (Turkey). This Islamic trend accepts the legitimacy of moderate secularism and the role of its advocates as partners in the political life of Islamic society.[27]

In *Dirāsāt Maʿrifiyyah fī al-Ḥadāthah al-Gharbiyyah* [Epistemological Studies in Western Modernity], Elmessiri deconstructs the mainstream understanding of Western secular modernity and defines it as the "use of value-free science and technology."[28] It is a form of comprehensive secularism which does not aim merely at the independence of science and technology from human subjectivity or the separation of church and state, but at "the separation of all values (be they religious, moral, human) not from only 'the state' but also from public and private life, and from the world at large. In other words, it strives for the creation of a value-free world."[29] Over and above, Elmessiri argues that modernism in art and literature, especially in its tragic and absurdist form, can be conceived as a critique of the contradictions of modernity, including the mechanistic tendencies of both capitalism and communism, and the shameful past of European expansive imperialism.[30]

In the introduction to the third edition of *Al-Ṣuhyūniyyah wa al-Nāziyyah wa Nihāyat al-Tārīkh* [Zionism, Nazism and the End of History], dedicated to the formerly Marxist French intellectual Roger Garaudy, Elmessiri expresses his astonishment at the fact that before the late 1980s, western scholarship had hardly recognized or approached Nazism and Zionism within the framework of a value-free, rationalistic and imperialistic modernity. Elsewhere Elmessiri mentions the way such ideologies were excluded from the map of secular modernity:

> The history of secularism is fragmented…for it was monitored by the Western social sciences in a piecemeal diachronic fashion: first humanism and/or the Reformation, the Enlightenment, rationalism, and totalitarianism; then the counter-Enlightenment, Romanticism, and Darwinism; then positivism, existentialism, phenomenology; and finally came the end of history and post-modernism. Racism, imperialism and Nazism were all seen as aberrations, having a history of their own, distinct from the history of secularism and modernity.[31]

Elmessiri, however, lavishes praise on Zygmunt Bauman's interpretation of modernity saying that his writings, particularly *Modernity and the Holocaust* (1989), are among the most important references he has drawn upon to develop his cognitive mapping of modernity.[32] Elsewhere he stresses that Bauman's writings are among the works he has read avidly as they uncover the dark sides that lie beneath the joyful glittering surface of modernity.[33]

The most remarkable feature of Bauman's critique is the invention or the introduction of new metaphors and concepts as one of the major mechanisms of the cognitive mapping of modernity. This study will attempt to show that Bauman's proposal of new tropes and concepts has much in common with Elmessiri's metaphor-based interpretation of modernity and secularism. Bauman's cognitive mapping depends on two key tropes: solid modernity and liquid modernity. Surprisingly enough, Elmessiri's cognitive mapping centres on almost the same tropes: rational solid materialism and non-rational liquid materialism. These major metaphors are based on the invention, or the collection, of sub-metaphors that are believed to have the potential of mapping the dominant motif of the secular modern. However, this study on Bauman and Elmessiri is not as much a question of influence but rather a search for common and opposing responses to specific questions concerning the use of hermeneutics in the interpretation of secular modernity.

In mapping secular modernity, Elmessiri went beyond capital as the only mechanism of the desanctification of man. More importantly, he realized that the definitions of secularism in dictionaries and encyclopedias either give conflicting meanings or reduce the term to the simplistic and popular formula of "the separation of religion and state." Ambivalent as it is in Western discourse, the term became more ambivalent and chaotic when it was transferred into the Arab and Islamic world.34 Elmessiri underlined a number of problems with the dominant definitions of secularism, many of which deal with the denotations and etymology of the word, ignoring its connotations and the development of its semantic field over centuries. Many of the definitions deal with the history of secularism in the West, but they ignore the actual crystallization of the comprehensive secular paradigm. In other words, all negative phenomena that accompanied secularism are excluded: imperialism, world wars, totalitarian movements, alienation, reification, commoditization, consumerism, anomie, nihilism and anarchy.35

In his attempt to go beyond these problems, Elmessiri stressed the metaphysical inferences and crystallizations of secularism as a "comprehensive epistemological vision of God, man and nature, one which constitutes a sequence that emerges in time and space with varying degrees and forms."36 The understanding of secularism as the separation of church and state should be replaced by a more complex representation of secular modernity as a comprehensive world out-look that operates on all levels of reality through a large number of mechanisms.37 Elmessiri does not claim that this paradigm is entirely new and he stresses that it has been introduced by Western intellectu-als, including Irving Kristol (secularism as a religious view deifying man); Agnes Heller (secularism as a pantheistic view); Max Weber (secularism as the disenchantment of the world); and Zygmunt Bauman (secularism as a compulsive modernization and a social production of moral indifference).38

The examination of cognitive mapping introduced by Zygmunt Bauman and Abdelwahab Elmessiri will be the major objective of this study, since both of them see the secular modern as a comprehensive vision of God, man and nature. Both of them use almost the same metaphors and paradigms, yet they offer different prescriptions to the crisis of the secular modernity. Neither Bauman nor Elmessiri embrace Marx's historical materialism or economic determinism; their fascina-tion with Marxism can be attributed to its strong emphasis on such human and political categories as political emancipation and social justice. It is true that both of them have drawn heavily on humanist Marxism, but they avoided the emphasis on class consciousness and the general obsession with the proletariat as a political category or as the right agency of effecting revolutionary ambitions or collective emancipation.

Unlike many intellectuals of Marxist background, Elmessiri and Bauman do not focus only upon social stratification, the suffering of the proletariat and their potential for revolutionary promise. Rather, they use the Marxist emphasis on social justice as a point of departure to comment critically on the human condition. Above all, they transcend the conventional capitalist/socialist dual classification and put the capi-talist and the communist systems in one and the same category. What united capitalism and communism, according to Bauman, is a shared emphasis on the promises and prospects of modernity, particularly the intensification of production, super-industrialism, rational manage-ment and the necessity of controlling nature and establishing the King-dom of Reason and the earthly paradise.39 Elmessiri puts it this way:

The secular paradigm includes both capitalism and socialism as materialist paradigms that organize human societies; both are variants of a deeper and more comprehensive paradigm, namely, comprehensive secularism (rationalistic materialism and materialistic monism as well). The paradigm of secularization is even used to explain many phenomena in the modern age, not only in the West but also all over the world; the prime manifestations of this paradigm are democracy, modern western philosophy, modernization, modernism and postmodernism.[40]

Though belonging to different religions, nationalities and cultures, Elmessiri (Arab–Egyptian former Marxist-Muslim) and Bauman (Polish–British former Marxist-Jew), have used the allegories of the Jew to approach much wider questions of secular modernity, including Nazism, racism, imperialism and the Jewish experience in modern Europe. The fact that Bauman comes originally from Poland gives this comparison a unique dimension, since when we talk about the Jews of the Western world, we are talking in fact, according to Elmessiri, about the Jews of Poland! It was only in the 1980s that Elmessiri came to realize that the vast majority of Jews in the West by the end of the eighteenth century were in Poland, and that they were divided among Russia, Austria and Germany by the division of Poland itself; thousands and millions of them emigrated to England, Austria, Canada, the United States, South Africa and Palestine.[41] It was also in Poland that the other face of secular modernity fully emerged; in Poland alone six Nazi concentration camps were established, of which the biggest and the most popular was Auschwitz. Reliable statistics, according to Gilbert Achcar, show that in 1948 almost 170,000 Jews from Poland constituted the largest segment of the community of Jews living in Palestine.[42] Bauman himself was forced to immigrate to Israel in the late 1960s, but he opted for England immediately after receiving a job offer from the University of Leeds.

With these facts in mind, Elmessiri embarked on developing new interpretative paradigms of secular modernity and its relationship with Nazism and Zionism. He drew heavily on Bauman's critical contribution and praised his cognitive mapping of modernity in his intellectual autobiography and in a number of his major Arabic publications, including *Al-Ṣuhyūniyyah wa al-Nāziyyah wa Nihāyat al-Tārīkh* [Zionism, Nazism and the End of History] (1997), *Mawsūʿat* (1999), and *Al-ʿAlmāniyyah al-Juzʾiyyah wa al-ʿAlmāniyyah al-Shāmilah* [Partial Secularism and Comprehensive Secularism] (2002). Here a Muslim Arab intellectual draws on the works of a Jewish European sociologist and attempts to integrate his discourse on secular modernity into contemporary Islamic discourse. Though representing a unique case of inter-textuality, Elmessiri and Bauman take different positions regarding the available options in western tradition and the possibility of an alternative worldview to the original project of secular modernity. Thus the study of Bauman's influence on Elmessiri goes beyond the search for specific words, images, terms and phrases that Elmessiri borrowed from Bauman. Rather, it underlines how this influence is the result of a common human consciousness, and how critics of the secular modern can use the same terminology to generate common maps with different prescriptions.

1.3 ZYGMUNT BAUMAN AND THE JEWISH EXPERIENCE

Bauman was born in Poland in 1925, and his family escaped to the Soviet zone of occupation, following the Nazi invasion of Poland at the beginning of the Second World War. By the late 1950s, Bauman, like Elmessiri, had been playing a significant role in humanist Marxism, remaining faithful to the major principles of Marxism and its repudiation of false consciousness. In the 1960s, Bauman became a member of the governing Polish United Workers Party, but he never approved of the practices of the communist regime. In the late 1960s, precisely in 1968, Bauman renounced his party membership and in the same year, in an anti-Jewish campaign, he, as well as many Jewish intellectuals, was driven out of Poland and stripped of his Polish citizenship on the accusation of fomenting student riots. Bauman had to go first to Israel where he stayed no more than three years. Janina Bauman, his wife, uncovers in a conversation with Madeleine Bunting the true reason behind their decision to leave Israel: "[I]t was a nationalistic country, and we had just run away from nationalism. We didn't want to go from being the victims of one nationalism to being the perpetrators of another."[43] In a conversation with Benedetto Vecchi, Bauman himself does not hesitate to say, "I suppose that my Jewishness is confirmed by Israeli inequities paining me still more than atrocities committed by other countries."[44]

The nationalistic drive that characterizes western modernity has a great impact on Bauman's mapping of modernity and postmodernity. The uniqueness of his critique came into prominence with the publication of his metaphorical trilogy: *Legislators and Interpreters* (1987), *Modernity and the Holocaust* (1989) and *Modernity and Ambivalence* (1991). Bauman has never abandoned his belief in the strong relationship between modernity and modernism, arguing that modernists gave their allegiance to the discoveries of modern science and developed their theories on scientific premises. He stresses that the impressionists took inspiration from optics, cubists from the relativity theory, and surrealists from psychoanalysis.[45] Elsewhere, Bauman argues that modernism would have never come into existence without the acceptance of the premises of modernity, especially the construction of contemptible people into a collective image of the bourgeois, philistines, or vulgar and uncultured masses.[46]

It is true that the Nazi Holocaust did not have a direct impact on Bauman's personal life, but his wife Janina had suffered as a young Jewish girl in the Warsaw ghetto. Janina wrote her memoirs *Winter in the Morning*, which aroused Bauman's interest in the Holocaust as a window to modernity or as one of its possibilities. More importantly, Bauman, in a conversation with Anver Shapira, criticizes the Israeli abuse and "privatization" of the Holocaust, arguing that the "Jews can be safe only in a world free of nationalisms, and that includes Jewish nationalism."[47] Bauman's anti-nationalistic stance shows in his membership in a well-known British group called Jews for Justice for the Palestinians. The group co-operates with other groups such as Writers against the Occupation and Jewish Students for Justice for Palestinians, all of which promote the idea that there is no hope for Israel without justice for the Palestinians. This is why they direct their efforts at building a broad-based End the Occupation campaign, one that

supports the rights of the Palestinians and condemns Israeli occupation, illegal settlement and the abuse of military coercive force and
violence against armless and impoverished Palestinians.

Bauman's exile from Poland played a crucial role in his mapping of
the consequences of modernity; it has given him the advantages of
marginality that led him to focus on the position of strangers, exiles and
outsiders. Bauman has intellectually led the nomadic existence of the
stranger, and he summarizes this intellectually fertile mode of existence
in the eloquent statements made by Frederic Raphael, George Steiner
and Ludwig Wittgenstein, respectively: (1) "The meaning of my
being a Jew is that I am everywhere out of place," (2) "My homeland is
my typewriter," and (3) "The only place where real philosophical
problems could be tackled and resolved is the railway station."[48]

In *Modernity and Ambivalence* (1991), Bauman traces the failure of
the liberalist utopia of western modernity and stresses that exclusivist
nationalism was not confined to Poland, since it manifested itself clearly
in the failure of the assimilatory ambitions in almost all European
countries. Phony assimilation, as Bauman describes it, involved the
dismissal of the mystical and messianic trends as un-Jewish, granting
credibility of cultural adjustment only to the relations of the *salon*: the
Bible of Luther, Hermann Cohen and Kant, Steinthal and Wilhelm
von Humboldt. The majority of the Jews were thus encouraged to
acquire "refined manners" and new standards of "cleanliness." The
call for physical and moral "cleanliness" was accompanied with a call
for linguistic cleanliness, and Yiddish, the language of the *Ostjuden*
(East European Jews from Russia, Poland, Ukraine and Galicia)
became a target of ridicule among German Jews. Like Yiddish, Polish
language was disdained as inferior to German. The *Ostjuden* were
conceived of as "disease and epidemic-carriers," "filthy, ignorant and
immoral savages," and "unwelcome strangers."[49]

Bauman's analysis of the history of Jewish assimilation in the West is
closely related and defined against the stereotype of the unassimilated
Ostjude, the Jew of East and Central Europe. Bauman holds that the
Holocaust had much sway on the meaning of Judaism because some
theologians viewed it as a sign of the "absence of God," the "failure of

God," the "Jewish exilic tradition" and the choice of the Jews as the "carriers of the truth" of modern civilization. Since the mid-nineteenth century, France, England and Russia directed their efforts at eliminating the increase in the numbers of the so-called poor, un-educated, backward and uncivilized Jewish immigrants who had two major options of salvation: Zionism and socialism. In Poland, the situation was much worse because there had been a strong belief that the Jews were an alien and poisonous body in the emerging Polish national organism.[50]

The saddest irony is that the success of individuals in almost all walks of life was not a sufficient guarantee of political equality and social acceptance. As a nation without a state, Jewish communities in Europe attempted to gain "a state-like sovereignty," but the failure of this ambition has led, in the final analysis, to the emergence of political Zionism and its programme of a new "Jewish liberal state":

> There is little doubt that the birth of political Zionism, most certainly in its most consequential, Herzl's version, was the product of the disintegration of assimilatory efforts, rather than a fruition of the Judaist tradition and the resurrection of the love of Zion.[51]

German Jews themselves saw the Zionist programme mainly as a solution to the *Ostjuden* problem; the suggestion made in 1914 that the Zionists themselves should actually go to Palestine "came as a shock to many philanthropic Zionist sympathizers who saw themselves as Germans."[52]

1.4 MODERN EPISTEMOLOGICAL BIAS

In spite of the differences in their religious, ideological and cultural backgrounds, both Elmessiri and Bauman devoted their critiques to the mitigation of the arrogance of secularism, especially its celebration of the nature-centred cosmology and the anthropocentric epistemology of natural sciences. Their critiques are accompanied with a serious call for establishing a new science which is given different designations, but whose target is almost same: critical sociology (Bauman) and *Fiqh al-Tahayuz* or the science of understanding bias (Elmessiri); both of which call for an ontological hermeneutics that goes beyond the objectivism/relativism dichotomy.

Throughout the 1990s, Elmessiri devoted much of his critical concern to the analysis of epistemological bias. In 1992, he managed to organize a conference in Cairo on the issue of bias in the different fields of knowledge. The conference papers, along with other studies, were published in a two volume work entitled *Ishkaliyyat al-Tahayuz* [The Problems of Bias]. The third edition of this work appeared in 1998 in seven volumes; the first volume is entitled *Fiqh al-Tahayuz*, and it constitutes a long introduction in which Elmessiri explains the dynamics of bias and the myths of both objectivity and subjectivity. Elmessiri also replaced the terms "subjective" and "objective" with the terms "more explanatory" and "less explanatory," thus making interpretation a continuous process of ijtihad (generative and creative interpretation). This new science, according to Elmessiri, neither aspires for a full control of human phenomena nor dismisses the ontological and epistemological dimensions of metaphoric language.[53] Elmessiri repeated this view and this call in a one volume work in English entitled *Epistemological Bias in the Physical and Social Sciences* (2006).[54]

Elmessiri's position is very close to that of Bauman who believes that the challenge of hermeneutics to social sciences consists of two problems: that of consensus and that of truth. Positive sciences established a disinterested commitment to truth and eliminated extra-scientific commitments on the ground they belong to the world of fantasy, unrealism, and utopianism.[55] Their success entailed an aggressive separation of scientific, moral and aesthetic discourses. The fascination with solid, objective and scientific facts is an attempt to exorcise "Descartes' malign genie," "the ghost of relativism" and the "inner demon" of uncertainty.[56] Bauman entirely rejects this "positivist restrictive epistemology" or "positivist imperialism," and has been critical of "neutral technology" and the authority of technical-instrumental interests which reinforce the already existing split between subjects and objects of action, the controllers and the controlled, the superior and the subordinated.57

Critical sociology, according to Bauman, undermines the analogy between a living organism and human society and dismisses the biological approach in the analysis of socio-cultural systems. Human societies and phenomena are neither biological organisms nor merely static or functional structures. It is hardly surprising that Bauman repudiates extremist behaviorism and fundamentalist sociology because their approach is based on the assumption that "human behavior posits no problems essentially different from those encountered...in the exploration of flies' conduct."58

Immanuel Kant, in Bauman's view, was the first to uncover the naïveté of the image of the mind as a *tabula rasa*, arguing instead that cognition is a creative work of reason in its encounter with reality. The subject of cognition is and must remain an active agent. Subjectivity is inseparable from cognition; and therefore, objective knowledge could be reached, if at all, only through it. Thus our understanding, in Bauman's view, should be viewed as a selective and an endless herme- neutical reflection and reassessment rather than a unilinear progress towards objective or absolute knowledge.59

Bauman argues that though the Kantian model recognized the indispensable role of the cognizing subject, it doubted the subject's disinterestedness and saw the cognitive framework as the distorting impact of prejudice and ideology. Critical theory, on the other hand, does not see the relation between reason and the world as a question of cognition but as the question of theory and practice, thus shifting the epistemological emphasis from the cognitive act to the social produc- tion of the cognized world. This perception, according to Bauman, is very crucial because it goes beyond two assumptions: (1) human beings possess everything in their minds and what is needed is only an encounter with the objects in reality and (2) the world itself (objects and outside reality) is absolutely true.60

Here Bauman stresses the role of critical theory which conceives of the liberation from the world and the emancipation of it as two inter- related and even inseparable tasks. In other words, the significance of critical theory lies in its repudiation of the defeatist withdrawal of the self and in seeing the possibility of the emergence of collective orientation and self-conscious history.[61]

Bauman's and Elmessiri's critical positions can be understood within the framework of the revolt against the domination of nineteenth-century positivism. This point is eloquently explained by the German-American political philosopher Eric Voegelin (1901–1985) who pointed out that the prominence of the natural value-free sciences led to the belief that they were models possessing some "inherent virtue." With the reign of this view, according to Voegelin, ontology became the scapegoat, and consequently ethics and politics could no longer be understood as sciences of the order in which human nature reaches actualization.[62] However, any analysis without an ontological orientation, in Voegelin's view, remains unscientific because political science goes beyond the validity of propositions to the truth of existence, and the prerequisite of analysis is still the perception of the loving openness of the soul to its transcendent ground of order.[63] The rejection of the this openness has led, in the final analysis, to the celebration of 'the death of God' and to a long process of imposition of meaning on history to the extent that we are confronted with the "anarchy of liberal and racist, of progressive and Marxist" and of many nationalist histories that "spelled the end of history as a science."[64]

1.5 MODERNITY AS METAPHOR AND NARRATIVE CATEGORY

Both Bauman and Elmessiri have embraced a metaphorical approach in their mapping of modernity and postmodernity. This methodological decision confronts a major challenge, especially when seen from a deconstructive perspective that considers truth an army of faded metaphors. According to both Nietzsche and Derrida, truth is described as "an army of faded metaphors;" concepts of reality as "effects of figurality" and the logocentric rationalism of metaphysics as a "carnival of figurative conceits."[65] This observation, however, does not necessarily entail the abandonment of the search for a degree of truth or the acceptance of the dominance of nihilistic tendencies in the processes of perception and interpretation. On the contrary, it uncovers a key aspect of cognitive mapping i.e. challenging and questioning the existing interpretations and representations because reality is complex and even unfixable. The history of truth is undoubtedly an "Error" or an "army of faded metaphors" in the sense that among the plurality of sentences, utterances, interpretations or modes of being, only one sentence, one utterance, one interpretation, or one mode of being is emphasized at the expense of other options and possibilities. This perception of the challenging relationship between truth and reality or between the world and the perception of the world acquired new significant implications with the publication of Thomas Kuhn's *The Structure of Scientific Revolutions* (1962). These implications are very crucial to the representation of both Bauman's and Elmessiri's metaphorical methodology.

Thanks to Kuhn, two key terms gained much popularity in western European discourse: "paradigm" and "paradigm shift." Kuhn's basic assumption is that science can not be seen only as a progressive accumulation of facts and data because it depends largely on the authority of scientific communities. Rather, scientific research should be seen as a process of "puzzle-solving" guided by a ruling paradigm (a body of intertwined theoretical and methodological belief shared by a community of scientists). As Kuhn suggests, when the scholars' confidence in the ruling paradigm is permanently shaken, they are expected to realize the presence of a crisis and the necessity of paradigm shift, a moment which is seen as a scientific revolution and a "Gestalt-switch."[66] This argument had far reaching consequences beyond the realm of natural sciences as it mitigated the authoritative position of science as the sole source of objective knowledge and provided the legitimation for the humanities.[67]

The terms 'paradigm' and 'paradigm shift' can be used to establish an "elective affinity" between Bauman's critique of modernity and Kuhn's argument. To put it differently, Kuhn's notion of paradigm can be employed to understand Bauman's call for a transition from modernity to postmodernity due to the realization of the contradictions inherent in the paradigmatic vision of modernity. Within this context, Bauman's critique of modernity uncovers a "paradigmatic crisis" that entails the necessity of emergence of a new interpretative paradigm to replace, or at least modify, the old one and the worldview it represented. The same "elective affinity" can be traced in Elmessiri's writings. However, Elmessiri's conception of paradigm is more comprehensive than that of Kuhn on the ground that it is neither limited to the natural sciences nor ignores the grand ontological issues of human existence.

Before examining Bauman's and Elmessiri's position towards the notions of paradigm and paradigm shift, it is extremely important to refer to Graham C. Kinloch who seems to have used Thomas Kuhn's notion of paradigm and applied it to the study of modern Western thought. In his book *Sociological Theory: Its Development and Major Paradigms* (1977), Kinloch argues that two significant paradigms can be easily traced in western thought: the organic paradigm and the conflict radical paradigm. The construction of these paradigms is based on a methodological decision that tends to over-emphasize the similarities between theorists and to ignore apparently conflicting details in favour of the prominence of one major dimension i.e. "paradigmatic foundation." Within the organic paradigm, society is conceived of as an integrated organism dependent on its division of labor. The conflict-radical paradigm has much in common with the organic functional paradigm, yet it views conflict, rather than integration, as central to the social system. Though different in assumptions, both the organic and the conflict radical paradigms belong to the organic, naturalistic, evolutionary and functional explanations of society. Kinloch does not hesitate to state that western civilization has been oscillating, since the Renaissance and the Enlightenment, between these major paradigms.[68]

Though the notion of paradigm, as introduced by Kuhn and manipulated by Kinloch, does not imply any suggestions of imperialistic monopolization of truth or objectivity, Bauman has remained suspicious of the excessive enthusiasm for this term, suspecting that it may be manipulated and misused to claim universal acceptance and exclusive superiority. This suspicion can be attributed to Bauman's faith in the fact that reality is "much more complex than even the best paradigm."[69]

Bauman nevertheless, has been using, consciously or unconsciously, the notion of paradigm in almost all of his English writings on modernity and postmodernity. A close examination of his writings shows that he uses the notion of paradigm; however, he used this analytical tool only by intuition and without much theorization.

It is true that Bauman distances himself from the term paradigm and its negative connotations, yet he uses other terms and phrases that are almost synonymous with the positive connotations of the term paradigm as manipulated by Kinloch and Elmessiri. Among the most recurrent terms in Bauman's writings on modernity and postmodernity are "world mapping," "pattern," "repeatable pattern," "mental setting," "central discourse," "theoretical model," "dominant ideology of the system" and the most "decisive feature." These terms are used in the same way Elmessiri uses such terms as theme, pattern, type, mental image, mental structure and cognitive map. All of them belong to a common semantic field that seeks to draw and re-interpret the ambitions of the past and the various, yet similar, roads taken to fulfill them without claiming that they represent definitive answers or the only valid interpretation. Bauman himself defines the nature of this semantic field when he refers to the role of intellectuals in the postmodern era. The task of the intellectuals is an interpretative, a "sense-making," a "world-mapping" knowledge that constructs a "mental setting in which decisions are taken and freedom of choice is exercised."[70]

A further example of Bauman's methodology can be traced in his analysis of the different visions of modernity introduced by thinkers like Max Weber (progressive rationalization), Freud (psychotic and neurotic ailment) and Nietzsche (the will to power). By putting all these examples into one and the same category, Bauman, implicitly and unconsciously, points out one of the major characteristics of the use of paradigms i.e. their tendency to go beyond intellectual differences, minute details and superficial oppositions in favor of the prominence of common and dominant features of discourse. Bauman emphasizes that it is due to a "new cognitive perspective" that the differences among the visions of modernity have begun to look less important, stressing instead a close kinship bond between the apparently antagonistic views.[71]

In one of his earliest writings on modernity, namely, *Socialism: the Active Utopia* (1976), Bauman saw modernity as a complex phenomenon that resists clear-cut definitions. He, however, attempted to associate it with such general and abstract patterns as the "technological revolution," the "human ascendancy over Nature" and the social systems associated with the rise of these patterns.[72] Elsewhere Bauman proposes to define modernity as "the time, or the way of life, in which order-making consists of the dismantling of traditional, inherited and received order; in which 'being' means a perpetual new beginning."[73] This definition is more than just a rhetorical and eloquent statement as it is based on the belief that the differences in approaches and opinions among writers and critics can be transcended in favour of discovering and establishing the "ideal type," the dominant motif or the most defining decisive feature of modernity. Bauman writes:

> Modern utopias differed in many of their detailed prescriptions, but they all agreed that the 'perfect world' would be one remaining forever identical with itself, a world in which the wisdom learnt today will remain wise tomorrow and the day after tomorrow, and in which the life skills acquired will retain their usefulness forever. The world depicted utopias also, expectedly, a transparent world – one in which nothing dark or impenetrable stood in the way of the eye; a world with nothing spoiling the harmony; nothing 'out of place'; a world without 'dirt'; a world without strangers.[74]

Elsewhere Bauman's definition of modernity is related to the notions of "cognitive map," "repeatable pattern" and what he refers to as the "decisive feature" and "the defining and permanent feature."[75] The belief in the superiority of the European modernity attracted and unified the contributions of intellectuals despite their apparently conflicting differences and political affiliations. Bauman puts it this way:

Introduction: Cognitive Mapping and Metaphoricity

I take here the concept of 'modernity' to stand for a perception of the world, rather than (as it has been misleadingly intimated) the world itself; a perception locally grounded in a way that implied its universality and concealed its particularism. It has been the decisive feature of modernity so understood that it relativized its (past and contemporary) adversaries and thereby constituted relativity itself as an adversary; as a spoke in the wheel of progress, a demon to be exorcized, a sickness to be cured.[76]

Bauman's emphasis on the difference between the "perception of the world" and the "world itself" is the basic mechanism of cognitive mapping because it focuses on "cultural logic," to borrow Fredric Jameson's term, rather than a diachronic unfolding over time. This crucial aspect of cognitive mapping, as well as its tendency to uncover the logic of narrative and storytelling, is celebrated in Jameson's unique study *A Singular Modernity: Essay on the Ontology of the Present* (2002). Modernity, within this approach, cannot be regarded as a historical period that can be periodized or as a concept, philosophical or otherwise, that can be easily defined but as a "narrative category," a "unique kind of rhetorical effect," and a "trope" which is entirely different in structure from the traditional figures and thus constitutes a "decisive break with the previous forms of figurality." It is precisely for this reason that what critics consider a theory of modernity is a "projection of its own rhetorical structure onto themes and content in question." This process involves a re-writing of the narratives of modernity; an act which cannot be considered fictive or unreal but one that transcends both conventional narratives and the "alleged insights of historical analysis."[77]

In mapping modernity and postmodernity, Bauman has decided to abandon the traditional vision and division of tropes of discourse and embraced metaphor as an analytical tool that has the potential to map the epistemological and ontological foundations of modernity, its ambitions and consequences. Thus in the present context, metaphor refers to all those tropes (metaphors, metonymy, synecdoche, etc) and abstract concepts that occur over time and discourses to express a worldview or a world-perception. In a private correspondence with the author of this book, Bauman stresses his belief in the cognitive capacity of metaphors and their ability to "to mentally map the lines of dependency too extended and too far reaching to be experienced 'at the first hand' and subjected to direct sensuous scrutiny." He stresses that metaphors are the "indispensable scaffoldings for imagination and perhaps the most effective tool of comprehension." Though fully aware of the methodological limitations of metaphors, particularly their "incurable non-comprehensiveness and non-finality," Bauman embraces metaphors as effective tools that can help us suggest and grasp similarity (resemblances or world perception) not identity (same meaning, world or reality). Here Bauman does not hesitate to uncover the bias of use of metaphor when it "prejudices the perception of the object it tries to comprehend." In other words, metaphors are by nature reductionist; nevertheless, they are necessary tools of approaching the human condition since human beings and the human condition "are not ideal objects for scientific treatment." The use of metaphors is a true indication of the "refusal to act under false pretences, to bid for greater authority than realistically can be claimed, and above all to distort the subject–object communication." Here metaphor is not only "a cognitive strategy; it is also…an ethical choice."[78]

Bauman's views on metaphor and its role in society are embraced by many writers and critics who still believe in the impossibility of doing without imagery and metaphysics. Iris Murdoch, for example, stresses that there is a "continuous breeding of imagery in the consciousness which is, for better or worse, a function of moral change. This slow constant genesis reflects and affects the quality of our attachments and desires."[79] Human beings live naturally and normally by metaphors to the extent that old associations are broken and new ones are created; we "live by developing imagery and also by discarding it. The 'modern crisis' can be seen as a crisis about imagery (myth, and metaphysics)."[80]

Bauman's metaphorical approach, according to Michael Hviid Jacobsen and Sophia Marshman, may potentially contain the seeds "not only of hermeneutical understanding but also of political mobilization and social transformation."[81] Bauman has never abandoned the explanatory power of metaphors and concepts in the interpretation of the human condition. In *Freedom* (1988), Bauman draws our attention to the fact that such concepts as class, domination, authority, ideology and culture have played a significant role in organizing the sociological map of the human world.[82]

Aware as he is of the effectiveness of metaphors as means of abstraction in the description and the explanation of the human condition, Bauman repudiates the reduction of metaphors to the simple process of a linguistic transfer of old lexical meanings to new objects. Commenting on one of the simplest metaphors, Bauman points out that "society," for example, can be conceived of as the prime metaphor that refers to an "abstract totality" and an "imagined community" under the protection of a nation-state. Metaphors have a cognitive function that lies, in Bauman's view, in its ability to "juxtapose the unclear with the obvious; it suggests thereby an affinity…between the two."[83]

The adoption of metaphor as a basic mechanism in cognitive mapping is based on a methodology that transcends the traditional approaches to tropes of discourse as emotive, decorative, aesthetic and rhetorical devices. The inclusion of metaphor in the terminology of discourse analysis and cognitive mapping is an integral part of serious scholarly attempts aimed at "sociologizing" metaphor. This approach is very close to the sociological call for a "metaphor-based sociology of knowledge" that views metaphors as effective elements in the interplay of knowledge and power. Metaphorical representation is expected to be one of the major mechanisms of cognitive mapping because it will help us understand how discourses, paradigms and world views are transformed or even overturned.[84]

Bauman takes the Enlightenment as the starting point of his metaphorical critique in order to uncover the crucial role played by *les philosophes* (the intellectuals of the Enlightenment) in creating a world-view that served the universalistic ambitions of the nation-state. The Enlightenment is represented by Bauman as a coalition between culture and power i.e. between modern intellectuals and modern rulers who are referred to metaphorically as gardeners and legislators in search of utopia and perfection. According to Bauman, European Jews were conceived of as stateless strangers and weeds that threaten the garden of modernity and the ideal of perfection. The task of modernity "consists of safeguarding the people from the overgrowth of the weeds."[85]

In this context, postmodernity was seen as a chance to recover modernity without any illusions or false consciousness regarding its destructive ambitions of universalization and intolerance to difference. This chance seemed possible because the role of the intellectuals is reduced to that of modest interpreters and semiotic brokers. The decline of the role of the intellectuals, however, has also been accompanied with a comprehensive process of liquefaction that dominates the scene to the extent that the term "postmodernity" itself can no longer uncover the dynamics of contemporary human condition. It is precisely for this reason that Bauman has introduced the metaphor "liquid modernity," one which celebrates two new sub-metaphors: sex and the body. This movement from solidity to liquidity is underscored in Elmessiri's cognitive mapping of modernity and post-modernity.

In his book, *Al-Lughah wa al-Majāz: Bayna al-Tawḥīd wa Wiḥdat al-Wujūd* [Language and Metaphor: Between Monotheism and Pantheism], Elmessiri explores his basic assumption that the use of metaphor is "inevitable in most processes of cognition and articulation, particularly highly complex phenomena."[86] The entire motif of modern secular western thought, according to him, can be grasped in two major metaphors: (1) the organismic metaphor and (2) the mechanistic metaphor; both, however, celebrate closed systems that deny transcendence and pluralism, thus reducing human beings and human existence into the dynamics of nature/matter in the philosophical sense of the word.[87]

Elmessiri's mapping of modernity, like that of Bauman, usually starts with a critique of the Enlightenment as the starting point of "solid rational materialism" that (mis)used science and philosophy to legitimize the construction of secular ideologies with a view to establishing an earthly paradise and realizing the end of history. The Enlightenment, as well as modernity at large, is seen as a secular worldview that celebrates the deification of man as the master of nature and the maker of history. Unlike the early Bauman who saw postmodernity as a chance to overcome the false consciousness of modernity, Elmessiri never saw postmodernity as an open system that promises pluralism, diversity and multiculturalism. Elmessiri, on the contrary, has been stressing from the outset that postmodernity or "liquid non-rational materialism" is not only an anti-metaphysical revolution but also a revolution against metaphysical materialism itself and the faith of humanism in the power of Reason to understand and change the world. Postmodernity is seen as a worldview that denies both history and referentiality because it declared the death of man in favour of such non-human categories as the market and power or in favour of such one-dimensional categories as the body, sex and pleasure.[88]

Like Bauman, Elmessiri used the notion of paradigm intuitively without any attempt at theorizing the term as an analytical tool, particularly in his early writings *The End of History* (1973) and *The Earthly Paradise* (1979). He, however, managed to develop this methodology through an extensive theorization and intensive elaboration on the meaning of paradigm and its elective affinity with metaphor as a trope of discourse in almost all of his later writings, particularly his eight-volume work *Mawsū'at*.

In almost all of Elmessiri's writings, the term paradigm is used, more often than not, in reference to an analytical tool and an immanent system through which people perceive and formulate their world. Like Bauman, Elmessiri does not equate the term paradigm with the world or reality because a paradigm "has no concrete existence and also because it is the fruit of a mental image, an intellectual system, a conceptual pattern, an abstract mental structure and a symbolic representation of truth."[89]

Aware of the fact that his manipulation of the term 'paradigm' stressed such terms as system and structure, Elmessiri emphasizes that he, unlike the structuralists, attempts to endow the human subject with an active role in the construction of paradigms and the process of interpretation. It is precisely for this reason that he always stresses that a paradigm is a mental construct or a cognitive map that the human mind abstracts from an enormous quantity of relations, details and facts.[90]

This process necessarily entails that the human mind is engaged in a serious process of inclusion, selection and exclusion so as to establish a general pattern that can stand as a valid interpretation of the relevant text, phenomenon or situation. In defining the term paradigm, Elmessiri equates the terms "cognitive" and "epistemological," especially when he maintains that a paradigm is "an epistemological map that the human subject abstracts…out of the events that he encounters, or the phenomena he examines, or the texts he reads."[91]

Commenting on the significance of the term "cognitive map," Elmessiri states that man is not simply a bundle of material desires, and that his mind is not a mere *tabula rasa* but a human being who is endowed with generative powers and a repository of many symbolic systems or a storehouse of conscious and unconscious images and memories. This map, like any paradigm, is not a fixed encrustation that does not change but a perception that can be challenged, thus giving rise to the possibility of a new vision or, to borrow Thomas Kuhn, a "Gestalt-switch."[92]

With his intensive elaboration on the meaning of paradigm, particularly in his *Mawsūʿat*, his intellectual autobiography and his book *Difāʿ ʿan al-Insān: Dirāsāt Naẓariyyah wa Taṭbīqiyyah fī al-Namādhij al-Murakkabah* [Defence of Man: Theoretical and Applied Studies in Complex Paradigms], Elmessiri has managed to distance himself from linguistic structuralism which attacks the notion of the subject, history and time in order to discover timeless, universal and absolute structures. Elmessiri always stresses that 'epistemological' and 'cognitive' paradigms revolve around three grand issues: (1) man and his relation to nature/matter, (2) the *telos* of existence and (3) the question of the ultimate point of referentiality.[93] With this conception of paradigms, not only has Elmessiri distanced himself from structuralism but also transcended Kuhn's definition of paradigm, endowing it with an ontological or even metaphysical dimension.

Here Elmessiri's contribution lies in his determination to ignore the western history of the term epistemology as he tends to equate it with both ontology and metaphysics. According to the *Oxford Companion to Philosophy* (2005), epistemology or the theory of knowledge is a branch of philosophy that explores the nature of knowledge, its possibility and general basis. Above all, epistemology is seen as the question of our cognitive stances and the right to our beliefs. Epistemology is usually explained by reference to the Cartesian method of doubt and the search for certainty. It comes as no surprise that Cartesian metaphysics was based on epistemological considerations. Ontology is concerned with the features of existence and Being. The question of metaphysics is also related to existence but in relation to the ultimate reality that transcends the boundary of possible experience. Both ontology and metaphysics were criticised by postmodernists and deconstructionists who favour cultural relativism rather than any objective conceptions of truth.[94]

Equating epistemology with both ontology and metaphysics can be attributed to the influence of the Islamic world view on Elmessiri's critique of modernity. This orientation can be seen as an inversion of the western world view and its 'epistemologically defined ontology.' In other words, the "ontologically determined epistemology" of the Islamic worldview, according to Ahmet Davutoğlu, can be seen as an alternative paradigm to the "epistemologically defined ontology" of the post-Renaissance western world view.[95]

But the dichotomy between Islam and western modernity cannot explain the nature and the dynamics of hermeneutics, especially hermeneutical ontology. Hermeneutical ontology or ontological hermeneutics, according to Stanley Rosen, can be defined as a method that "treats the text, whether a philosophical essay, a work of art, or a dream, or a sign, not of its own sense, but of some comprehensive theory of human existence, even of Being."[96]

Elmessiri's emphasis on the ontology of paradigms raises a very old hermeneutical problem. According to Paul Ricoeur, there has been a constant tendency to reduce fiction to illusion, thus closing the way to any "ontology of fiction."[97] However, the goal of metaphor is to shatter "not only the previous structures of our language, but also the previous structures of what we call reality....With metaphor we experience the metamorphosis of both language and reality."[98] Elmessiri's basic methodological assumption is that a paradigm is almost synonymous with the major and abstract theme or the major metaphor that endows a literary work (fiction in Ricoeur's terminology) with its unity and coherence. Metaphor thus becomes a paradigm for the explanation of the literary work since readers can "construct the meaning of the text in a way which is similar to the way in which we make sense of all the terms of metaphorical statement."[99]

Elmessiri's metaphorical methodology can be best introduced through a stimulating example. According to Elmessiri, when a critic approaches Shakespeare's *Macbeth*, he/she can trace the most significant metaphor i.e. the blood metaphor. This recurrent metaphor is used in reference to Macbeth's and Lady Macbeth's sense of guilt due to the crime they have committed as well their failure to conceal this unbearable feeling. The metaphor reaches its climax with Lady Macbeth committing suicide and Macbeth throwing himself into the "laps of determinism" and drowning in "seas of blood."[100]

Here one can argue that the terms metaphor and paradigm are almost synonymous with the Aristotelian *mythos*, which is, according to Paul Ricoeur, "the principal 'part' of the tragedy, its 'essence'; all other parts of the tragedy – the 'characters,' the 'thoughts,' the 'diction,' the 'spectacle' – are connected to the mythos as the means or the conditions of the performance of the tragedy as *mythos*."[101]

This methodology poses a challenge and requires us to raise the following questions: Does this definition of paradigm mean that we are going to approach western modernity as a metaphor, a play (as a tragedy to be more precise), a poem (an elegy perhaps), or a movie that has a certain beginning and well-known end? Is it all possible to use this methodological instrument in the fields of politics, philosophy, religion and sociology? Are paradigms nothing but closed systems that deprive western man, this abstract entity, of all potentials for transcending this text, movie or play, thus reducing him/her to our tragic hero Macbeth and/or our tragic heroine Lady Macbeth?

In Elmessiri's thought, paradigms cannot be equated with the world, truth, or reality because they are modest interpretative tools. Western man is approached as an abstract entity and a cohesive image consisting of a set of characteristics that are gradually engraved on the person's mind, heart and even the unconscious to the extent that he would be unable to see reality except through it.[102] In approaching modernity, it seems impossible, in Elmessiri's view, to do without such abstract categories as "man," "modern western civilization," "modern English civilization," "the Industrial Revolution" or the "Enlightenment," though we are fully aware that we are referring not to real referents residing in the world but to metaphorical expressions that can help us communicate and narrate the story. This methodology offers a modest product of a human perspective that aspires to reach only a degree of truth and not the whole truth because absolute objective knowledge is not only an impossible dream but also a terrible nightmare.[103]

This methodology is very close to Richard Bernstein's suggestion that our contemporary intellectual discourse attempts to go beyond the objectivism/relativism dichotomy. In his book *Beyond Objectivism and Relativism* (1983), Richard Bernstein points out that there has been a growing atmosphere of confusion, uncertainty and skepticism about foundations, methods and rational standards of explanation and interpretation of historical narratives, literary texts and the overall human condition. This state of confusion has given rise to an extreme version of relativism, one which frequently leads to cynicism and absurdism. Above all, the state of confusion becomes more complex due to the floating of such signifiers as "rationality," "objectivity" and "realism" as well as the difference in the fundamental attitudes of the interlocutors towards these signifiers and their explanatory or dogmatic power. Bernstein, however, argues that our intellectual discourse has been attempting to go beyond the opposition between objectivism and its connotations of foundationalism and scientific rationalism on the one hand and relativism and its connotations of skepticism and nihilism on the other. This orientation repudiates both absolutism and subjectivism in favour of a sophisticated form of "fallibilistic objectivism" or a "non-subjective conception of relativism."[104]

Here another stimulating example of Elmessiri's paradigmatic or metaphorical methodology can be introduced to highlight the modest aspirations as well as the explanatory power of the formulation of cognitive paradigms. Elmessiri used his skills in literary criticism to trace the change of characterization in different literary genres to explain the idea of paradigm and paradigm shift. He holds the view that against the paradigm of complex and heroic, though tragic, characters portrayed in eighteenth and nineteenth-century literature is set the modernist paradigm of anti-heroes suffering from loneliness and alienation as in T.S. Eliot's poem *The Waste Land*; from complete surrender to determinism as in Kafka's novels and from absolute absurdity as in Samuel Beckett's play *Waiting for Godot*.[105]

This conception of paradigm and paradigm shift echoes Georg Lukács in analysis of the ideology of modernism. The transformation of the image of man in literature, according to Lukács, is not just a change in artistic technique but a change in a worldview, especially the Heideggerian ontology of *Geworfenheit* (thrownness), which is used consciously or unconsciously by modernist writers who portrayed man as if he were "by nature solitary, asocial, unable to enter into relationships with other human beings" and as if this nightmarish and neurotic state is "an immutable *condition humaine*."[106]

The cognitive and interpretative function of paradigms has much in common with that of tropes of discourse, particularly metaphors and their ability to articulate complex relations that are difficult to be expressed in literal language or semi-algebraic terms. Elmessiri does not hesitate to define analytical cognitive paradigms as "intensive metaphors open unto reality."[107] This belief encouraged him to conclude that it is possible to examine the history of ideas and cognitive paradigms through a selective and exclusive examination of the development and the transformation of cognitive metaphors.[108]

This emphasis on the significance of metaphors can be traced in Elmessiri's *Al-ʿĀlam min Manẓūr Gharbī* [The World from a Western Perspective] in which he refers to the influence of the New Criticism on his thought. Elmessiri embraced the New Critical notion that poetry and metaphor are issues related to our human existence and that "close reading" could result in the imposition of a certain meaning on the text, a meaning that has never been intended by the poet or the author.[109]

The analysis of metaphors plays a crucial role in this process since the adoption of a specific metaphor is not only an act of linguistic criticism but also a process of identification with a specific worldview. In the introduction to *Epistemological Bias in the Physical and Social Sciences*, Elmessiri stresses that the metaphors that dominate western thought cannot be approached as neutral descriptive figures of speech because the use of the adoption of a particular metaphor creates an "elective affinity" between the scholar and the worldview represented by the metaphor.[110] Elsewhere Elmessiri underlines the fact that his metaphorical methodology can be attributed partly to his study of Romantic theory and poetry, both of which see the truth not as a thing added to phenomena and reached by reason but as something inherent in the phenomena and felt by the human subject.[111] It is interesting also to note that the house in which Elmessiri lived in Damanhur followed the design of Art Nouveau, an architectural design which appeared in Europe between 1890 and 1910 as a "part of the Western man's Romantic revolution against an industrial and mechanical society."[112]

Elmessiri insists that human language, unlike the language of algebra and geometry, is not an unbiased tool, which can adequately describe the world of unbiased facts.[113] Though aware of the modest role of interpretation, Elmessiri has great expectations similar to those of Maasen and Weingart who stress that metaphor analysis might uncover "paradigm shifts, the emergence of a new *Zeitgeist*, or the rise and fall of general world views."[114] Metaphors cannot be reduced to the process of transferring old lexical meanings to new objects because they are literally "ways whereby societies 'build' webs of collective meaning; create...*cultural cosmologies* or meaning-worlds that, once built, for better or worse become the 'homes' in which we reason and act, places that constrain without determining any of our particular conclusions or actions."[115]

Within this methodology, metaphors are viewed as a fertile source of cognitive mapping, since they enable us to uncover similarities, relationships and structures between various categories and phenomena. Metaphors are ubiquitous because they dominate our conceptual system and structure our worldview and the very understanding of human existence.[116] Metaphors have an epistemological authority, one which shows clearly in the metaphors of wholeness, extending "not just across domains of nature and culture, but into domains of pragmatic politics as well."[117] The transferability of metaphor is traced from the scientific discourse of biology to the discourse of politics and every day communication (and vice versa) or, to borrow Friedrich Engels, from "natural history" into the "history of society." This process may involve a deliberate misuse of metaphors, especially when ideologies are "elevated to the level of scientific truths."[118] The transfer of Darwin's oft-quoted metaphor "struggle for survival" is often mentioned in connection with the German context where 'struggle for existence' was translated to "*Kampf ums Dasein*" and had a devastating role in the politics of Germany up to the Second World War.[119]

II

Radical Enlightenment

THE term Enlightenment found its way to English discourse only in the nineteenth century, though there were remarks made by English writers and poets during the eighteenth century, celebrating the metaphor of light as in Alexander Pope's oft-quoted lines: "Nature and Nature's laws lay hid in night/God said, let Newton be! And all was light." The same motif had been celebrated in the French *Lumiere* (light), the Italian *Illuminismo*, the German phrases *Aufklärung und Licht, Freiheit und Licht* (Enlightenment and Light, Liberty and light). The light metaphor covered a wide range of positive connotations, including the discovery of the hidden laws of Nature, scientific rationalism and freedom.[1] This chapter is devoted to the light metaphor, the role of intellectuals of the Enlightenment and the term Nature as the code of secular modernity.

2.1 *SAPERE AUDE!* AND THE LIGHT METAPHOR

'*Was ist Aufklärung?*' ('What is Enlightenment?') was the question raised by the monthly periodical *Berlinische Monatsschrift* in 1784. The question was answered by Immanuel Kant in an article that bears the same interrogative form. The main argument in his answer to this question is rendered in only two words: *Sapere aude!* i.e. "Have the courage to use your own reason!" The Enlightenment is thus seen as man's release from his self-incurred tutelage, which is nothing but the inability to make use of his understanding without direction from others.[2]

But neither the Kantian *Sapere aude* nor the light metaphor has an explanatory power that can render the cognitive mapping of the Enlightenment as a complex narrative category. The Enlightenment, according to the *Encyclopedia of Philosophy* (1967), is a mental construct or an abstract idea that designates a long historical period, roughly eighteenth-century Europe. In most western languages, the French philosophers of the period were known as *les philosophes*, not philosophers, on the ground that they were not systematic philosophers but intellectuals who admired the natural sciences and showed a considerable contempt for metaphysics. They were influenced by seventeenth-century philosophers like Bacon, Descartes, Locke and Newton. The Enlightenment as an abstract paradigm is often approached as a cluster of three major ideas, namely, Nature, Reason and Progress; all of which refer to the standards and laws that can establish a rational and progressive system as opposed to the "unnatural," and "irrational" burdens imposed by Judeo-Christian traditions. Unlike the latter, the rational Enlightenment envisaged the possibility of reaching a state of perfection without waiting for a second coming of Christ and the Garden of Eden. In this sense the Enlightenment is related to the ideals of rationalism, humanism and the optimistic faith in man's ability to achieve happiness and paradise on earth via a strong belief in science and reason as the fundamental instruments of salvation and human progress.[3]

The Enlightenment is also associated with Cartesian rationalism, which came later to signify the establishment of universal, essential and ideal standards of science, art and aesthetics. These standards can be seen as a typical representation of the myth of Prometheus, which celebrates the self-sufficiency of human power and the urging drive to place man at the centre of the universe, signalling his ability to discover the laws of Nature and his determination to achieve progress without any reference to teleological or metaphysical terms.

Bauman traces this Promethean idea and points out that it derives its power from Hesiod's poem and Aeschylus's play. The former attributes Prometheus's punishment to his arrogant attempt to change the pre-established order by cheating the gods in the division of sacrificial meat. The latter, on the other hand, relates his punishment to his brave initiative that made the arts of life, including medicine and mining, available to all human beings. Aeschylus's Prometheus is not represented as a criminal but as a "persecuted hero" who stands for the advance of humanity. He stands for the courageous act that has strengthened the belief in man's ability to control both time and place.4

The domination of nature and the rational conquest of space, according to David Harvey, were seen as an integral part of the modernizing project and even a necessary or perhaps a sufficient condition of human emancipation. But the organization of both space and time was not meant to reflect the glory of God but to "celebrate and facilitate the liberation of 'Man' as a free and active individual, endowed with consciousness and will."5

Bauman argues that this process involved a relentless war against the tropes of the Other of order: undecidability, incoherence, incongruity, incompatibility, illogicality, irrationality, ambiguity, confusion, undecidability, ambivalence. The war against ambivalence, as Bauman calls it, is the most decisive defining feature of modern life, politics and intellect. The attempt to overcome ambivalence becomes almost synonymous with the attempt to intensify progress, viewed as an 'obsessive [materialist] movement forward' or as the '[materialist] movement with a pointer.' What is common among these metaphors is the emphasis that the western notion of progress is nothing but a linear 'unstoppable movement' against ambivalence and all its negative connotations as if "full clarity means the end of history [and the establishment of the Earthly paradise]."6

The metaphor of progress has turned metaphysical eschatology into a secular version immanent in history. *Les philosophes* were obsessed with the idea of progress, and their excessive materialist philosophy usually led to comic reductionism of the complex humanity. D'Holbach, for example, conceived of human history as part of the biologically and chemically determined *histoire naturelle*, arguing the spread of Islam can be attributed to Prophet Muhammad's (ṢAAS)[*] physiology i.e. the particles of his blood, the texture of his fibres, the salts and the proportion of fluid in his system.[7]

2.2 GARDENERS AND LEGISLATORS

The emphasis on rationalism, science and Reason has led Bauman to look for a new metaphor that can be contrasted with the metaphor of the gamekeeper which he used to describe the pre-modern or traditional role of human beings. The advent of modernity required a new metaphor that can describe the new emerging reality. Bauman introduces the "gardener" metaphor to characterize the new role assigned to human beings. Against the traditional role of the game-keeper is set the modern secular role of the gardener who stands for modern man's effective intervention and the determination of the human will to create paradise on Earth. As Bauman suggests, "modern culture is a garden culture. It defines itself as the design for an ideal life and a perfect arrangement of human conditions."[8] Modernity, unlike the long rule of Christianity, "rebuffed the obsession with the afterlife, focused on the life 'here and now,' redeployed life activities around different narratives with earthly targets and values, and all–in–all attempted to defuse the horror of death."[9] Modernity required adven-turous or even rebellious 'gardeners' rather than mere humble game-keepers because a gardener

> assumes that there would be no order in the world at all, were it not for his constant attention and effort. Gardeners know better what kind of plants should, and what sort of plants should not grow on the plot entrusted to his care. He [sic] works out the desirable arrangement first in his head, and then sees to it that this image is engraved on the plot. He forces his pre-conceived design upon the

---

[*] (ṢAAS) – *Ṣallā Allāhu ʿalayhi wa sallam*: May the peace and blessings of God be upon him. Said whenever the name of the Prophet Muhammed is mentioned.

plot by encouraging the growth of the right type of plants and uprooting and destroying all the others (now re-named 'weeds'), whose uninvited and unwanted presence disagrees with the overall harmony of the design.[10]

Keith Tester argues that the word 'gardening' was coined by Ernest Gellner (1925-1995) and extended by Bauman as a metaphor for the modern strategies of improvement introduced by the political and the intellectual discourse in the course of the eighteenth century in the attempt to establish a "new and self-sufficient social life."[11] The garden metaphor, however, is as old as history itself. Almost a century before Gellner was even born, T.H. Huxley (1825-1895) accepted the Hobbesian interpretation of Darwinism and used this metaphor in his comparison of the ethical process to the work of the gardener. Richard Hofstadter puts it this way:

> Instead of encouraging, horticulture restricts multiplication of the species. Like horticulture, human ethics defies the cosmic process; for both horticulture and ethical behaviour circumvent the raw struggle for existence in the interest of some ideal imposed from without upon the process of nature.[12]

However, unlike T.H. Huxley, Gellner embraced neither the assumptions of Hobbes nor those of Darwin. On the contrary, he represented the garden metaphor in an extremely ironic tone:

> Cultures, like plants, can be divided into savage and cultivated varieties. The savage kinds are produced and reproduce themselves spontaneously, as parts of the life of men.... Cultivated or garden cultures are different, though they have developed from the wild varieties. They possess a complexity and richness, most usually sustained by literacy and by specialized personnel.[13]

Bauman maintains that this orientation can be best described through the metaphor of the "geometric grid," one which he regards as the ruling trope that underlines the intensity of the project of modernity and its attempt to squeeze the world into "geometrically inspired grids."[14] It comes as no surprise then that the designers of utopias chose architecture and urban planning as both the "vehicle and the master-metaphor of the perfect world that would know of no misfits and hence of no disorder."[15] The metaphors of "architecture" and "urban planning" are used to suggest that the intellectuals and the nation-state were determined to view the material and the social space as a vacuum to be shaped and manipulated effectively. The saddest irony, in Bauman's view, is that the process of getting rid of ambivalence leads to an endless state of ambivalence and an infinite process of inclusion and exclusion:

> Order is continuously engaged in the war of survival. The other of order is not another order: chaos is its only alternative. The other of order is the miasma of the indeterminate and unpredictable. The other is the uncertainty, that source and archetype of all fear. The tropes of the other of order are: undecidability, incoherence, incongruity, incompatibility, illogicality, irrationality, ambiguity, confusion, undecidability, ambivalence.[16]

The emergence of western modernity is seen as a marriage of convenience between what Richard Rorty refers to as "foundational politics" and what Bauman refers to as "foundational philosophy;" both aspired to establish unshakable truth, full clarity and absolute perfection. Foundational modernity set its epistemological grounds in all realms of human existence, including politics and the theory of knowledge. Bauman puts it this way:

> In the political realm, purging ambivalence means segregating or deporting strangers, sanctioning some local powers and delegalizing the unsanctioned ones, filling the 'gaps in the law.' In the intellectual realm, purging ambivalence means above all delegitimizing all grounds of knowledge that are philosophically uncontrolled or uncontrollable. More than anything else, it means decrying and invalidating 'common sense'– be it 'mere beliefs,' 'prejudices,' 'superstitions' or sheer manifestations of 'ignorance.'[17]

The absolute monarch, according to Bauman, was the first model of the modern state as he transformed the inhabitants from feudal subjects into citizens. The "legislating," "crusading," and "missionary" authority of the state was so absolute that the king played the "role of God" and both scientists and intellectuals conceived of the society as a "free, unoccupied space," "a sort of a political no man's land" and an "empty land to be colonized, given laws, knitted into a selected pattern."[18] Elsewhere Bauman introduces a key metaphor that shapes his understanding of foundational modernity: "[M]odern rulers and modern philosophers were first and foremost legislators; they found chaos, and set out to tame it and replace it with order."[19] The legislators are not ordinary human beings but supermen who can transcend the existing reality and examine it from the outside using their God-like gaze. They included:

> [T]he benevolent despot; the Legislator; the Philosopher; the Scientist – all of them belonged to the family of Supermen who by dint of miraculous power, omnipotent technology or ability to wrench its secrets from History, were able to unravel and bring to their less endowed fellows the ideas which, in a sense, were 'not from this world.' This answer is still very much with us, deep down in the common-sense of the twentieth century, manifesting its presence in whatever has been left of our almost uncritical faith in the ability of science and the scientists to pave the way to a better and more congenial future: though, to be sure, it posed in this latter version a new, but equally vexing and antinomial question of how science, this completely technical-instrumental venture, can possibly tell good from evil.[20]

Bauman traces the role of the legislator back to Plato's *The Republic*, emphasizing that the attempt to perform this role is a permanent pattern that culminated in the modern age. Philosophers imagined that unless human beings comply with the world designed according to their "canvas of imaginary bliss," they will never enjoy absolute peace and the world will become nothing but a "lunatic asylum."[21] Unlike Socrates who chose to play the modest role of the interpreter to improve the citizens' *doxa* through dialogue, Plato, according to Hannah Arendt, aspired to educate the citizens, denouncing *doxa* and assuming the role of the legislator who sets absolute standards, rules and yardsticks.[22]

In order that Bauman thickens the metaphor of the legislators, he traces other significant metaphors introduced by influential figures in European intellectual history. Thomas Hobbes, for example, introduced the metaphor of "the state of nature" in connection with the nasty and brutish life in which the dominant atmosphere is one of "war of all against all" or a struggle of wolves attacking one another; *homo homini lupus*. According to Bauman, this image has a tremendous impact on the last three centuries of European intellectual history as it had been used, more often than not, to justify the discourse on the opposition between nature and passions on the one hand and culture and reason on the other. One of the major consequences of this metaphor, in Bauman's view, is the "recasting of the way of life of the poor and lowly as a product of human animal nature, inferior to, and at war with, the life of reason"; and therefore, humans are justified to become "objects for cultural gardeners."[23] The "gardener" and the "legislator" metaphors are meant to highlight the intricate relationship between culture and power. Richard Kilminster and Ian Varcoe uncover this motif in Bauman's works, showing how he sees modernity as a general structuring or ordering drive, and how the urge to structure has always created new "problems."[24]

Bauman stresses that Reason was embraced by the intellectuals of the Enlightenment in order to promote human emancipation and to eliminate prejudice, ignorance, superstition and dogmatism. The saddest irony is that it has led, in the final analysis, to "a new bondage," "terror," and "monopolistic knowledge."[25] The liberal vision of cultural assimilation, Bauman believes, is one of the main contradictions of modernity because "the game of emancipation was in fact the game of domination." The irony that lies at the heart of this matter is that emancipation was not a call for diversity, cultural exchange, cultural diffusion or pluralism but a call for uniformity, homogeneity and comprehensive unification of the population. This orientation led to a growing atmosphere of "intolerance to difference."[26]

The saddest irony is that man became an object of disdain and contempt. The contempt for the people, Bauman argues, is a recurrent motif in the writings of de Tocqueville, Diderot, D'Alembert and

Voltaire. In an ironic tone, Bauman affirms that the image of man as a selfish beast "was very much an axiom to *les philosophes*, who never neglected an opportunity to manifest their disdain for the ignorant, mentally inept masses."[27] This perception of the Enlightenment deconstructs the light metaphor and uncovers the radicalism of *les philosophes* who "saw in the unenlightened world nothing but error, superstition, darkness and barbarism."[28]

Bauman reveals the stimulating idea, contrary to dominant secular western and Arab beliefs, that the Enlightenment project was not a noble dream of spreading the light of wisdom and freedom. Rather, it aimed at promoting the ambitions of the state and creating a "social mechanism of disciplining action."[29] The word culture itself became the "master metaphor for the new mechanism of social reproduction – both designed and centrally operated."[30] The Enlightenment is not seen as a metaphor for light, liberty, illuminating reason and freedom. The Enlightenment mapped by Bauman unmasks "instrumental and terroristic reason" as well as "racism of the intellectuals."[31]

2.3 *LES PHILOSOPHES*: ADVOCATES OF ENDARKENMENT

Like Bauman, Elmessiri was interested in the other face of the Enlightenment. The light metaphor is not different from mainstream metaphors in Western philosophy and politics; it hides more than it reveals. Elmessiri puts it this way:

> Light in human consciousness is the opposite of darkness in the same way good is the opposite of evil. Thus the Enlightenment metaphor (light-like thought which forces dark-like ignorance to disappear) does not differ from other common metaphors in philosophical and political discourses that see the world through a set of simplistic and inflexible binary oppositions, such as pigeons/hawks, civil state/religious state, and mechanism/organicism.[32]

Elmessiri, unlike Bauman, does not refer metaphorically to the intellectuals as legislators. Rather, he explicitly refers to *Les philosophes* as "advocates of endarkenment" and "seductive carriers" of simplistic mechanistic and/or organismic ideas.33 Unlike Bauman, who puts François Voltaire (1694-1778), Jean Jacques Rousseau (1712-1778), Denis Diderot (1713-1784), Jean le Rond D'Alembert (1717-1783), Paul d'Holbach (1723-1789) and Alexis de Tocqueville (1805-1859) in one and the same category on the ground that their contempt for the masses is a recurrent motif in their writings, Elmessiri goes beyond this simple issue and attempts to relate the role of the intellectuals to the ontological and epistemological foundations of modernity. In his attempt to discover the paradigmatic foundation of western modernity, Elmessiri does not hesitate to put Niccolò Machiavelli (1469-1527), Thomas Hobbes (1588-1679), John Locke (1632-1704), Baruch de Spinoza (1632-1677), Isaac Newton (1643-1727), Jean Jacques Rousseau (1712-1778) and many others in one and the same category. The whole philosophical and scientific output of each one of them is discussed in reference to an oft-quoted word or phrase (usually a metaphor) so as to discover the paradigmatic foundation of modernity. The logical consequence is that we will be presented with a seemingly consistent map but one which is also acknowledged to be subjective and biased; especially when no reference is made to the wide interest in developing medicine, physics, mathematics, mechanics and law. The map of the modern world as drawn by Bauman and Elmessiri does not stress the revolutionary republican ideas, the development of the theory of the separation of powers or the advocation of tolerance among religious beliefs. The comprehensive worldview of the Enlightenment is seen as more important than its details and procedures.

Elmessiri conceives the Enlightenment as "the philosophical basis of comprehensive secularism."34 Like Bauman, he believes that the roots of the Enlightenment can be traced back to the age of reason in the seventeenth century and the beginnings of the eighteenth century, especially in the writings of Francis Bacon (1561-1626), Thomas Hobbes (1588-1679), Rene Descartes (1596-1650), Spinoza (1632-1677), John Locke (1632-1704), Isaac Newton (1642-1727), and Leibniz (1646-1716). The movement was not confined to a single country and was prominent in France, Germany, England and the United States, respectively: Jean Jacques Rousseau (1712-1778),

François Voltaire (1694-1778), Montesquieu (1689-1755), Denis Diderot (1713-1784), Julien La Mettrie (1709-1751) and Paul d'Holbach (1723-1789); Christian Wolff (1679-1754), Moses Mendelssohn (1729-1786), Gotthold Ephraim Lessing (1729-1781), Kant (1724-1804) and Johann Herder (1744-1803); Joseph Priestley (1733-1804), Jeremy Benthem (1748-1832), and Adam Smith (1723-1790); Thomas Paine (1737-1809), Thomas Jefferson (1743-1826) and Benjamin Franklin (1706-1790).35

Elmessiri, however, argues that the Enlightenment reached its paradigmatic, monistic and rationalistic moment in the thought of the eighteenth-century French *encyclopédistes*. Not surprisingly he focussed only on their materialist philosophy which reflected the mechanistic and/or organismic paradigms of the Enlightenment. In other words, the manifestations of radical Enlightenment are discussed in reference to the writings that celebrate the world as a mechanistic and/or organismic existence: La Mettrie's *Histoire Naturelle de l'Âme* (1745) and *L'Homme Machine* (1748); Claude Adrien Helvétius's *De l'esprit* (1758) and *De l'homme* (1773); Paul d'Holbach's *Système de la nature ou des loix du monde physique & du monde moral* (1770); Pierre Jean Cabanis's *Rapports du physique et du moral de l'homme* (1802); and Marquis de Condorcet's *Esquisse d'un tableau historique des progrès de l'esprit humain* (1795).36

According to Elmessiri, Rousseau and *les philosophes* tried to seduce man into believing that the state of nature is actually a state of human bliss, a secular Garden of Eden. This vision is seen as a result of, or an interaction between, the metaphorical perception of man in the sixteenth and seventeenth centuries:

> Hobbes and Machiavelli cautioned us from the outset that man is…a wolf…Spinoza compared man to a piece of stone thrown by a powerful hand…Newton compared the whole world to a perfect machine, a watch that keeps on ticking endlessly and uniformly without any divine or human intervention…Locke compared the mind of man to a *tabula rasa* that indiscriminately registers all sense data.37

Elmessiri uses the Enlightenment as his point of departure in the critique of modernity in order to show that all the above-mentioned metaphors had a significant impact on the deconstruction of man as promoted by other western leading figures, including, to mention but a few, Adam Smith (1723-1790), Charles Darwin (1809-1882), Sigmund Freud (1856-1939) and Ivan Pavlov (1849-1936). Here Elmessiri resumes his argument:

> All of this gave rise to Adam Smith's image of man as living in a world regulated by an invisible hand, and a market regulated by the mechanical laws of supply and demand.... Darwin pointed out that Rousseau's Garden of Eden is not machine-like; it is a jungle that achieves harmony through the invisible hand of the struggle for survival and the survival of the fittest.... Freud came along and proved...that the jungle is actually within. Pavlov experimented on dogs, and applied his findings on man.... Man is thereby completely deconstructed.[38]

This metaphorical mapping is based on the assumption of uninterrupted continuity of the intellectual foundations of modern western thought. Elmessiri is aware of the existence of differences, discontinuities or ruptures but he attempts to go beyond them to find a paradigmatic foundation that supports his major distinction between man and Nature. It is true that Elmessiri's cultural bias as an Egyptian Arab Muslim who is fully aware of the atrocities of the West and its imperial legacy in the Middle East is a key element in the inclusion or the exclusion of details in the representation of the Enlightenment. However, Elmessiri's mapping of the Enlightenment can draw support from twentieth-century western historiography and from western revisionist critics and historians. In other words, it is true that subjectivity and ideology cannot be erased in the process of interpretation, but they are not obstacles to introduce more explanatory and more interpretative paradigms.

The Enlightenment as a metaphor for light, reason and freedom is mitigated and modernity at large is represented as a secular transgression against both God and man. Though aware of the existence of differences, discontinuities and ruptures, critics and historians attempt to go beyond them to find a paradigmatic foundation that supports their thesis. According to Jonathan Israel, there were two trends in the Enlightenment movement: Radical *philosophes* and moderate *philosophes*. The latter attempted to counter the former's ambitions to put an end to the entire system of social pressures by making Reason and Nature the ultimate points of reference but the radical mainstream dominated the intellectual scene. The Enlightenment moderate trend "simply proved unable clearly and cogently to win the intellectual battle."39

Elmessiri's critique of the Enlightenment has much in common with the fierce attack launched by twentieth-century historiography against the materialists in general and Julien Offray de La Mettrie (1709-1751) in particular. *Les philosophes* as a group have been accused of being responsible for the rise of the totalitarian state, the ills of the twentieth century and nihilism which denied man a special place in the universe. The Enlightenment legacy is reduced to a materialist view that shows perfectly in La Mettrie's fundamental works on the philosophy of nature: *L'Histoire naturelle de l'âme*, *L'Homme machine*, *L'Homme plante* and *Le Système d'Épicure*. The repudiations of materialists as "purveyors of scandalous ideas" are attributed to the fact that they were singled out by Karl Marx, thus making it easy for historians to hold them accountable for the ills of the twentieth century, the practices of communist regimes, the rise of totalitarian governments and even the Holocaust.40

This view might be seen as nothing but a reduction of modernity to the "dark side of modern society" which was anticipated by Max Horkheimer and Theodor Adorno in *Dialectic of Enlightenment*, originally published in 1944 under the title *Philosophische Fragmente*. This critique was later taken to an extreme by Herbert Marcuse in his *One-Dimensional Man* (1964). Elmessiri might be easily accused of being influenced by the tragic and pessimistic cultural critique of the Frankfurt School, the Weberian critique of rationalism and the metaphors of the 'iron cage' of modernity and the 'disenchantment of the world.' As Bernstein suggests, we can see clearly that twentieth-century critiques of the Enlightenment and rationalism "can be understood as variations of Weberian themes."⁴¹ It comes as no surprise then that Elmessiri has devoted an entire chapter his book *Epistemological Studies in Western Modernity* to the representation and analysis of Weber's theory of rationalization. Elmessiri is thus close to all western critiques that prophesied that the twentieth century would be the era of rationalization that colonizes and reshapes our everyday life.

The rational materialism of the Enlightenment makes man and/or Nature as the ultimate point of reference. It is attributed to a western discourse promoted by well-known intellectuals who perceived of nature as *kosmos* or *natura*, one which presupposed teleological and anthropic as well as physical meanings. As Dupré suggests, there had been a radical break once the human subject became the source of meaning, reducing nature to 'subordinate' and 'instrumental' position. Alchemists saw the possibility of reshaping 'parasitical growth into organic matter' and mechanist philosophers promoted the belief in the atomistic nature of the universe, the general passivity of matter and the self-supporting and self-moving cosmos.⁴²

Though aware of the Greek legacy of the aesthetic vision of nature as a form of perfection, Elmessiri has decided to represent it as the passive/active 'matter' that signals either man's power to be a superman who can reshape reality or nature's potential to transform man into a sub-man who cannot transcend its physical and materialist laws. Elmessiri's argument is based on his belief that with the advent of modernity the idea of nature has been embraced as the ideology of progress rather than an aesthetic form reflecting the perfection of a divine paradigm. This shows in a number of metaphors that can be easily traced and analysed to map the foundations of modern western thought or what he refers to as 'solid rational materialism': the human mind as *tabula rasa* (John Locke); the absolute state as the *Leviathan* or a raging dragon (Thomas Hobbes); the world as a machine (Issac Newton); the state as an absolute god (Friedrich Hegel); the world as an iron cage (Max Weber); the world as a botanical organism (Talcott Parsons); and man as Prometheus, Faust, Napoleon, and Tarzan (Nietzschean *Übermenschen*). According to Elmessiri, all the aforementioned western metaphors are sub-metaphors that have to be weaved into two major paradigms or metaphors: the mechanistic and the organismic.[43]

Elmessiri's argument has its roots also in western self-scrutiny discourse. According to *The Encyclopedia of Philosophy* (1967), a close examination of the history of western philosophy shows that it has been characterized by the oscillation between the mechanistic and organismic metaphors. Descartes, for example, conceived of animals as pure machines and men as machines with minds, thus making a compromise between his scientific aims and his Christian view of man. It was John Locke, however, who managed to go beyond this mechanistic philosophy and demarcate man from animals, on the ground that animals lack the powers of abstraction and articulation, though possessing some sensory ideas and a degree of reason. Erasmus Darwin, however, introduced a new speculative theory of evolution as a process of filamentation through all plants and animals to man. Later the mechanistic metaphor was reinforced by La Mattrie in his controversial book *L'Homme machine* (1748), which mitigated the Cartesian ethical and theological aspects of the human mind. With Charles Darwin, the story of the organismic metaphor reaches its climax, declaring that man is a part of nature, precisely a part of the animal kingdom.[44] Living organisms and machines are seen as closed, self-sufficient and self-referential systems. This perception precludes not only transcendent metaphysics but also the advocation for a special method to deal with uniquely human phenomena.[45]

Elmessiri rejected both organismic and mechanistic visions and included them among the metaphors of immanence, which is inconsistent with a monotheistic worldview that espouses the idea of transcendence. Elmessiri emphasizes that the original intention of the Enlightenment was to emancipate man from the shackles of ignorance, to place him at the centre of the universe and to stress his freedom, transcendence and mastery over nature. Ironically, the proponents of the Enlightenment were convinced that man is also an organic part of organic nature and thus governed by the same materialistic laws governing physical phenomena. Hence, no wonder perhaps that the attempt at transcendence has been transformed into immanence, and the aspiration for freedom has turned into biological and physical determinism. In short, human beings were not conceived as unique human individuals and were conceived instead as the children of nature.[46]

Elmessiri argues that the metaphor of organismic and mechanistic progress has been transformed into a real driving force of human history. "The advocates of Endarkenment" come to believe that progress is capable of answering almost all questions related to human existence and the ultimate goals of life. More importantly, they tried to impose on the rest of the globe this worldview on the ground that Europe is the best, if not the only, model of progress and the ultimate point of reference against which all other temporalities and human modes of existence are measured. This is why universality and homogeneity were declared to be the ultimate goals of progress and human existence itself. Elmessiri, like Bauman, comes to the realization that progress is almost equated with a movement with a direction towards full clarity, full control, perfect harmony, earthly felicity and, in short, the end of History:

> All materialistic utopias (technocratic utopias)…celebrate an entirely idealistic image of man, one who is as perfect as bees, ants and highly systematic animals [an organismic metaphor]. The latter are organisms living logically and mechanically like robots [a mechanistic metaphor] indulged in materialistic rationalization from head to toe…. They do not bear any moral burdens, since they behave according to their mechanical nature, one that recognizes neither good nor evil, neither anxiety nor the grand issues of human existence.[47]

In materialistic utopias, the metaphor of progress has become an essential ingredient of western modernity. The cultural bias of this metaphor shows in denial of the right of traditional localities and foreign cultures to difference and even existence, since the West represents modern culture and the rest stands for so-called pre-modern cultures that are given only three options: colonization, assimilation or extermination.

Les philosophes or the Enlightenment intellectuals turned meta-physical eschatology into a secular version immanent in history; they were obsessed with the idea of progress and an excessively materialist philosophy. They, especially Diderot, regarded themselves as educators who are capable of teaching magistrates the meaning of justice, the soldiers the meaning of patriotism and the priests the nature of God.[48]

Not surprisingly, Elmessiri saw the myth of Prometheus as the fundamental secular metaphor that can truly describe the orientation of the Renaissance and the Enlightenment. Prometheus, in Elmessiri's view, is the "symbol of man who rebels against metaphysical powers, rejects their domination, develops science to defeat nature and becomes himself a self-sufficient god."[49] Elmessiri, however, under-scores the main contradiction in the Enlightenment, affirming that its idealistic vision was accompanied, paradoxically, with the perception of man as a child of nature. In a private conversation with the author of this book, Elmessiri puts it this way:

> The dream of the human self that can apprehend, dominate and reshape reality was replaced by a self that had been deconstructed and reduced to material elements. Man becomes an indivisible part of a material becoming with no fixity, unity, transcendence or meaning.... [M]aterialist rationalism leads, in the final analysis, to materialist irrationalism."[50]

2.4 NATURE: THE CODE OF MODERNITY

A close examination of the critiques introduced by Bauman and Elmessiri shows that both of them see Nature as the major cultural concept whose thematic content constitutes the code of secular modernity. In other words, the Enlightenment and secularism can be understood only when the term Nature is decoded.

One of Bauman's earliest critical writings is *Towards a Critical Sociology: An Essay on Common Sense and Emancipation* (1976), which is a unique critical attempt at deciphering the term Nature as the basic code of secularism. The relevance of the term Nature to secularism is traced back to Francis Bacon who grasped, four centuries ago, the elusive dialectics of nature: Nature is only subdued by submission. In order that Bauman explains this struggle between man as the subject and Nature as the object, he introduces the metaphor of the sculptor (man/the subject) and the stone (nature/the object):

> Men experience nature in the same dual, equivocal way in which the sculptor encounters his formless lump of stone: it lies in front of him compliant and inviting, waiting to absorb and to incarnate his creative ideas – but its willingness to oblige is highly selective; in fact, the stone has made its own choice well before the sculptor grasps his chisel. The stone, one could say, has classified the sculptor's ideas into attainable and unattainable, reasonable and foolish. To be free to act, the sculptor must learn the limits of his freedom: he must learn how to read the map of his freedom charted upon the grain of the rock.[51]

According to Bauman, when this metaphor is extended so as to embrace the totality of the human condition, life then becomes the art of the possible, and science as the elimination of the impossible, the suppression of the unrealistic and the exclusion of morbid questions. This understanding of the relation of science to nature is extended by Bauman to the realm of human action in view of Max Weber's analysis of the necessary rules and laws of the bureaucratic machine that confronts individuals as a true reflection of a merciless and unchangeable Nature:

> In as much as science eliminates questions which lead to God, the scientifically informed action eliminates acts which lead to irrationality. Both employ nature, or nature-like necessity, as their lever. The price they willingly pay for the gain in efficiency is the agreement never to question its legitimacy. To be sure, this legitimacy cannot be questioned by science, just as it cannot be challenged by a rational action. Both are what they are in so far as nature remains the realm of omnipotent and unchallengeable necessity.[52]

In this context, Bauman refers to the conclusions reached by Comte de Buffon and Denis Diderot, respectively: (1) "Everything that can be, is" and (2) "opposed to nature, opposed to reason." These statements, in Bauman's view, do not just equate Nature with the inevitable and the unavoidable but also with the appropriate, the apposite, the good, the sacred and the undefiable:

> Nature supplies not just the boundaries of reasonable action and thought: it supplies reason itself. All valid knowledge is a reflection of nature. The power of man consists in his ability to 'know' what he cannot do. Science is there to teach him exactly this. This is the only way in which science 'is' power.[53]

Western modern thought, at least since Rousseau, has applied this concept of Nature to society. The latter became the locus of highest authority, the supra-human power, the Sovereign, the Ruler and the Legislator in charge of crushing the resistance of selfish bestiality. This image of man as a selfish beast to be tamed was an axiom to *les philosophes* whom Bauman compared to legislators in charge of setting the rules of secular truth-seeking and of legitimizing the centralized power of the state and its civilizing mission.[54] As modernizing elite, they launched a "cultural crusade" to redefine all cultural values and styles that they saw as signs or stigmas of backwardness, retardation or, in extreme cases, of insanity.[55] *Les philosophes* aspired to establish "the kingdom of Reason," but their "enlightened radicalism is revealed as the drive to legislate, organize and regulate, rather than disseminate knowledge."[56] The Enlightenment was thus very crucial to the "enthronement of the new deity, that of nature, together with the legitimation of science as the only orthodox cult, and scientists as its prophets and priests."[57]

The deification of society was complete with the emergence of sociology as the theory of modernity, especially in the writings of Emile Durkheim. This deification came within the context of the rapid secularization of French social and political life, a process which was so thorough that the will of society became "sufficient 'ratio' for moral commandments." Society became the only foundation, measure, and authority behind morality. The "liberating surrender" to God was replaced with the liberating surrender to the domination of society.

God is not quite dead in this context as Nietzsche would have it; He is just marginalized and replaced by a new authority.[58]

Like Bauman, Elmessiri argues that secularism in its solid phase is characterized by a struggle between two worlds: homo-centric or man-centred world and nature-centred world. In the liquid phase of secularism, the struggle ends in favour of the nature-centred world. The following comparison underlines Elmessiri's mapping of the central tendencies of the two overlapping worlds:[59]

Man-centred world	Nature-centred world
Man as the centre of the universe	Nature as the centre of the universe
Man as a subject	Man as an object
Nature as useful instrument	Man as an instrument of Nature/matter
Humanistic secular absolutes	Materialist secular absolutes
Imperialistic Reason (science & ethics without metaphysics)	Pragmatic Reason (functional & one-dimensional man)
Superman (Hitler, Stalin, etc.)	Subman (Adolf Eichmann)
Humanistic socialism	Scientific socialism
Humanistic utopia	Bureaucratic machine
Freedom in socialism and capitalism	Unfreedom in socialism and capitalism

Solid modernity, in Elmessiri's view, secularized Christian and non-Christian value systems, and it was characterized by a fierce struggle between these two paradigms, thus giving rise to humanistic secular absolutes (the movement of history, the will to power, the will of the people, the spirit of the people, the organic people or *Volk*, the white man's burden, the civilizing mission and the absolute state), and materialistic secular absolutes (historical determinism, ethnic determinism, the law of supply and demand, market/factory, interest or pleasure, laws of nature, ethnicity, class, and economic interests). God was thus replaced with different secular absolutes, including "Logos," "society" and "the proletariat." As for the metaphysical notions of the Hereafter, Resurrection and the Day of Judgment, they were replaced with such secular notions as "the verdict of History," "the end of History," "the technocratic utopia" and the "Earthly Paradise."[60]

In the liquid phase of secular modernity, the idea of transcendence is entirely eradicated, since the struggle between the subject and the object ends. The subject dissolves in the object, and the object dissolves in the subject. Causality, according to Elmessiri, is replaced with discontinuity, chance, and indeterminacy. The centrality of man and nature ends in favour of the centrality of perpetual becoming; all centres are deconstructed. This new condition might be seen as a sign of perfect pluralism, yet it is in fact a process of atomistic fragmentation that underlines the reign of relativism and the disappearance of such notions as truth, goodness, right and beauty. It is a transformation from "solid monism" (whether man-centred or nature-centred) to "comprehensive liquid monism" which recognizes no limits or constraints. According to Elmessiri, the possibility of transcendence as a result of the struggle between a man-centred world and nature-centred world is marginalized and even eliminated in "the age of liquid and comprehensive immanence."[61]

Elmessiri was so obsessed with decoding the term "nature" that he regarded it as his major philosophical question in decoding the essence of secular modernity. In the mid-1960s, Elmessiri wrote a study in English entitled "Competitive Capitalism and the Natural Man," which underlined the role capitalism played in transforming man from a complex human being into a mechanical being governed by the laws of nature and consumption.[62] When Noam Chomsky visited Cairo in 1994, Elmessiri admired his humanistic discourse, yet he did not accept his conclusions because they implicitly reduce man to the world of nature/matter. It is precisely for this reason that Elmessiri asked Chomsky the following rhetorical questions: "What is Nature? Do human beings have something that distinguishes them from Nature or are they merely part of it and cannot transcend it?"[63] On another occasion, in Berlin at *Haus der Kulturen der Welt*, Elmessiri had a heated debate with Mohammed Arkoun. The latter was advocating the dominance of the natural sciences whereas Elmessiri saw this dominance as a sign of the loss of man, stressing instead the need to emphasize the distinction between the natural sciences and the humanities. Elmessiri used this occasion to lavish praise on Immanuel Kant and representatives of the Frankfurt School who advocate the duality of man and nature. He even concluded his talk with the following strong statement: "I, as a Muslim intellectual, find myself a rightful heir to Kant and the Frankfurt school."[64] The contribution of the Frankfurt school in decoding the term "nature" helped Elmessiri decipher the term nature; and therefore, he did not hesitate to describe this critical school as the "best critique of comprehensive secularism and relativism."[65]

Though the idea of nature can be represented, from an Islamic perspective, as an aesthetic form reflecting the perfection of a divine paradigm, it is coded and decoded here as the ideology of progress. This act renders the terms "nature" and "matter" (thus naturalism and materialism) in a negative light and prepares the reader to suspect this ideology which, according to William Connolly, places both human and non-human nature at the disposal of humanity as material to work on.[66]

Elmessiri argues that modernity oscillates between two major paradigms or metaphors: the mechanistic and the organismic. The former represents the world as a machine whose motion is given by an external force whereas the latter portrays the world as a living organism whose growth is directed by an internal force. Both of them, however, exclude human potential for transcendence and celebrate the world of matter/nature. The "dominant paradigm" in modern western civilization oscillates between these two major metaphors.[67]

This view is also dominant in western critical discourse, especially when the rise of mechanistic philosophy went beyond the metaphysical connotations that Aristotle and the Scholastics attached to matter and nature. This philosophy, according to Louis Dupré, did not attempt to appeal to teleological arguments or final causes, emphasizing instead mathematical deduction. In other words, mechanism is a closed, autodynamic and self-generating system indifferent to any external influence, even though all that occurs within it is effected by a transcendent source of motion. The significance of this philosophical orientation lies in the fact that it conceived of the possibility that the human mind as the single source of meaning can capture all reality, one which is governed by identical mechanistic laws.[68] The turning point in the intellectual history of the West, according to Hannah Arendt, came when the image of organic life development emerged in place of the image of the watchmaker. This image led to the disappearance of the split between subject and object, one which is inherent in human consciousness and in the Cartesian opposition of man to a surrounding world.[69]

The focus on these changes in perception and worldviews is meant to show that the appearance of secularism is related to a deep structural and epistemological transformation of western societies and their perception of man, nature and history. Elmessiri's aim is to show that neither the mechanistic paradigm nor the organismic one is consistent with an Islamic worldview:

> The mechanistic metaphor cannot express the monotheistic vision as it assumes that the universe is nothing but a machine running [by an external force] aimlessly and without any purpose. Even the organic metaphor (the world as a plant or an animal) is impossible to be in harmony with monotheism as it sees the world as a closed and coherent totality [functioning by its inner laws] with no *lacunae* separating its constituent parts [only absolute and solid causalities], that is, as a self-sufficient and self-referential world.[70]

Elmessiri rejects the solid and absolute causalities of the comprehensive organic and mechanical paradigms because they aspire to control human existence and to put an end to History in the same way a merchant deals with the market or a scientist deals with the materials of his experiment:

> Both [mechanistic and organismic] paradigms help to generate a kind of knowledge that allows for an entire control of and mastery over reality ('imperialistic

knowledge'); such knowledge resembles the merchant's knowledge of the market which helps him predict the prices and the dynamics of the market. It also resembles the knowledge of a scientist who cannot carry out any experiment unless he entirely controls all variables and excludes uncontrollable factors. The knowledge sought by both paradigms is non-human; it aspires to explain everything, it leaves no spaces for other possibilities, and its results must be scientific or virtually final and absolute.[71]

In his attempt to uncover the cultural prejudice and epistemological bias of the metaphor of mechanistic and organismic progress, Elmessiri argues that it presupposes the existence of a linear universal human history and introduces the accumulation of knowledge and the control of human resources as the *telos* of human existence. Neither mechanical movement nor organismic growth is goal-oriented or teleological; both are monotonous operations indifferent to the unique notions of value, success, failure and choice.[72] Progress is almost equated with a movement with a direction towards full control, perfect harmony, earthly felicity and, in short, the end of History. This perception is not restricted to capitalist societies as it has also penetrated the worldview of Marxists, socialists and communists. Not surprisingly, Elmessiri, the formerly Marxist intellectual, draws our attention to the horrible fact that Marx, who repudiated injustice and exploitation and whose writings are littered with expressions and terms such as "human essence," "alienation" and even "transcendence," applauded the British colonization of India, and that Engels applauded the French colonization of Algeria. Elmessiri's critique of the notion of progress in both its capitalist and Marxist versions distances him from his former affiliation with Marxism and brings him closer to cultural bias as an Arab Muslim amidst western imperial legacy and Israeli occupation. It is hardly surprising that Elmessiri does not exclude Zionism from the ideology of materialist progress, especially when its adherents claimed that they had turned the desert green, thus justifying the injustice and oppression of the entire Palestinian nation.[73] Elmessiri's position led many of his disciples, friends, colleagues and Arab scholars to identify him as a proponent of a new Islamic discourse, a defender of Arabs and Muslims on the fronts of imperialism and Zionism. In 2004, this view was endorsed by many of Elmessiri's critics, disciples and friends in a two volume-work published in Cairo and entitled *Fī ʿĀlam Abdul Wahāb al-Mesīrī: Ḥiwār Naqdī Ḥaḍārī* [In the World of Abdelwahab Elmessiri: A Critical Civilizational Dialogue]. The same reception can be traced in another work published in Damascus in 2007 under the title *Abdul Wahāb al-Mesīrī: Fī ʿUuyūn Aṣdiqāihi wa Nuqādihi* [Abdelwahab Elmessiri in the Eyes of his Friends and Critics].

As we mentioned before, the same critique of the idea of progress is embraced by Bauman, thus distancing himself from his former affiliation with Marxism. The socialist critic of capitalism, in Bauman's view, was "modernity's most faithful and effective friend" and whatever the ugliness of its capitalist edition, modernity need not be disparaged. This ideology of progress is closely related to the end of History thesis; it is nothing but a linear "unstoppable movement" against ambivalence as if "full clarity means the end of history."[74] It represents a "radical break in universal history" and became "the reference point for the interpretation of the *telos* of history" giving itself the legitimacy and the right to "colonize the future in the same way it had colonized the surrounding space;" all other temporalities are seen as "retarded, underdeveloped, immature, incomplete or deformed, maimed, distorted and otherwise inferior stages or versions of itself."[75]

The progress metaphor is a major tool of mapping the mechanism of secular modernity, its ambitions and consequences. This metaphor, according to Eric Voegelin, played a significant role in the modification of the Christian idea of perfection, which is no longer conceived as a supernatural realm that can be reached only through grace in death by the sanctification, a notion which is clearly related to the notion of the pilgrim's progress. The progress metaphor and its utopian implications have been celebrated in Western discourse: Immanuel Kant (the unending progress of mankind); Nicolas de Condorcet (the unending progress of history and its acceleration through a directorate of intellectuals); Thomas More (the notion of utopia); Auguste Comte (the idea of a final state of industrial society under the temporal rule of positivist intellectuals); and Karl Marx (the notion of a final state of the classless realm of freedom through the rise of the communist man).[76]

Though Elmessiri did not refer to Eric Vogelin and his critique of the progress metaphor, it is still possible to trace his influence on Elmessiri. The first Western critic Elmessiri refers to in his search for revisions of secularism is the American Jewish writer Irving Kristol, dubbed as the "godfather of neoconservatism." Kristol is the missing link between Elmessiri and Voegelin. It is Kristol who turned to Voegelin's works to support his attacks on liberalism and the secular view of history. Secularism, according to Kristol, is more than science; it is a "religious view" which proceeds to make "metaphysical and theological inferences." By embracing this secular religion (*Ersatz Religion* or alternative religion in Voegelin's terminology), man can make or create himself (the deification of man). Playing the role of God, man can understand natural phenomena, control them and use them rationally to develop his condition on Earth. This is how this secular religion, according to Elmessiri, developed the idea of progress and became the ultimate framework of both liberalism and socialism.[77] As we will see in the next chapter, the critiques introduced by Voegelin can be regarded as Elmessiri's starting point in representing modernity as a gnostic narrative.

III

Modernity as a Gnostic Narrative

FREDRIC Jameson stated four key maxims or theses of modernity: (1) one cannot periodize; (2) modernity is not a concept but rather a narrative category; (3) subjectivity is unrepresentable and thus only situations of modernity can be narrated and (4) no 'theory' of modernity makes sense today unless it comes to terms with the hypothesis of a postmodern break with the modern.[1]

The four maxims stated by Jameson summarize the mechanism of cognitive mapping and its relationship with metaphorical paradigms. These maxims are very crucial to the metaphorical representation of the two major narratives of secular modernity as mapped by Bauman and Elmessiri: (1) gnosis and salvation, and (2) gnosis and utopia.

3.1 GNOSIS AND SALVATION

In *The Human Condition* (1958), Hannah Arendt points out that the dominant paradigm of academic philosophy has been celebrating the "never-ending reversals of idealism and materialism, of transcendentalism and immanentism, of realism and nominalism, of hedonism and asceticism."[2] Idealism and transcendentalism, as opposed to materialism and immanentism, have a long history in European and American philosophies. According to *The Encyclopedia of Philosophy* (1967), transcendentalism is often conceived of as the most remarkable American intellectual movement of the nineteenth-century and Ralph Waldo Emerson is regarded as one of its most influential advocates. The proponents of the movement were extremely influenced and inspired by Platonism, Indian mysticism and the writings of many romantic idealists like Samuel Taylor Coleridge, Immanuel Kant, and Fredrich Schelling. The movement repudiated 'psychological subjectivity' and placed a great emphasis on Reason as a form of conscience, subjective intuition and personal insight in establishing a rational system of moral idealism. Materialism and immanentism, on the other hand, do not refer to a psychological disposition to pursue money and private property but rather to a family of theories that give 'matter' a primary position. In their extreme versions, they assert that the world consists of material things; and therefore, it is seen as an attempt to create "metaphysics without ontology" with the "omnicompetence of natural science" in place of the "omnipotence of God."3

The metaphors of transcendence and immanence have been also a recurrent motif in the writings of influential twentieth-century figures. In *The Idea of the Postmodern* (1995) Hans Bertens stresses that these metaphors are central to the thought of Eric Voegelin who conceived modernity as a form of secular Gnosticism, and Ihab Hassan who depicted postmodern literature as Neo-Gnosticism.4 The metaphors of immanence and transcendence, according to George Siedel, have also been one of the major preoccupations of influential feminists, especially Simone De Beauvoir who attempted in *Le Deuxième Sexe* to introduce a "feminist epistemology" in which transcendence becomes simply the phallus, and immanence becomes nothing but the passive female virgin who is ready to be penetrated.5 So while Hassan's and Beauvior's bipolar metaphors of transcendence and immanence are very limited in their scope, (postmodern literature and feminist epistemology respectively), Voegelin's philosophy has a broader perspective. It is precisely for this reason that the best angle from which we can approach Bauman's and Elmessiri's interpretation of modernity as a Gnostic narrative is the bipolar metaphors of immanence and transcendence as interpreted by Voegelin.

Voegelin's understanding of gnosticism and/or immanence as the essence of modernity was first introduced in his book *The New Science of Politics* (1952) and was later deepened and extended in *Science, Politics and Gnosticism*, which first appeared in German in 1959, and was later translated by Henry Regnery in 1968. In the introduction to a new edition of *Science, Politics and Gnosticism* (1997), Ellis Sandoz states the two leading features of modern Gnosticism as understood by Voegelin: (1) immanentist programs to transform the world; and (2) the deification of man as superman, master of nature, and maker of history in the wake of the death of God. Voegelin's major argument, according to Sandoz, is that modernity did not do without the metaphor of transcendence but reversed its direction instead, thus transforming transcendence into gnosticism (the worship of knowledge). Vertical or otherworldly transcendence is renounced whereas horizontal transcendence or worldly salvific doctrines are proclaimed as the ultimate truth.[6]

Gnosis or knowledge becomes the only instrument of salvation and the establishment of a perfect earthly paradise. Unlike ancient gnosticism, in which deliverance is accomplished through faith in an alien and hidden God, modern gnosticism sees gnosis itself as the instrument of salvation and escape from the sickness and confusion of the world. Our understanding of modernity, according to Voegelin, will gain a new depth, if we can understand the contemporary critical struggle between modern ideologies and Christianity not as a struggle between 'modern' ideas and Christianity but as a renewal of the old struggle between Christianity and heretical Gnosis.[7]

Among the most significant movements that Voegelin labelled as gnostic are progressivism, positivism, Marxism, psychoanalysis, communism, fascism and National Socialism. Voegelin avoided the trap of tracing the origins of gnosticism and sought instead to explore its most decisive features: (1) a state of dissatisfaction with one's situation, (2) a belief in the poor or even wicked organization of the world; (3) a belief in the possibility of salvation from the evil of the world; (4) a belief in human action as the vehicle of change in the order of being and (5) the construction of a formula for self and world salvation. Voegelin's contribution lies in his attempt to trace this motif in the writings of major western philosophers, arguing that this aspiration for a final perfect world shows in the philosophy of Thomas More (1478-1535) and the ideal design for perfection; Thomas Hobbes (1588-1679) and the idea of the *Leviathan*; Immanuel Kant (1724-1804) and the unending progress of history; Marquis de Condorcet (1743-1794) and the immediate progress through a directorate of intellectuals; Friedrich Hegel (1770-1831) and the revelation of God in History; Auguste Comte (1798-1857) and the dominance of the positivist man; and finally Karl Marx (1818-1883) and the emergence of the communist superman.[8]

As Gerard Delanty points out in his unique study *Modernity and Postmodernity* (2000), a close examination of Bauman's critique of modernity shows clearly that it has much in common with that of Voegelin who saw modernity as the growth of gnosticism, a process or an orientation that necessarily deifies man and leads to the "immanen-tization of the Christian eschaton," giving rise to every modern movement from the Reformation to German National Socialism and even communism.[9] Modernity is seen by Bauman as an act of ontolog-ical separation, or rather an ontologically inauthentic escape from our worldliness or *Dasein* (being-there), that has led, in the final analysis, to the indifference to the sacred and more generally to our concern with other-worldly eternity.[10] This may seem to be a trivial and irrelevant indulgence in a theological dispute but it is actually the starting point of what Elmessiri also refers to as "immanentization" (God being incarnate in human beings, in one man, in an idea, in *einem Volk* or in an interpretation). Bauman refers to this idea of immanence as the celebration of the '*one and onliness*,' affirming that the death of God thesis has given rise to new secular Gods, such as Nature, Laws of History, Reason and Progress.[11] Human beings as moral subjects, according to Bauman, are expected to play a positive role against these notions: "It is solely in the struggle against such one and onliness that the human individual, and the human individual as a moral subject, a responsible subject and a subject taking responsibility for his responsi-bility, may be born."[12]

Though aware of the fact that the invention of new secular Gods aimed at constructing a utopian vision, Bauman never abandoned his belief in utopia as a dynamic force that enables us to go beyond the harsh realities of the human condition. Bauman views utopianism as the fountain of transformation, transcendence, and critical activity as opposed to the celebration of order, rigidity and structure that western modernity has been striving to achieve.[13] Aware of the consequences of modernity, Bauman criticizes the modern utopian project as it has reversed the direction of transcendence and thus transformed the metaphor of transcendence into a metaphor of transgression. Like Voegelin, Bauman sees this reversal as one of the central ambitions of the modern project, namely, the realization of self-transcendence and self-perfection in human beings. Bauman determines two closely related features of the modern spirit: (1) the urge to transcend and (2) the concern with the ability to act, even if this transcendence is transformed into a form of gnostic immanence or an act of transgression.[14]

This vigorous task of transformation is set in a sharp contrast with what Bauman refers to metaphorically as the traditional role of the "gamekeeper," one who stands for the fierce defence against human interference and all attempts at violating or disturbing God's perfect design. Due to traditions and a wide range of beliefs, human beings, especially within the framework of religious and theological paradigms, conceived of the end of history in the form of apocalypses and the last judgment. Tradition, according to Anthony Giddens, played a key role in "articulating action and ontological frameworks" and in creating a "sense of firmness of things that typically mixes cognitive and moral elements;" and therefore, there was an obvious lack of obsession with replacing the existing forms of life and people. Modernity, on the other hand, is a "post-traditional order" in which self-identity becomes a "reflexively organized endeavour" within impersonal organizations.[15]

Contrary to the foundations of modernity, the existence and the task of the "gamekeeper," in Bauman's view, derived their *telos* from God as the transcendental locus of all authority on the ground that the world is a "divine chain of being." Bauman uncovers the significance of the metaphor of the "gamekeeper," stressing that the services of the gamekeeper

> rest on the belief that things are at their best when not tinkered with; that the world is a divine chain of being in which every creature has its rightful and useful place, even if human mental abilities are too limited to comprehend the wisdom, harmony and orderliness of God's design.[16]

Bauman's metaphor of the "gamekeeper" echoes Hannah Arendt's elaborations on the old interpretations of the term *vita activa* and its negative connotations of complete human stillness and contemplation, whose justification rested on the conviction that no work of human hands can equate in beauty and truth to the physical cosmos. With the advent of modernity, according to Arendt, this term acquired new positive connotations or a "Promethean revolt," since it came to refer to the transformation of man from a mere *animal laboran* to a *homo faber* who conducts himself as "lord and master of the whole earth."[17]

Elmessiri, like Bauman, repudiates the ambitions as well as the consequences of the search for exclusive interpretation, absolute certainty and universal homogeneity, all of which are obvious manifestations of reductionist and monistic paradigms that attribute the movement and the end of history to only one force, whether spiritual (God-the *Führer*-the revolutionary mind-the greatest conspiracy) or materialist (the laws of dynamics-economy-body-sex). In short, Elmessiri, like Bauman, repudiates all worldviews that either reduce human reality to "nature/matter" or ignore the multiplicity and variety of our modes of being-in-the-world. This critical stance shows that Elmessiri's perception of modernity as a Gnostic narrative has striking similarities with Bauman's mapping of modernity as the monopolization of power, truth and existence within the "death of God" thesis.

Elmessiri's understanding of western modernity as almost synonymous with materialism in the philosophical sense is based on his celebration of the distinction between the metaphors of transcendence and immanence. This distinction is intimately tied to the former Muslim Bosnian President Alija Izetbegović's critique of western modernity. Izetbegović approaches western modernity as a monistic philosophy that takes the existence of matter as its starting point. This conception is set in a sharp contrast with the most central feature of Islam i.e. "bi-polarity": spirit/body, religion/science and culture/ civilization.[18]

Elmessiri uses the term "duality" to refer to the same conception of "bi-polarity," and he tries to introduce a new critique of western modernity on the assumption that western civilization lacks this aspect of bi-polarity or duality i.e. it is governed by a one-dimensional and one-sided materialist paradigm that gives priority to the triangle: body/science/civilization. Elmessiri calls this orientation "monistic materialism," a vision that ignores the distance between the two main bi-polarities, namely, the Creator and the created, man and nature. It is precisely for this reason that Elmessiri always emphasizes in all of his writings that the dissolution of the distance between these bi-polarities leads ultimately to the emergence of "the natural man" or what Herbert Marcuse refers to as the "one-dimensional man."[19]

In *Al-Ḥadāthah wa mā Baʿda al-Ḥadāthah* [Modernity and Post-modernity], Elmessiri points out that the dominant western paradigm celebrates nature/matter as the moving force of history and the uni-verse. This materialist paradigm has been dominating not only the public and the private spheres but also almost the "entire cognitive map" through which western man perceives the world and his salva-tion. Elmessiri, however, does not deny the existence of alternative paradigms but he always emphasizes that they fail to pose a challenge to the dominant paradigm because they lack the same centrality and effectiveness in society.[20]

3.2 GNOSIS AND UTOPIA

In his childhood, Elmessiri used to go to the library, and he first saw the word "Gnosticism" in one of Abdul Rahman Badawi's books. The tone and strangeness of the word made him tremble to the extent that he kept thinking of it throughout his life. In the second volume of *Mawsūʿat al-Falsafah* [The Encyclopedia of Philosophy], Badawi included entries on monism and pantheism and devoted a four-page entry on Gnosticism, which he defines as a "mystic religious and philosophical orientation…. Gnosis of God is the way to salvation because God is man; the basis of gnosis is man's realization of himself as God; this knowledge leads to man's salvation."[21] Perhaps this definition helped Elmessiri distance the Islamic worldview from Gnosticism, throwing modernity and secularism back to the legacy of heresiology in ancient Christianity.

Elmessiri saw Gnosticism as the most prominent form of both immanentism and pantheism; both of which are represented as inconsistent with a purely monotheistic worldview. Elmessiri puts it this way:

> 'Immanent' means 'indwelling,' 'inherent,' 'operating from within.' Therefore, anything that is said to be self-contained, self-operating, self-activating, self-explanatory could be described as 'immanent,' since its laws are inherent to it and its operating force is internal. The world of immanence, therefore, is a highly unified organic world, with no space separating one of its constituent parts from the others.[22]

Immanence is almost synonymous with pantheism, and Elmessiri sees no fundamental difference between them, yet he opts for each word according to the context:

> Despite the near synonymity, I prefer to use the term 'pantheism' when the organizing principle dwelling in man and/or nature assumes the name of God, or any variations thereon, since it contains the suffix 'theism' from theos, meaning 'God.' I use the term 'immanence' when the organizing principle assumes a materialist or a quasi-spiritual name.[23]

Gnosticism, in Elmessiri's view, started as a form of spiritual pantheism till the eighteenth century and then transformed into materialist pantheism in the Kabbalah, the philosophy of both Spinoza and Hegel and contemporary comprehensive materialist secularism. In the early stages of writing his *Mawsūʿat*, Elmessiri devoted only a few lines to the

Spinoza entry, but when the paradigm of immanentism was crystallized in Elmessiri's mind in the 1990s, the Spinoza entry was enlarged and extended into many pages. "Gnostic heresies" in ancient Christianity, according to Elmessiri, were resurrected with the Reformation and the rise of extremist Protestants along with the spread of Kabbalah. This argument is very close to that of Voegelin who launched his attack against the proponents of the Reformation and prominent protestant figures such as Luther and Calvin. Unlike Voegelin, who referred *en passant* to the Israeli idea of the chosen people, Elmessiri stressed the role of the Kabbalah and argued that it transformed Judaism from a monotheistic into a Gnostic and immanentistic system that puts an end to the distance between God and nature, signaling the end of history and the immanence of God in the Jews as the chosen people. Even Jewish mysticism is said to have been transformed into a Gnostic and immanentistic aspiration to be one with God.[24]

Elmessiri's argument and terminology, except for the part on Judaism, are very close to Voegelin's general revolt against modernity in the early 1950s. Elmessiri seems to side with Voegelin in his approval of the role of the Catholic Church in the battle against its enemies when it realized the danger of "heretic Gnosticism," especially against pagan and Jewish doctrines of millenarianism. Like Voegelin, Elmessiri usually refers to Saint Augustine and his fight against such immanentistic perceptions of history, though introducing a temporary immanentistic moment (the coming of Christ, his crucifixion, his rise to Heaven, and the emergence of the Catholic Church as the spiritual Kingdom of Christ but within a normal, undetermined track of history till the second coming).[25]

One can also argue that Voegelin had much sway on Bauman's cognitive mapping of modernity as a Gnostic worldview. As mentioned above, this fact has been underlined by Gerard Delanty who stresses that Bauman's critique has much in common with that of Voegelin who saw modernity as a process or an orientation that necessarily deifies man and leads to the "immanentization of the Christian eschaton," giving rise to every modern movement from the Reformation to Nazism and communism.[26] The death of God thesis and the "so-called secularization" have given rise to new secular gods, including not only the Nietzschean superman but also Nature, Laws of History, Reason and Progress. The signifier "God" acquired new implications and connotations that go beyond the theological dispute on the existence or non-existence of God. God has not been secularized, and he has incarnated in such non-personal categories as Reason, the laws of History, the invisible hand or Historical Inevitability.[27] Monism and monopoly of Truth have never left the scene:

> God stands for the idea of the 'one and only,' for the 'thou shalt have no other gods before me' idea in all its countless renditions and costumes: of ein *Volk*, ein Reich, ein *Führer*, of one party, one verdict of history, one line of progress, one way of being human, one (scientific) ideology, one true meaning, one proper philosophy. In all such cases 'one and only' conveys the one and only message: the right to the monopoly of power for some, the duty of total disobedience for others.[28]

Like Voegelin and Bauman, Elmessiri saw modernity as a paradigmatic sequence that starts with partial immanentism (partial secularism) and culminates with comprehensive immanentism (comprehensive secularism). He repudiated all reductionist and monistic paradigms that attribute the movement and the end of History to only one force, whether spiritual or materialistic. Elmessiri saw the whole process of immanentization/modernization/secularization in terms of secular incarnations of God in mankind as a whole (humanism and the solipsistic subject); in one people (racism and imperialism); in one leader (fascism); and in nature (pantheism), affirming that there is no lack of other incarnations and signifiers.[29]

Elmessiri, Voegelin and Bauman repudiated all nationalistic and ideological movements as forms of immanentization and organismic/mechanistic paradigms. Elmessiri's position and analysis, however, are more explicit, decisive and comprehensive when he affirms that such movements promise their adherents the "end of struggle and the establishment of a technocratic utopia, whether in Zion, the Third Reich, the Welfare society or the communist society."[30] Modern ideologies are depicted as expressing nothing but the "realm of human action" and "will to immanentization" because all gnostic movements attempt to abolish the constitution of being, with its origin in the divine, transcendent being, and to replace it with a world-immanent order of being.[31]

Elmessiri's and Bauman's positions are close to that of Voegelin who understood the modern age as the definite breakdown of imperial Christianity and the rise of national states. The domination of the organic metaphor reached its climax by the end of the eighteenth century when the concept of the natural organism could be applied to the state which could be seen, in Voegelin's view, as "bearing its formative principle within itself just like a living being, and thus the state was completely detached from the unity of the *corpus mysticum*." Solidarity among members of the Christian community was thus perceived only within the secular context of the nation.[32]

The secular modern, in Voegelin's view, is not a single sudden explosion that led to the separation of state and religion but a long process that developed from the "partial immanentism" of the fifteenth humanism to the "total immanentism" of the twentieth century.[33] Immanentism is set in a sharp contrast with the emphasis on transcendence, that is, the relevance of a transcendent ground of being. Profane history, according to Voegelin, does not have an essence or direction; it is a "waiting for the end; its present mode of being is that…of an age that grows old."[34]

This perception of history is very close to the Islamic worldview, and it anticipates a convergence of the Islamic and Christian view of the modest role of man on Earth. Voegelin was impressed by St. Augustine's theoretical distinction between transcendental history and profane history. This distinction kept human beings, to borrow Bauman's metaphor, "gamekeepers" rather than "gardeners and legislators." Eschatological fulfillment is confined to the transcendental history whereas profane history lacks such a direction. The projection of a radically immanent fulfillment, in Voegelin's view, grew slowly, in a long process roughly called "from humanism to enlightenment." This process reached its radical point in the nineteenth century; Feuerbach and Marx interpreted the transcendent God as "the projection of what is best in man into a hypostatic beyond; for them the great turning point of history, therefore, would come when man draws his projection back into himself, when he becomes conscious that he himself is God, when as a consequence man is transfigured into a superman."[35]

Voegelin rejected all biological and organic doctrines of community and opposed it to the *Corpus mysticum* or the mystical body in Christianity. The idea of the mystical body is "not simply a metaphor, not merely a symbol, but a real idea."[36] If Christ is the head, Christians are the members of the body. The members are the church, thus Christ and Church are one and the same thing. *Corpus mysticum* is also a "comprehensive organism [that] has a rank for the rich and the poor, for the priest and the layman, for the prince and the subject, for the educated and the uneducated, for the heroic ascetic and the weak sinner, for the warrior, the tradesman, and the peasant. By virtue of this comprehensiveness the church could penetrate a civilization with its spirit."[37] All modern post-Christian community development, in Voegelin's view, followed the schema of particularist community, a chosen community, possessing not just blind faith but also all scientific insight to launch its 'just' and 'true' war against the evil enemies, spirits and criminals who fail to adapt to its norms or those who show resistance.[38]

Elmessiri's understanding of western modernity, as well as his dualistic understanding of the distinction between immanence and transcendence, is based on his repudiation of pantheism, which appears in different names in Arabic and Islamic lexicon, including *wiḥdat al-wujūd* (the unity of being), *ḥulūl* (indwelling) and *fanā'* (literally annihilation), all of which aim at the "complete absorption of the human into the divine," a stage that Elmessiri describes as the "embryonic state" and the ultimate "organic monism" as opposed to the state of full and complex humanity.[39] Elmessiri refers to these variations as the unconscious, yet pleasurable mode of being, which stands for the biological and utopian comfort of the mother's womb. The problem is that the contours between the microcosm (fetus-placenta) and the macrocosm (political structures) are blurred. Elmessiri does not hesitate to describe political and technocratic utopias as a "real and sincere desire to find final solutions to all problems, to create a worldly paradise and put an end to history."⁴⁰

The devastating consequences of modernization and rationalism, according to Elmessiri, have given rise to Romanticism and absurdist modernism. The latter protested against the alienation of modern man and the disappearance of a solid logo-centric human potential for transcendence. However, the protest of romanticism and modernism remained marginal, transient, and insignificant. Romanticism, on the contrary, celebrated an organismic paradigm and informed many racist nationalistic movements with ideologies that celebrate an immanent organic trinity (God, territory and the people), which became the most fundamental element in secular organic nationalisms.⁴¹

In his critique of the modern absolute state, Elmessiri sometimes refers to Bauman who described it as a gardening state, a therapeutic/surgical state, a space-managing state.⁴² Elmessiri has devoted almost two pages to illustrate how Bauman's metaphors map very well the nature of modern secular states, and how modern man has been submitted to such secular absolutes as "*raison d'etat,*" "the interest of the state" and "the will of the *Volk.*"⁴³ The state became the "secular absolute itself in both the literal and the metaphorical sense."⁴⁴ This point is also underlined by Bauman who suggested that the advent of modernity witnessed the "birth of the (un) holy trinity" (territory, nation and state). These three allies, in Bauman's view, had to be seen as one organic unit, or one God, so as to achieve the "arrogant" ambitions of modernity.⁴⁵ Like Bauman, Elmessiri holds that the emphasis on the notions of *Blut, Boden und Volk* as sacred and absolute facts is a good example of immanent materialist monism, one which is reminiscent of the pantheistic immanent trinity: God-Nature-Man. One of the most devastating consequences of this worldview is that non-national nations or nations without a state are viewed as strangers, vagabonds, pariahs and even sub-men.⁴⁶

The absolute state is conceived metaphorically as a gardener who gives only useful plants the chance to thrive and condemns harmful weeds to death so as to guarantee the highest degree of order and the best quality of production. Unlike Bauman who argues that the best image that can be used to describe the existential nature of Jewish communities within modernity in both capitalist and communist societies is that of the "prismatic group,"[47] Elmessiri opts for the metaphor "functional group" as a more explanatory paradigm of the emergence of non-national nations. In the Third Reich, Jewish communities were described by both the Nazis and Zionists as pests, bacteria and pariah *Volk*. Zionist literature itself is loaded with metaphors intended to "productivize" the Jews in order to make them "less parasitical," "less marginal" or "less dependent."[48] Both Nazism and Zionism seek to make Europe *Jundenfrei* (having no Jews). The only difference, however, is that Zionists prefer Balfour-like solutions to the Hitler-like final solution for the Jewish question.[49]

Science played its role in the aspiration for a utopian world. Indeed, the determinism that dominates phrenology and physiognomy, according to Bauman, gave rise to scientific racism.[50] It was aggravated by the advent of the modern nationalistic state and the emergence of the "stateless person," the *sans papiers*, the idea of *unwertes Leben* (useless life or being), and the later-day reincarnation of the ancient institution of *homo sacer* (Latin for 'the accursed man'), whose destruction is devoid of all ethical or religious significance.[51]

As designers of the perfect society, the Nazis conceived of *'unwertes Leben'* as the fundamental target that had to be distanced from the *lebensraum* or even exterminated.[52] *Unwertes Leben* included the Gypsies, communists, the mentally-retarded and all those who were perceived as harmful weeds threatening the harmony of the garden of modernity; the six million Jews were among the more than twenty million people annihilated at Hitler's behest. Not surprisingly, Bauman does not conceive of the Holocaust as a Jewish affair or a German problem but as one of the possibilities of modernity at large; it is more than a "cancerous growth on the otherwise healthy body of the civilized society."[53] Other victims of the Holocaust, according to Janina Bauman, are thrown into oblivion simply because they lack the means to publicize their cause. The Gypsies, unlike the Jews, did not have many professors, writers and journalists to highlight their suffering and advocate their rights.[54]

Mapping the Consequences of Modernity

REFERRING to Theodor W. Adorno's and Max Horkheimer's study of the *Dialectic of Enlightenment*, Bauman points out that one of the major consequences of the Enlightenment and the modern spirit has been the emergence of a "culture of the universal taboo." In this culture, everything that shows deviation from or resistance to *naturalization*, routinization and schematization is repressed in practice and banned in theory.[1]

4.1 THE REINCARNATION OF *HOMO SACER*

The advent of the modern state as a nationalistic gardening entity was accompanied with the re-emergence of the ancient institution of *homo sacer* ('the accursed man'). The latter refers metaphorically to an absolutely alien Other who can be stripped of all human rights, even the right to exist. Bauman maintains that the *homo sacer* as an alien Other has been usually associated with the

ultimate embodiment of the sovereign right to exempt and to exclude such human beings as has been cast off the limits of human and divine laws; to make it into a being that can be destroyed without punishment but whose destruction is devoid of all ethical or religious significance.[2]

According to Bauman, the advent of western modernity was conceived of as a "radical break in universal history." The West, this abstract entity, viewed itself as the "reference point for the interpretation of the *telos* of history" giving itself the legitimacy and the right to colonize "the future in the same way it had colonized the surrounding space." All other spaces and temporalities become mere objects to be moulded, shaped, educated and cultivated. This mission derives its force and continuity from the assumption the all other temporalities are "retarded, underdeveloped, immature, incomplete or deformed, maimed, distorted and otherwise inferior stages or versions of itself."[3]

Bauman repudiates the western imperialistic vision that attempted to transform the "virgin lands" into a "dumping ground for those unwanted" and into a "promised land" for the proponents of progress. The populations of conquered, invaded and colonized lands were recast as a "collective *homo sacer* of the metropolis."[4] Science and technology promoted a strong belief in the superiority of western modernity and its inevitable ascendancy i.e. a conception of modernity as the highest point of development as opposed to the idea of static cultures. This cognitive map made western modernity the transcendental locus of all authority i.e. it became autonomous, self-contained, self-referential and self-validating.[5]

One of the most devastating consequences of drawing this cognitive map is the emergence of a long list of structural binary oppositions, setting the superiority of Europe against the inferiority of the rest of the world. Bauman puts it this way:

> Western civilization has articulated its struggle for domination in terms of the holy battle of humanity against barbarism, reason against ignorance, objectivity against prejudice, progress against degeneration, truth against superstition, science against magic, rationality against passion. It has interpreted the history of its ascendance as the gradual yet relentless substitution of human mastery over nature for the mastery of nature over man.[6]

Within the imposition of an artificial dichotomous map, progress, development; science; reason; objectivity; truth; health; civilization;

and sanity are drawn into a sharp contrast with retardation, backwardness; religion; superstition; subjectivity; prejudice; illness; barbarism and insanity, respectively. The logical conclusion to be inferred from this set of binary oppositions is that the dominant paradigm in the West celebrates the "kingdom of Reason and rationality" whereas other temporalities and other ways of life are conceived of as "wanting in both respects."[7]

In this process, the nation-state as a socio-political entity, according to Antony Giddens, played a very significant role because it possessed "specific forms of territoriality and surveillance capacities, and monopolises effective control over the means of violence."[8] This fact had been underlined by Bauman when he stated that the emergence of the nation-state as the new absolute power was expected to universalize the cognitive and behavioural patterns so as to create an imagined community that enforces ethnic, religious, linguistic and cultural homogeneity. Science and nationalism reinforced each other, and both of them aspired to put an end to ambivalence and indeterminacy.[9]

Bauman repudiates the ambitions of the nation-state, and he even compares its determination to impose uniformity to the dogmatism of the church which "forces the prospective flock to practice the cult."[10] In other words, secularism did not aim at replacing the state and the church but at the emergence of a central secular bureaucratic state that could replace the authority of the church and its monopoly of human existence. Bauman puts it this way:

> What was truly new in the modern figuration was the secularization of the pastoral and proselytizing techniques, the techniques themselves were not new, but their emancipation from the hierarchical body of the Church and their redeployment in the service of the state was.[11]

The absolute state is conceived metaphorically as a gardener who gives only useful plants the chance to thrive and condemns harmful weeds to death so as to guarantee the highest degree of order and the best quality of production:

The design, presumed to be dictated by the supreme and unquestionable authority of reason, supplied the criteria to evaluate the present-day reality. These criteria split the population into useful plants to be encouraged and tenderly propagated and weeds – to be removed and rooted out.[12]

Bauman's metaphoric mapping of modernity as a narrative category is not always an abstract representation of the Imaginary; it does not lose its intimate relation with reality. In order that Bauman explicitly uncovers the significance of these metaphors he refers not only to Jewish communities in Europe but also to all human beings who were regarded as sub-men and who were expelled from their land due to the emergence of a new power. In the following quotation Bauman does not refer explicitly to western imperialism and its support of Zionism; and therefore, some explanations within the quotation are required:

As it transpired, the admittedly unruly and anarchistic Jewry was one of the many weeds which inhabited the plot marked for the carefully designed garden of the future. But there were other weeds as well – carriers of congenital diseases, the mentally inferior, the bodily deformed. And there were also plants [perhaps the Palestinians?] which turned into weeds [now colonized Palestinians or Palestinian refugees and asylum seekers?] simply because a superior reason [perhaps Britain and the United States as well as other western imperial powers?] required that the land [Palestine?] they occupied should be transformed into someone else's garden [the Zionists' garden?][13]

More explicit references to the gardener metaphor in relation to western imperialism become more obvious in Bauman's later writings but without much emphasis on Zionism. In *Europe: An Unfinished Adventure*, Bauman argues that the gardener metaphor was not restricted to the geographical contours of Europe, and therefore, the western adventure, at the zenith of its expansive imperialism, saw the whole globe as nothing but "vast lands...waiting to be discovered," "an empty planet," "an empty playground," "an empty stage for countless heroic exploits and glorious unheard-of feats" and "no man's deserted, underpopulated, fallow and undercultivated land." Thus under the pretext of the "civilizing mission" and the meta-narratives of the Enlightenment, the rest of the world was transformed into a "vacuum" that should be "discovered" and then designed in the best way.[14] With these facts in mind, Bauman describes modernity as an "intrinsically expansive and transgressive civilization" in search of new adventures:

> On the map of the modern world, there was profusion of blank spots marked (provisionally, of course!) 'ubi leones,' and waiting to be spattered with new towns and crisscrossed with new road networks. For almost two centuries, those distant blank spots were safety valves letting out the steam and protecting the metropolis from overheating. There were a lot of places for the adventurous to seek adventure, for the gamblers to try their luck and for the defeated to attempt reversal of bad fortune.[15]

Here it is clearly obvious that Bauman's critique is very comprehensive, and his ethnic background as a Jewish intellectual does not stand between him and a serious, yet implicit, critique of western imperialism and atrocities inside and outside Europe.

4.2 MODERNITY, THE JEWS AND THE HOLOCAUST

In order that Bauman supports this metaphorical interpretation of the consequences of modernity, he uses the Jews as the group whose modern historical conditions can best reflect the tendencies and consequences of secular modernity.

As we mentioned in the first chapter, most of the Jews in the Western world had been living in Poland; and therefore, the understanding of conditions of the Jews in Poland can help us understand the Jewish Question and its relevance to the consequences of modernity. Bauman uses two major studies to analyze this crucial point: (1) Anna Zuk's "A mobile Class. The Subjective Element in the Social Perception of Jews: The Example of Eighteenth-century Poland"(1987), and (2) Joseph Marcus's *Social and Political History of the Jews in Poland 1919-1939* (1983). As we will see under the last heading of this chapter, Elmessiri's formulation of the paradigm of the "functional group" can be understood in view of these studies and Bauman's analysis of their arguments.

In eighteenth-century Poland, Polish Jews were "servants of nobility and gentry," since they performed all sorts of functions that the political and economic domination of landed nobility required. In other words, Polish Jews served as a "middle man" and as a "shield, for the real lords of the land." The nobility saw them as social inferiors and as uncivilized, dirty, ignorant and greedy people who should be kept at a distance. Lower and oppressed classes, on the other hand, saw them as the enemies, the ruthless exploiters and the ruling classes. Not surprisingly, Polish Jews were the objects of two contradictory class antagonisms.[16]

With the advent of modernity and the prominence of Polish Jews on both the economic and social levels, an anti-liberal and anti-capitalist impulse among the established classes and nobility emerged. The Jews were thus seen as groups that undermined the dominant order and the once close co-ordination between the scale of prestige and that of influence. The established classes were surprised that a "servant group" could reach positions of power "while climbing a ladder it picked from the junk-heap of discarded values." There was also, according to Bauman, an endemic tendency in the socialist movements of Europe to conflate Judaism with money and power and with the ills of capitalism. The Jewish attachment to the liberal heritage of the Enlightenment was also seen in these terms; the Jews were the most prominent group that benefited from the citizenship that liberalism promoted. As a "non-national nation," the Jews mitigated the distinction between hosts and guests, natives and the foreigners, thus reinforcing the opacity of the world fighting for clarity and the ambiguity of the world lusting for certainty. It is in this sense that racism against the Jews was in perfect harmony with the worldview and practice of modernity. And it is also in this sense that the Holocaust is consistent with modernity and its tendencies.[17]

The term "Holocaust" was not used in the different expulsions that Jewish communities faced in Europe, whether the expulsion from England in 1290, from France in 1340 or from Spain in 1492. Those expulsions were seen only as a disaster of oppression that could be avoided by converting to Christianity. In *Theoretical Interpretations of the Holocaust* (2001), Dan Stone points out that since the 1960s, the term Holocaust became the most widely used name to refer to the genocide of the Jews. The use of the term began in the late 1950s, displacing such terms as "catastrophe," "disaster" and even "genocide." The meaning of the Holocaust, however, differs from one writer to another because "all writing on the Holocaust is unavoidably an instrumentalization of it."[18]

Though Jewish assimilatory problems were obvious all over Europe, the pressure exercised on German Jews is always emphasized. The history of German Jewish communities, in Bauman's view, is conceived as the focal case in the exploration of Jewish assimilation for a number of reasons: (1) All Jewish heroes of modern culture wrote their seminal contributions to modern consciousness in German; and therefore, their biographical experience throws light on Jewish experience in Germany; (2) German-speaking Jewish communities occupied a pivotal position in the economy, culture and ideology (Moses Mendelssohn's match-making between Judaism and Enlightenment as well as Theodor Herzl's marriage between Jewishness and modern nationalism); (3) German Jewry occupied a borderline position between the affluent Jewish communities of the West and the vast expanses of impoverished East-European Jewry; and (4) It was in Germany and the German speaking lands that modernization was first lived as a conscious and motivated process.[19]

Bauman, however, argues that the significance of the Holocaust for sociology will be belittled, misjudged, and thus instrumentalized, if the Holocaust is seen as "something that happened to the Jews," as "an event in Jewish History" or as one of the "many similar cases of conflict or prejudice or aggression."[20] More importantly, Bauman underlines the fact that German anti-semitism alone cannot be a sufficient explanation of the Holocaust. According to Bauman, the term anti-Semitism, which was coined and came into general use toward the end of the nineteenth-century, cannot provide a complex explanation of the Holocaust; it lacks historical or contemporary evidence:

Long before the Weimar Republic put the finishing touches to the long process of Jewish emancipation, Germany was widely conceived by international Jewry as the haven of religious and national equality and tolerance. Germany entered this century with many more Jewish academics and professionals than contemporary America or Britain. Popular resentment of Jews was neither deep-seated nor widespread. Hardly ever did it manifest itself in outbursts of public violence, so common in other parts of Europe. Nazi attempts to bring popular anti-Semitism to the surface by staging public spectacles of anti-Jewish violence proved counter-productive and had to be foiled.[21]

Prejudice and hatred cannot explain modern genocide; irrational and barbaric emotions were neither the major causes nor the means of the Holocaust. The ultimate aim of Nazism was a utopian world and a perfect design. The perfect society or design in the case of the Holocaust was the thousand-year Reich or the kingdom of the liberated German Spirit.[22] Modern science, technology and bureaucracy, rather than irrational emotions, were all employed to realize this goal:

The Hobbesian world of the Holocaust did not surface from its too-shallow grave, resurrected by the tumult of irrational emotions. It arrived (in a formidable shape Hobbes would certainly disown) in factory-produced vehicle, wielding weapons only the most advanced science could supply, and following an itinerary designed by the scientifically managed organization. Modern civilization was not the Holocaust's sufficient condition, most certainly its necessary condition. Without it, the Holocaust would be unthinkable.[23]

Drawing on Max Weber's analysis of bureaucratic and rationalized culture, Bauman underlined the "bureaucratic rationalization" of the Holocaust; the official name of the Department in the SS headquarters in charge of the destruction of the Jews was "the Section of Administration and Economy." The very idea of the Final Solution (*Endlösung*) was "an outcome of the bureaucratic culture;" the Nazis thought of exterminating the Jews only when they failed to find a "dumping ground for the Jewry" inhabiting Europe, whether in Nisko, Madagascar or beyond the Archangel-Astrakhan line. Bauman repudiates the notion that the Holocaust was an "irrational outflow of the not-yet-fully-eradicated residue of pre-modern barbarity," arguing instead that it was a "legitimate resident in the house of modernity." To support this argument, he refers to the line of defence adopted by Dr. Servatius who was Adolf Eichmann's counsel in Jerusalem during his trial in 1961: "Eichmann committed acts for which one is decorated if one wins, and goes to the gallows if one loses." In other words, bureaucratic and rational actions in the map of the modern world "have no intrinsic moral value," and moral evaluation is something "external to the action itself."[24]

The very myth of the European civilizing mission is based on the emancipation of rationality from ethical norms or moral inhibitions; and therefore, all human beings can be victims of this worldview: "it is therefore possible to be a pilot delivering a bomb to Hiroshima or to Dresden, to excel in the duties assigned at a guided missile base, to design ever more devastating specimens of nuclear warheads – all this without detracting from one's moral integrity and coming anywhere near moral collapse."[25]

Scientific institutes under Nazism were established to investigate the 'Jewish question' and to provide rationally designed solutions. The elimination of the Jews was referred to as *Gesundung* (healing) of Europe, *Selbsttreinigung* (self-cleansing), *Judensäuberung* (cleansing-of-Jews), hygienic prophylactic, and *eine Frage der politischen Hygiene* (a question of the political hygiene). The murder of the Jews was thus portrayed as an "exercise in the rational management of society" and a "systematic attempt to deploy in its service the stance, the philosophy and precepts of applied science."[26] The authority of science, however, was not confined to Germany. German universities, in Bauman's view, were like their counterparts in other modern countries, all of them "carefully cultivated the ideal of science as an emphatically value-free activity."[27] Science as a body of ideas and a network of institutions "cleared the way to genocide through sapping the authority, and questioning the binding force, of all normative thinking, particularly that of religion and ethics."[28]

According to Anna Harrington, the authority of metaphor reached its climax when European Jews were viewed as the ultimate form of inauthenticity, chaos and mechanicism (liberalism, fragmentation, chaos and revolution) in contrast to the German organismic world-view that places a great emphasis on unity, wholeness, pacification and life.[29]

In order that Bauman establishes the development of the metaphors of chaos and inauthenticity, particularly in relation to the ideology of the modern state in the 1930s, he traces its manifestations in the writings of the Nazi Minister of Agriculture R.W. Darre, the world-famous biologist Erwin Bauer and his colleague Martin Stämmler. What is common among these figures and scientists is the use of a basic organismic metaphor that compares society to a garden; individuals to plants, weeds and animals; the state and the scientists to gardeners and breeders. These organismic tropes are not explored to uncover the scientists' ideological conceptions but to emphasize determination of modernity to fight what was regarded as "inherently chaotic natural forces" and "dangerous weeds" that threaten the "carefully designed garden of the future."[30] It is precisely for this reason that Bauman refuses to attribute modern genocide and atrocities to barbarism or irrationalism, and he always emphasizes that they are "legitimate off-spring of the modern spirit, of that urge to assist and speed up progress of mankind towards perfection."[31]

However, Bauman's thesis repudiates the perception of the Holocaust as a purely German problem. Eugenics and its ambitions were pioneered simultaneously in several European countries, and English scholars, like their German colleagues, strived for superiority and success. British scholars and politicians celebrated the racist discourse of eugenics, particularly its fierce drive to eliminate "genetical deficiency," "degenerate stock," "submen," "low-grade types" and the "biologically unfit." The United States was no exception. Between 1907 and 1928, twenty-one states, in the name of progress and the elimination of genetical deficiency, enacted eugenic sterilization laws, covering "criminals, rapists, idiots, feeble-minded, imbeciles, lunatics, drunkards, drug fiends, epileptics, syphilitics, moral and sexual perverts, and diseased and degenerate persons."[32]

According to Sabine Maasen and Peter Weingart, this worldview cannot be regarded as a German invention, since its epistemological foundations can be traced back to a major English biological metaphor (the struggle metaphor in Thomas Hobbes and Charles Darwin) that was later transferred to different European territories including Germany (the *Kampf ums Dasein* metaphor). Seen from the perspective of a metaphor-based interpretation, the entire history of the notions of "the struggle for survival" and the "survival of the fittest" can be traced back to the Hobbesian theory of *bellum omnium contra omnes* (the war of all against all) as well as the Hobbesian statement *homo homini lupus* (man is a wolf to his fellow man). In other words, the genocidal tendency of modernity was not a German monopoly or invention.[33]

Ian Varcoe holds that Bauman's major argument is set in sharp contrast with the *Sonderweg* thesis which cites and asserts that Germany underwent "a series of structural and cultural factors for a divergence from the western European path of development."[34] Bauman, on the other hand, rejects the assumption that the history of Germany constitutes a deviation from the normal liberal, humanistic and enlightened European civilization. What is at stake here is that the ambitions of eugenics were not a German monopoly, since they were born in many western countries before Hitler and his vision of the Thousand-Year Reich. Bauman's position is of great significance because it comes from a Jewish thinker who affirms that the Holocaust is neither an absolutely incomparable crime nor a result of the particularities of German history.[35]

The significance of Bauman's argument lies in the fact that it repudiates the assumption that the Holocaust is a Jewish affair, a German problem, a Nazi invention or a product of National Socialism. Rather, it is one of the possibilities of the instrumental rationality of modernity; one which is politically and morally neutral. In "Sociology after the Holocaust" (1988), an early version of the introduction to *Modernity and the Holocaust* (1989), Bauman argues that the Holocaust is a rationally calculated activity that cannot be reduced to a merely uncontrolled outburst of passions. Modernity, in Bauman's view, aspired for a state of ultimate and stable perfection, even though this aspiration might entail the suppression or neutralization of individual action as well as the universal domination of system and the absence of man. It comes as no surprise then that Bauman also repudiates the interpretation of the Holocaust as the culmination of European-Christian anti-semitism or as an interruption caused in the normal flow of history by German anti-Semitism and Nazi bestiality. Bauman's humanistic vision reaches its climax when he repudiates Israel's abuse of the Holocaust and its tragic memories as a certificate of Israeli political legitimacy and as an advance payment for the injustices it might itself commit against Palestinians in particular and the Arabs in general. The Holocaust, in Bauman's view, was not the result of irrational Hobbesian emotions but the product of the most scientifically advanced and sophisticated weapons and the most scientifically managed organization. It is true that instrumental rationality cannot be regarded as the Holocaust's major cause but it was a necessary condition.[36] Bauman, however, conceives of the Holocaust neither as the normal state of modernity nor as its paradigmatic moment. Rather, he represents it as one of the possibilities of modernity, a window to modernity and more generally the test of modernity that the West avoids to confront:

> The unspoken terror permeating our collective memory of the Holocaust...is the gnawing suspicion that the Holocaust could be more than an aberration, more than a deviation from an otherwise straight path of progress, more than a cancerous growth on the otherwise healthy body of the civilized society; that, in short, the Holocaust was not an antithesis of modern civilization and everything...it stands for. We suspect (even if we refuse to admit it) that the Holocaust could merely have uncovered another face of the same modern society whose other, more familiar, face we so admire. And that the two faces are perfectly comfortably attached to the same body. What we perhaps fear most, is that each of the two faces can no more exist without the other than can the two sides of a coin.[37]

4.3 *UNWERTES LEBEN*, VAGABONDS AND STRANGERS

The metaphor of the *unwertes Leben* (useless being) is prominent not only in the European discourse of eugenics but also in the American popular imagery that depicted the Japanese as "diseased organisms," "submen," "little yellow beasts," "lice," "rats," "bats," "vipers," "dogs" and "monkeys." Bauman holds that the modern role of racism is the "forceful removal of the *unwertes Leben*;" scientific racism, of eugenics, phrenology and physiognomy, informed the Nazi worldview and helped the Nazi designers of the perfect society to split human life into worthy and unworthy; "the first to be lovingly cultivated and given *Lebensraum*, the other to be 'distanced,' or – if the distancing proved unfeasible – exterminated."38 Hitler himself embraced the same orientation in dealing with the Jewish question when he declared that his mission was the extermination of the pest. Stripped of his humanity and redefined as a vermin, the Jew is no more an object of moral evaluation.39

As these examples clearly show, human beings – not only the Jews – can be easily dehumanized and exterminated under the pretext that they are mere animals or objects that disturb the harmony of human existence. The Jews were equated figuratively with the *Ungeziefer* (insects, pests and vermin). The motif of this organismic metaphor is also underlined when Bauman draws readers' attention to the biological origin of the term "assimilation," which was first used in the sixteenth century in reference to the processes of absorption and incorporation performed by living organisms. The term was then used metaphorically in the eighteenth and the nineteenth centuries to refer to the processes of "making like," and "becoming like." Bauman believes that the metaphorical use of this term has a new social function as it reflects a "comprehensive cultural crusade." Bauman's thesis is that assimilation was an integral part of the liberal process and it came in the disguise of such humanistic ideals as tolerance, enlightenment and progress. Hence while the modern "civilized state" was setting the rules of the game and the "measures of progress," strangers and minority groups had nothing to do but to "wash off the stigma of foreignness" otherwise they would be accused of backwardness, inferiority and illegitimacy.[40]

With the advent of modernity, the annihilation of vagabonds and strangers, according to Bauman, was seen as a process of "creative destruction" because they did not fit the "cognitive, moral, or aesthetic map of the world."[41] Vagabonds were people who "appeared and disappeared from sight without warning; they stubbornly remained strangers and vanished before the community could absorb them by subjecting them to its all-penetrating gaze."[42] Dangerous, masterless and rootless are the frequent epithets used in connection with vaga-bonds and strangers. More importantly, any reference to these groups was usually associated with an organismic metaphor; and therefore, they were, more often than not, compared to parasitic insects such as cockroaches, flies, spiders, mice, carpet mites, bacteria and viruses. What is common among these nominations is an organismic metaphor that represents strangers as parasitic organisms or carriers of disease; and therefore, it reflects a growing atmosphere of insecurity and fear that haunt "purity seekers" in the presence of strangers and foreigners.[43]

The dynamics of metaphor were not played only on the intellectual stage, they also found their way to the realms of legislation and prac-tice. The Enlightenment, in Bauman's view, was not "a collection of ideas" but "a mode of life."[44] Two important acts are cited by Bauman to underline the exclusivist tendency of western modernity. First, the act of 1531 defined the vagabond as "any man or woman being whole and mighty in body and able to labour, having no land, master or using any lawful merchandise, craft or mystery whereby he might get his living." Second, the act of 1604 instructed that the mark be "so thoroughly burned and set on upon the skin and flesh, that the letter 'R' be seen and remain for a perpetual mark upon such [a] rogue during his or her life."[45] Modern order-building under the aegis of the modern state is represented by Bauman as a war of attrition waged against the strangers and the strange. Not surprisingly, modern society conceived cultural and/or physical annihilation of strangers and of the strange as a creative destruction. Typical modern strangers were regarded as the waste of the State's ordering zeal.[46]

Mapping the Consequences of Modernity

The friends/enemies dichotomy, according to Bauman, is always expected to separate "truth from falsity, good from evil, beauty from ugliness." And thus friends are called into being by the "pragmatics of co-operation" whereas enemies are called into being by the "pragmatics of struggle." The strangers, however, refused to split neatly into 'us' and 'them,' 'friends' and 'foes.'[47] They bring "the outside into the inside, and poison the comfort of order with suspicion of chaos."[48] Modern society had two solutions to the problem posed by strangers: the anthropophagic and the anthropoemic. Bauman puts it this way:

> The first solution boiled down to 'eating the strangers up.' Either literally, in flesh – like in cannibalism allegedly practiced by certain ancient tribes, or in a more sublime, modern metaphorical re-make, spiritually – as in the power-assisted assimilation practiced almost universally by nation-states so that the strangers are ingested into the national body and cease to exist as strangers. The second solution meant 'vomiting the strangers' instead of devouring them: rounding them up and expelling…either from the realm of the state power or from the world of the living.[49]

Using post-structuralist terminology, Bauman describes strangers as one member of the family of the undecidables; it is like a *pharmakon* (remedy and poison), *hymen* (fusion of self and other) and *supplement* (neither a plus nor minus). In short, they stand for the "horror of inde-termination and uncertainty" and the lack of "cognitive clarity."[50]

Bauman's analysis of "strangerhood" is indebted to Georg Simmel's "The Stranger." According to Simmel, the trader epitomizes the stranger *par excellence*, since he can be represented as the "potential wanderer" known usually for his "mobility," "objectivity" and "estrangement." In European history, the Jew represents the classical example of the stranger who had his social position "as a Jew, not as the individual bearer of certain objective contents." Simmel states that strangers represent an awful "synthesis of proximity and remoteness" as well as a synthesis of moral and contractual relationships, participation and detachment, involvement and indifference.[51] The Jews, in Bauman's view, were "the very epitome of Simmel's strangers – always on the outside even when inside, examining the familiar as if it was a foreign object of study, asking questions no one else asked, questioning the unquestionable and challenging the unchallengeable."[52]

Bauman describes the stranger as "the bane of modernity," "the archetypal example of Sartre's *le visquex* or Mary Douglas's the slimy," the "embodiment and the incurable sickness" of "multiple incongruity."[53] This is due to the fact that he is an ambivalent entity and a tempting object of stigma, permanent exclusion, cultural isolation or even genocide. It comes as no surprise that strangers often suppress their identity; otherwise they will be regarded as "cultural inferiors," "eternal wanderers," "homeless adventurers" and "natural nomads." Thus the existential situation of the stranger was almost reduced to a "nomadic existence."[54] And because the Jews were always on the move, they became a figure of strangeness, separation and exile. Not surprisingly, the comprehensive segregation and isolation of the Jews reached its climax when the Jew was transformed into an eternal symbol of the failure of any German attempt at a unified national culture and a German collective identity; he was conceived of as a vermin feeding upon the German organism.[55]

According to Bauman, the universalizing, absolutist, all penetrating and monopolistic ambitions and tendencies of the "high-handed" nationalist state power are the most prominent features of all modernization. The rational thrust of modernity was set in sharp contrast to the irrational and "unscathed ghetto conditions" of the Jews. The Jews did not adhere to the "new universal codes" and thus their communal and juridical autonomy was seen as deviation from the norm. Hence in the name of equality, rationality and universalism, legal privileges were abolished and their identity was suppressed and de-legitimized. Here Bauman stresses the "illiberalisms of the Liberal era":

> Modernization was also a cultural crusade; a powerful and relentless drive to extirpate differences in values and life-styles, customs and speech, beliefs and public demeanour. It was, first and foremost, a drive to redefine all cultural values and styles except those endorsed by the modernizing elite (and particularly the values and styles that resisted the *Gleichschaltung* process) as inferior: signs or

stigmas of backwardness, retardation, mental impairment or, in extreme cases of insanity.[56]

It is true that the Jews tried to assimilate into the fabrics of modern life, yet their attempts at assimilation could be compared to a "Sisyphean labour."[57] Even in communist Eastern Europe, and in spite of the comprehensive assimilation in language, customs and life-styles as well as the tremendous success in commerce, banking, the press, liberal professions and politics, the Jews were regarded as subordinated nations that have "no territorial claims" and as the archetypal case of the denial of "all and any national self-assertion."[58]

Since the advent of modernity, the existential situation of human beings in general and the Jews in particular has been oscillating between the metaphors of the pariah and the parvenu or the victim and the hero with no chance to overcome his growing sense of existential fear and anxiety for a single moment:

> Modernity was...the hope of the pariah. But the pariah could stop being a pariah only by becoming – struggling to become – a parvenu. And the parvenu, having never washed out the stain of his origin, laboured under a constant threat of deportation back to the land he tried to escape. Deportation in case he failed; deportation in case he succeeded too spectacularly for the comfort of those around. Not for a moment did the hero stop being a potential victim. Hero today, victim tomorrow – the dividing wall between the two conditions was but paper-thin. Being on the move meant belonging nowhere.[59]

Though Bauman focuses on the Holocaust, his vision is more comprehensive and humanistic. He repudiates the abuse of the Holocaust by Israeli politicians to legitimize the atrocities they commit against the Palestinians. Bauman refers *en passant* to the catastrophic presence of thirteen to eighteen million refugees, of them three million Palestinians in the Middle East.[60]

The reference to the Jews and their centrality in the interpretation of modernity is not made as an attempt to glorify the Jews or to stress the "privilege" of Jewishness. Bauman puts it this way:

It is not a specifically Jewish phenomenon, this elective affinity…. To emphasize: I am not ascribing a special mission to Jewishness – I am simply saying that, by accident of history, it so happened that the Jewish experience had a special significance for understanding the logic of modern culture.[61]

The existential mode created by modernity can be rendered in the metaphors of the *homo sacer, unwertes Leben* and the *Muselmann* (Muslim; pl., *Muselmänner*, a slang used in Auschwitz for a prisoner in starvation and near death). These metaphors, or rather real collective entities, are not to be regarded as the most truly original contribution of the Third Reich but as products of western civilization and its monopolistic vision of existence. They epitomize the real essence of strangerhood, exclusion and the justification of genocide. As Simon Clarke argues, the stranger becomes a psychic entity or a construction that stands for our fears and anxieties; he is the one who has been persecuted as Jew, as a Gypsy, as a Muslim, as a victim and as a potential victimizer.[62]

Victimization gives rise to what Nietzsche calls the slave morality, he associates its origins with the Jews and describes its driving force as the feeling of *ressentiment*.[63] The irony is that the experience of injustice does not give rise to the aspiration for justice but to the morality of vengefulness, even though it is directed into the wrong direction and the false enemy. As Bauman suggests, the ethical code of the defeated who went through a long process of suffering and misery remains so low that he cannot differentiate between punishability and immorality:

The memories of the Holocaust firm the hand of the Israeli occupiers of the Arab lands: mass deportations, roundings-up, hostage-taking and concentration camps are well-remembered as cost-effective. As history progresses, injustice tends to be compensated for by injustice with-role-reversal. It is only the victors, as long as their victory stays unchallenged, who mistake, or misrepresent, that compensation as the triumph of justice. Superior morality is always the morality of the superior.[64]

4.4 SUPERMEN, SUB-MEN AND FUNCTIONAL GROUPS

Bauman's exploration of the metaphors of the *homo sacer, unwertes Leben*, strangers and vagabonds had a great impact on Abdelwahab Elmessiri's mapping of the consequences of modernity. Elmessiri argues that the early phase of modernity may be represented as a heroic or promethean secular project that started with the deification of both man and nature yet ended, paradoxically, with man's tragic alienation and defeat.[65] With the advent of heroic or promethean modernity, God disappeared, or at least was marginalized whereas man and nature come into centre stage as the ultimate source of meaning and truth. This phase of western modernization may be referred to as the time of "imperialist accumulation" and "heroic materialism." The devastating consequences of modernization and rationalism led to the rise of Romanticism. Also the abuse of science and technology gave rise to 'absurdist modernism' which protested against the alienation of modern man and the disappearance of solid logo-centric human potential for transcendence. However, the protest of modernism, according to Elmessiri, remained marginal, transient, and insignificant.[66] This idea is eloquently explained by Georg Lukács when he stresses that the protest of modernism against modern reality ignores the corrupt society of capitalism and presents the escape into psychopathology as a mere abstract representation:

> The rejection of modern reality is purely subjective. Considered in terms of man's relation with his environment, it lacks both content and direction. And this lack is exaggerated still further by the character of the *terminus ad quem*. For the protest is an empty gesture, expressing nausea, or discomfort, or longing.... These [modernist] writers are not wholly wrong in believing that psychopathology is their surest refuge; it is the ideological complement of their historical position.[67]

Neither Romanticism nor absurdist modernism can claim a central or an effective role in the confrontation with the dominance of the materialist paradigm. This view has been embraced and advocated by many western scholars. It is argued that the ambivalence of many western intellectuals towards modernity and modernization was reflected in a nostalgic sense of "paradise lost" but by the mid-twentieth century this ambivalence had dissipated.[68]

Elmessiri's main argument is that the original western project of humanism has proved to be a form of "naturalistic anti-humanism" or "materialist monism." The anti-humanistic tendencies of materialism have become the "epistemological basis for a process of deconstruction, neutralization, depersonalization and desanctification not only of nature but also of man."[69] Elsewhere, Elmessiri places a great emphasis on the same argument and attempts to trace the lost expectations of humanism, particularly the attempt to construct a new *logos* and *telos* i.e. the establishment of absolute secular ethical systems that emphasize man's uniqueness from the world of nature/matter.[70] Elmessiri does not hesitate to refer to western civilization in its phase of "solid materialism" as nothing but a tragic and imperialist worldview governed only by the Nietzschean "will to power," the Freudian pleasure principle epitomized by Dr. Faustus, Macbeth, Don Juan and Casanova.[71]

As Elmessiri suggests, the devastating consequences of the rationalistic and mechanistic paradigm gave rise to Romanticism which celebrated an organismic paradigm based on the immanent unity, order, and wholeness of living organisms which have an intrinsic order, a self organizing potential or inherent design to reproduce life. Romanticism informed many nationalisms with 'unscientific' ideologies that eventually gave rise to racism in general and anti-Semitism in particular. This point is stressed in Elmessiri's writings, especially when he argues that organismic metaphors had been extended by Friedrich Hegel (1770-1831) to a metaphysical concept of *Volkgeist* which was employed in part to promote a totalitarian nationalism. Based upon the pantheistic implications of God as a cosmic *Geist* (spirit) that must embody itself in nature and human history as an evidence of moral and cultural progress of human existence, Hegel's philosophy, according to Elmessiri, is based on an illusory dialectic that aspires to unite the subject and the object, the absolute and the relative i.e. the comprehensive totalitarian organic point where materialistic pantheism meets with spiritual pantheism. The immanent organic trinity (God, territory and the people) became the most fundamental element in secular organic nationalisms.[72] In a private conversation with the author of this book, Elmessiri pointed out one of the most remarkable ironies of Hegelianism:

> [T]he Absolute Mind will be embodied, and even incarnated, in nature and the general law is realized in history, a time which will mark the end of dialectics and of human suffering, when man will find final solutions to all his problems and fully control all things. However, one of the ironies of this situation is that the moment of total control is itself the moment that will mark the victory of simplism over complexity, of one-dimensionality over multi dimensionality, and of the natural over the human.[73]

According to Elmessiri, the promethean heroic phase of solid materialism witnessed the emergence of secular nationalisms and absolutist centralised nation-states that placed great emphasis on the notions of national past, identity, common good and good society. The saddest irony, however, is that this phase ended with Nazi tyranny, Stalinist terrorism, the destruction of Hiroshima and Nagasaki, the war in Vietnam and the establishment of the Zionist State in Palestine. In the phase of solid rational materialism, western global imperialism, according to Elmessiri, has transformed the entire world into "utilizable matter" in the name of "the white man's burden," "the *mission civilatrice*," and "the manifest destiny."[74]

In mapping the consequences of modernity, Elmessiri is critical of all closed systems that seek full control and absolute perfection: Marxism and its call for a communist society devoid of any manifestations of conflict and contradiction; liberalism and its desire to employ science and technology in gratifying people's desires; Nazism and its dream of full control and perfect rationalization; the New World Order and its ambitions of reaching a universal natural law that ignores the differences among cultures; and finally Zionism and its deification, like Nazism, of *Blunt, Boden und Volk*. Here the Zionist vision and praxis are always perceived within the context of western materialism and imperialism. Elmessiri's cognitive map always associates Israel with western imperialism because he belongs to geographical, historical and cultural circumstances that witnessed the British support of Jewish communities at the expense of Palestinian and Arab interests (the Balfour Declaration of 1917), the Anglo-French support to Israel in the 1956 aggression on Egypt and the current American occupation of Iraq and Afghanistan as well as the blind support of Israeli occupation of Palestine.

Elmessiri, like Bauman, emphasizes that a modern absolute nation-state does not simply mean a totalitarian and authoritarian state. Rather, it refers to the monopoly of truth and interpretation as it becomes the "only ultimate point of reference," "the *telos* of human existence" and the "ultimate point of freedom." The deification of the state reaches its climatic moment when Hegel emphasized and even justified the necessity of wars as a means of maintaining state sovereignty and *raison d'etat*, rejecting the Kantian notion of perpetual peace and celebrating instead the absolute sovereignty of the state. As for the deification of man, Elmessiri holds that Hitler can be regarded as the paradigmatic figure of the Nietzchean *Übermensch* (superman) who epitomizes the will of the absolute state i.e. a self-sufficient, self-referential superman bounded by no historical, social, ethical or aesthetic constraints. Elmessiri, however, stresses that the emergence of the superman went hand in hand with the creation of *Untermenschen* (sub-men governed by organismic laws or civil servants governed by bureaucratic orders) like Adolf Eichmann, who represents the "paradigmatic civil servant;" one who believes blindly in the authority of the state and faithfully carries out the *Führer*'s orders.[75]

Like Bauman, Elmessiri focused on the Holocaust as the "paradigmatic moment" of solid rational materialism which has given rise to a universal human condition that can be grasped in Elmessiri's metaphor of the "functional group." This metaphor is very close to Bauman's metaphors of strangehood and vagabondage. Elmessiri refers to key Western figures and their influence on his understanding of the role of functional groups; among them are Georg Simmel, Karl Marx, Max Weber and Werner Sombart.[76] Elmessiri, however, criticized western scholarship for its failure to incorporate the stranger metaphor into a more comprehensive interpretative paradigm. Replacing the stranger metaphor with the metaphor of "functional group," Elmessiri attempts to introduce a more comprehensive paradigm that can cover a wide range of people who are either imported from outside society or recruited from within its ranks and who are generally defined in terms of a definite function rather than their complex humanity.

Among the major characteristics of functional groups are utility, neutrality; rationalization; instrumentalization; isolation; alienation; powerlessness; double standards; and mobility. According to Elmessiri, this new metaphor as well as its relevant connotations are applicable to a wide range of groups in history, including, to mention but a few, the Gypsies in Europe and in Egypt; Armenian merchants in the Ottoman Empire; Mamluks in Egypt and the Samurai in pre-modern Japan. Elmessiri, however, holds that the Jews are the prime example of functional groups throughout history. This metaphor, however, is not a unique product of modernity, but it is modernity that makes it a universal human condition.77

The highly loaded metaphor of the stranger with its humanistic implications of misery and suffering, fear and anxiety is now replaced by a more comprehensive metaphor that attempts to map one of the major consequences of modernity i.e. the transformation of community into a purely functional and bureaucratic society i.e. a society of civil servants who lack any human bonds. The functional group metaphor, however, lacks the humanistic aura of strangers as *heimatlos Dasein* (diasporic being) and not only as *obdachlos Menschen* (homeless people) i.e. as human beings who are forced to play this role while yearning for their true humanity wherever they are forced to go, though Elmessiri had these connotations in mind when he theorized the paradigm of the functional groups.

Elmessiri's use of the functional group metaphor echoes Ernest Gellner's celebration of the *Mamluk* as the best metaphor to describe the universal existential consequences of the emergence of modernity and rational bureaucracy:

When everyone has become a *Mamluk*, no special mamluk class predominates in the bureaucracy. At long last the bureaucracy can recruit from the population at large, without needing to fear the arrival of dozens of cousins as unwanted attachments of each single new entrant.[78]

Elmessiri sees this universal situation as a result of a long process of secular rationalization that sets a wide range of binary oppositions: traditional versus complex and rational societies; community (*Gemeinschaft*) versus society (*Gesellschaft*); and affective versus contractual relationships. This issue of the isolated modern individual is as old as history and it takes roots in classical sociology, most memorably in Ferdinand Tönnies's famous distinction between *Gemeinschaft* and *Gesellschaft*. According to Karel Dobbelaere's analysis of secularization, it is the rationalization process in the economic order that has brought about huge bureaucracies resting on mechanistic foundations in which individuals are reduced to being role players in *gesellschaftliche* relationships.[79]

Here it is extremely important to contrast the metaphor of the stranger as introduced by Bauman and Elmessiri in relation to modernity and the Jewish communities. Bauman argues that the best image that can be used to describe the existential nature of the Jews is that of the "prismatic group":

Depending on the side from which the Jews were looked at, they – like all prisms – unwittingly refracted altogether different sights; one of the crude, unrefined and brutal lower classes, another of ruthless and haughty social superiors.[80]

Unlike Bauman, Elmessiri opts for the metaphor 'functional group' as a more explanatory paradigm of the existential nature of the Jews. Instead of seeing the Jews as *heimatlos Dasein* or even Jewish communities, Elmessiri argues that modernity has reduced them to functional groups, not only in modern liberal society but also within western feudal system. As Elmessiri points out, the Jews were landless, and by the 13th century they became intermediary groups to their Christian hosts who used them in the military, commercial and financial sectors.

Elmessiri affirms that the Jews in pre-modern Europe were part of the King's property and were not a force of production, but rather a means of production.[81] This point is also emphasized by Bauman when he refers to the fact that both the position and definition of the Jews throughout the pre-modern history of Europe were determined by the body politic: "The Jews were *König juden*, property and wards of the King, of the Prince, or the local warlord, depending on the stage or variety of the feudal order. Their status was politically born and politically sustained."[82]

The metaphor of functional group, in Elmessiri's view, finds its best expression in anti-Jewish discourses through the use of other sub-metaphors and terms, all of which belong to almost the same semantic field. Parasitism, abnormality, slime fungus, vampires and *Luftmenschen* were usually used in connection with the Jews in general and *Ostjuden* in particular. The image of parasitism has a long history and it refers to the thesis that Jews threaten the moral and economic order and that they pursue wealth at the expense of all moral obligation.[83]

As Bauman suggests, the proponents of National Socialism identified modernity as the "rule of economic and monetary values," and they assumed that Jewish racial characteristics were the major reason behind the disappearance of "the *volkisch* mode of life and standards of human worth."[84] It is precisely for this reason that they were conceived of as leeches and vampires, sucking the lifeblood from others; and therefore, they deserve death without redemption. The saddest irony, according to Elmessiri, is that the abstraction of the Jew into a permanent victim or a permanent parasite in Zionist discourse is countered by an equal, and even injust, abstraction of the gentile into a "permanent wolf."[85]

Like Bauman, Elmessiri repudiates the notion that the Holocaust is a deviation from western modernity. He also rejects the theological interpretations that attempt to explain the Holocaust in metaphysical terms that ignore the complexity of human reality. It is precisely for this reason that Elmessiri rejects all manifestations of what he calls "iconization," a method that strips a human phenomenon of its historical nature and presents it as *sui generis*, a *mysterium tremendum* to be discussed, if at all, only in the most sophisticated forms of eschatological discourse.[86]

In an attempt to create a more comprehensive paradigm that goes beyond the Holocaust as a paradigmatic moment in the history of modernity, Elmessiri argues that western civilization as a whole, including Nazism, can be viewed as "the civilization of transfer" on all levels. "Transfer," in Elmessiri's view, is not just a political concept but also an "essential and structural component of comprehensive secular-ism and value-free modernity."[87] According to Elmessiri, the earliest transfer was the linguistic transfer that took place in the Reformation era when Protestant Reformists transferred the religious concepts from the metaphorical level to the literal level, thus transforming the signifier "Zion" into a geographical land called Palestine and the reli-gious love of Zion into a movement towards settling in it. The same process shows in the transfer of the signifier "Jerusalem," the heavenly city of God, which has been transformed into the worldly Jerusalem.[88]

As for political transfer, Elmessiri refers to the emergence of nine-teenth-century "Darwinian utilitarianism" which celebrated racist and imperialist terminology, including "human material," "human surplus," and "useful matter."[89] Elmessiri argues that the earliest historical transfer was the deportation of political opponents, religious extremists and criminals to North America and the extermination of American Indians. This process was followed by other, yet more violent, transfers, including the transfer of the European armies to the whole world to transform it into a "utilizable matter;" the transfer of western human surplus to western settlement enclaves (as was the case in Algeria, South Africa and Palestine); the transfer of minority groups to other countries (the Chinese to Malaysia and the Jews to Argentina); the transfer of Asians and Africans to the Americas; and last, but not least, the transfer of the Jewish question from Europe to the Middle East. Elmessiri cites the Balfour Declaration as an example of political transfer as it aimed at transferring the remaining Jews from Europe to Palestine "in a bid to employ them in the service of the interests and the ends of western civilization."[90]

In all these examples human beings are viewed as utilizable, trans-ferable and disposable matter. It is precisely for this reason that Elmessiri insists that the Nazi genocide was not a mere aberration of the history of neither Germany nor the modern West.[91] Nazism, according to Elmessiri, represents the paradigmatic moment of west-ern civilization. The Nazis, as always, Elmessiri suggests, were keen on using such objective and neutral terms as transfer, resettlement, final solution, racial hygiene and euthanasia, all of which led to the neutral-ization of perception, particularly the perpetrator's perception of the victim as an object or utilized matter.[92] The Holocaust, however, did not only target the Jews but also other human beings, including the mentally retarded, old people, Slavs, communists, criminals and drug addicts, all of whom were viewed as "transferable and disposable matter."[93]

V

Bauman and the Postmodern Secular Dilemma

THE transition from modernity to postmodernity is represented metaphorically in Bauman's and Elmessiri's writings as an inherent transformation from solid modernity or solid rational materialism (reason, science, nation/state, families, and factories) to liquid modernity or liquid non-rational materialism (body, sex, global markets and consumption). This chapter approaches the mapping of this transformation in Bauman's writings, and the last chapter will trace Elmessiri's mapping of this transformation with particular emphasis on its convergence with, and divergence from, that of Bauman.

5.1 END OF INTELLECTUAL IMPERIALISM

Bauman assumes that there is a "genetic bond" between modernity and postmodernity. "Solid modernity" aspired to establish

> a fully rational perfect world, rationally perfect, or perfectly rational.... The most powerful thinkers were convinced that it was a matter of acquiring enough information, enough knowledge, and enough technological skills in order to achieve such a perfect world. Change was seen as temporary until we construct a world which won't require further change.[1]

This utopian urge, however, has not been fulfilled, and new conditions have been emerging. Understanding the nature of these conditions can be grasped only if compared to the utopian ambitions of modernity. The basic assumption of *les philosophes* was that more education would necessarily entail more rationality and tolerance. However, this assumption, according to Karen Armstrong, "proved to be as utopian as any of the messianic fantasies," and secular ideologies "proved to be just as murderous as the old religious bigotry, as become clear in the Nazi Holocaust and the Soviet Gulag."[2] Bauman underlines the ironic transformation of the basic assumption of the Enlightenment, and modernity at large, by drawing our attention to the two Greek lexemes of the word "utopia": eutopia (a good society) and outopia (nowhere).[3]

The term postmodernity, in Bauman's view, underlines the defining traits of the conditions that emerged throughout the affluent countries in the course of the twentieth century, and took its present shape in the second half of that century.[4] Postmodernity was seen by the early Bauman as a new human condition resulting from the divorce between culture and power or the nation-state and the authority of intellect. In the new condition, intellectuals no longer play the role of the legislators and their position is reduced to the modest role of the "interpreters" and "semiotic brokers." Though the intellectuals may remain loyal to their elevated and lofty ideals of freedom and justice, they have abandoned "the universalistic ambitions" of modernity. And even if they still maintain such ambitions, their opinions are set on the same level of any other ordinary citizens. The postmodern political state is hardly in need of intellectual mobilization, and it relies instead on the rational techniques of coercion, panoptical control and the seduction of the market; and therefore, culture is no longer expected to be the intellectuals' monopolistic domain of authority.[5]

The postmodern world, in Bauman's view, celebrates the "political dispossession of the intellectuals" and the end of their "intellectual imperialism."[6] Unlike the age of the Enlightenment and the era of solid modernity which represented a glorified image of *Les philosophes*, the postmodern worldview conceives of the intellectuals as mere "semiotic brokers with the function of facilitating communication between communities and traditions."[7] Bauman does not hesitate to claim that the "universalist, imperialist, and assimilationist ambitions of the modern state are resented everywhere."[8] The role of the intellectuals becomes a target of ridicule in postmodern times because history has become nothing but scattered details and phenomena dominated by the reign of relativity. The realm of art is no exception, since the boundaries between art and non-art are blurred in the same way the boundaries between truth and falsity, justice and injustice are blurred. Over and above, postmodernity witnesses the dissolution of the signifier and the signified as well as the distortion of communication. Here the decline of the position of the intellectuals is eloquently described by Bauman in a series of rhetorical questions:

> How ridiculous it seems to try to change the direction of history when no powers give an inkling that they wish to give history direction. How empty seems the effort to show that what passes for truth is false when nothing has the courage and the stamina to declare itself as truth for everybody and for all times. How farcical it seems to fight for genuine art when one can no more drop anything incidentally without the dropped object being proclaimed art. How quixotic to debunk the distortion in the representation of reality once no reality claims to be more real than its representation. How idle it seems to exhort people to go there rather than somewhere else in a world in which everything goes.[9]

Though Bauman conceives of postmodernity as a chance to open the closed systems of modernity and to transcend the universalistic ambitions of the intellectuals as legislators, he is also aware of the dilemmas of postmodernity, particularly its tendency to challenge all foundations and any points of referentiality. Bauman refers to the domain of art and literature as obvious examples that reflect the end of the ambitions of legislation in postmodernity; there are no longer any explicit and determined rules that govern or control the discourses of taste and artistic judgment. The best metaphor that can reflect the state of contemporary art, in Bauman's view, is that of the rhizome, a metaphor which is very close to Jacque Derrida's metaphor of the zigzag movement that characterizes the infinite, unexpected and undetectable direction of the process of both artistic creation and aesthetic interpretation. Caught in a state of "perpetual present," art and literature do not conform to any vision of development or rules, embracing instead the absence of all referential frameworks. It is precisely for this reason that postmodern art can be conceived of as a state of protest against the notions of mimesis and its negative connotations. This postmodern orientation, however, has its promise of creativity as well as its threat of radicalism.

Postmodernist theories, in Bauman's view, can be conceived of as an explicit declaration of the mitigation of the ambitions of modernist art and critical reception; it is a call for the end of political or missionary ambitions of art, of artistic canons, and of interest in aesthetic grounds. In short, it is a declaration of the "impossibility of legislating the rules" that distinguish between true art on the one hand and non–art or bad art on the other.[10]

Bauman's attitude is influenced by the views of Walter Benjamin, particularly his reference to what Marcel Duchamp had already shown in 1919. Andreas Huyssen refers to Benjamin's lamentation on the loss of the aura of artistic creation and reception, including *l'art engage* and critical realism:

> By iconoclastically altering a reproduction of the Mona Lisa and, to use another example, by exhibiting a mass-produced urinal as a fountain sculpture, Marcel Duchamp succeeded in destroying what Benjamin called the traditional art work's aura, that aura of authenticity and uniqueness that constituted the work's distance from life and that required contemplation and immersion on the part of the spectator.[11]

Bauman refers to this act as one of the most "scandalous" acts of "ostensible radicalism," foreshadowing the anarchy that dominates the creation and the perception of art at present:

> Post-modern art (which truly took off, according to most analysts, only in the 1970s) has gone a long way now from the iconoclastic gesture of Marcel

Duchamp, who sent to an art exhibition a urinal dubbed 'Fountain' and signed 'Richard Mutt,' with the explanation that 'whether Mr Mutt with his own hands made the fountain or not has no importance. He *chose* it.'[12]

It seems that Bauman is shocked with this vulgarity of non-art, and one wonders what his reaction and comment would be if he were acquainted with Vanessa Beecroft's latest public performance which transformed the pictorial tradition of idealized fantasy of feminity and the world of naked bodies into reality. According to Luke Harding, the performance featured one hundred women standing still in Berlin's *Neue Nationalgalerie* for three hours, each woman oiled from the waist up and wearing nothing but a pair of pantyhose. The performance was said to be an attempt at the exposition of "naturalness," since these naked bodies were expected to do nothing on stage but to react "naturally" to their physical feeling in the form of physical actions as standing, sitting, lying and yawning.[13]

5.2 PROMISE AND RISK OF POSTMODERN ETHICS

The state of confusion in mapping postmodernity becomes very obvious when Bauman introduces many definitions to cover the newly emergent human condition. Here he does not define postmodernity as the situation created by the divorce between the state and the intellectuals but as

the state of mind of philosophers, social thinkers, artists – all those people on whom we rely when we are in a pensive mood or just pause for a moment to find out whence we are moving or being moved.[14]

Philosophers, social thinkers and artists are expected to articulate the new emergent reality and its orientation. However, the cognitive mapping of postmodernity presupposes a state of confusion not only in the world around us but also in the way a critic or a philosopher attempts to determine the contours or the significant signs of such a map. In other words, the state of confusion does not exclude the philosophers, the artists and the intellectuals who attempt to map this confusion because they themselves are, as cartographers of the post-modern, like nomads in uncharted space.

The state of confusion, if not inconsistency and ambiguity, is enhanced by the fact that it is very difficult for Bauman to determine the significant difference between modernity and postmodernity, especially when he stresses that the postmodern mind is the radical victory of modern critical culture over the modern society it aimed to improve through throwing it wide open to its own potential.[15] It comes as no surprise then that Bauman does not provide a clear-cut definition of postmodernity. Rather, he takes refuge in metaphors so as to uncover the complexity of the new emergent reality.

Like Jameson, Bauman is aware that no theory of modernity makes sense today unless it comes to terms with the hypothesis of a postmodern break with the modern. The dominant paradigms of modernity, as Bauman suggests, celebrated a shared vision of modern history as a movement with a direction by means of universalization, rationalization or systemization. None of those concepts can be upheld in the light of postmodern experience, and new metaphors are required to describe the newly emergent phenomena and their point of convergence with and divergence from the original project of modernity. Not surprisingly, Bauman holds that it is necessary to discard the metaphor of progress and the conception of society as an organismic or mechanistic metaphor because all order that can be found is a local and transitory phenomenon whose nature can be grasped by a metaphor of a whirlpool appearing in the flow of a river, retaining its shape only for a relatively brief period and only at the expense of constant renewal of content.[16]

This metaphoric representation, in Bauman's view, signals the movement from the closed systems of modernity to the open systems of postmodernity i.e. from a uni-dimensional mode of existence and a singular modernity to a multiplicity of being-in-the-world and alternative modernities. Within the postmodern worldview, the very image of society as the human body or the *telos* of progress (the organismic metaphor) or as the system and machine (the mechanistic metaphor) are no longer operative because agency and habitat have become more important as unpredictable and complex systems.

In an attempt to trace the most decisive difference between modernity and postmodernity as understood by Bauman, Peter Beilharz argues that the postmodern worldview gives priority to localism, relativism, plurality of models, communities of meaning and hermeneutic interpretation over the universalistic ambitions of intellectuals, the obsession with mastery over nature and social engineering.[17] According to this explanation, postmodernity can be seen as a critique of culture rather than a new vision that entirely breaks with modernity; and therefore, the nature and the contours of postmodernity cannot be fully determined, giving rise to a state of confusion, ambiguity and ambivalence that can be expressed only in metaphors. Vit Vanicek attributes Bauman's metaphorical approach to postmodernity to the fact that metaphorical expressions try to capture the "elusive nature of post-modernity," providing the reader with the realization that such metaphorical language is inevitable for reinforcing the way the new human condition is being presented.[18]

A close examination of Bauman's early understanding of postmodernity shows that he bases his perception of postmodernity on a call for the abandonment of the "ontological and epistemological premises of modernity."[19] Postmodernity called into question the premises of social reality, including art, the nation-state, society, ethnicity, race, family, gender and religion. Thus an adequate theory of postmodernity was expected to be constructed only in a "cognitive space organized by a different set of assumptions; it needs its own vocabulary."[20]

But Bauman's faith in the achievements of the Enlightenment and modernity leads him into a state of confusion in mapping postmodernity. In other words, it is extremely difficult for a European intellectual to abandon the legacy of Western modernity, one which is seen as, to borrow Bauman, an "incomplete adventure" or, to borrow Habermas, an "incomplete project." It is precisely for this reason that Bauman finds it difficult, paradoxically, to abandon modernity; and therefore, he defines postmodernity as "modernity conscious of its true nature," "modernity for itself" and "modernity emancipated from false consciousness"[21]

Though aware of the fact that postmodernity is an inherently poly-semic and controversial idea, Bauman has attempted to describe its main tenets and its expected roles. Five major tenets and roles can be detected in Bauman's writings on postmodernity: (1) the acceptance of the plurality of the world; (2) the resolute emancipation from the modern drive to overcome ambivalence; (3) the admittance of the non-feasibility of the original project of modernity; (4) the belief in the possibility of peaceful coexistence rather than a temporary equilibrium of hostile powers; and (5) the celebration of a new trinity: liberty, diversity and tolerance as opposed to nation, blood and territory.

Bauman, however, is not idealistic, and he believes that if the aforementioned ambitions fail to materialize, postmodernity will be another version of "adolescent modernity." Here the state of confu-sion in cognitive mapping is clear because we are confronted with a state of fluidity and uncertainty that defies predication or clear-cut definitions. Though aware of the social and moral consequences of the "collapse of grand narratives," "the death of God," "the death of man" and the "disappearance of all sacred and secular authorities," Bauman is still optimistic, and he attempts to dismiss our exaggerated "popular fear of the void," "anarchy" and "universal carnage."[22]

Bauman is aware of the fact that postmodernity is characterized by the dominance of relativity, especially when subjectivity becomes the only ultimate authority and when postmodernity "proclaims all restrictions on freedom illegal, at the same time doing away with social certainty and legalizing ethical uncertainty. Existential insecurity – ontological contingency of being – is the result."[23]

According to Richard Bernstein, it is true that the ambitions and the intentions of postmodernists are good, particularly their critiques of logo-centrism, Euro-centrism, humanism, and the Enlightenment legacy. They, however, are believed to be obsessed with a "relentless questing of any appeal to *archai* or foundations."[24]

In both *Modernity and the Holocaust* (1989) and *Postmodern Ethics* (1993), Bauman attempted to show that technological and bureaucratic efficiency and state monopolization of action are the major forces that disrupted the possibility of transcendence and the recognition of the humanity of all human beings. Killing at distance within a closed and rationalized system turned the intersubjective relationship among human beings into a subject-object relationship that discards all implications of guilt and responsibility. The liberation of means from ends is seen as a major mechanism of modernity, one which has led to the marginalization of God, and thus "sapped the most solid of grounds on which moral instruction rested in the past," promoting contractual obligations and even replacing "being for the other" with "being for oneself."[25]

In order that Bauman overcomes the vacuum created by rationalistic materialism he takes refuge in the philosophy of Emmanuel Lévinas (1906-1995), particularly his notion of the ethic of care for the Other. Bauman's reference to Lévinas is interpreted by Keith Tester as an attempt to recover ethics from the vacuum "created by metaphysical and historical rebellion when they are combined with the modern instruments of rationality."[26]

Ross Abbinnett holds that the centrality of the concept of the care for the Other can be seen as response to the negative consequences of modernity in general and the Holocaust in particular. Emmanuel Lévinas attempted to introduce a transcendental philosophy based on the experience of the encounter with the Other i.e. the face-to-face encounter with the Other-than-self rather than the legislative structures of law, contractual obligations and economic necessity. This encounter is a metaphysical, though non-ontological, tendency towards transcendence and responsibility for the Other.[27]

Lévinas himself maintains that his philosophy is based on a "phenomenology of sociality" that takes the face of the other man as the starting point of transcendence. It is a form of transcendence based on an intersubjective relationship among human beings rather than on ontology or formal legislation (perhaps a Kantian universal moral law). The transcendence of the self in the face of the other, or the situation of becoming oneself as another, is seen as the locus of transcendence as it creates the fear of rejecting, excluding, exiling or killing the Other.

Transcendence, Lévinas holds, becomes a never-ending process in which the human subject questions itself whether the *Da* (there) of *Dasein* (being-there) is not the usurpation of someone's place.[28] Here transcendence is almost synonymous with the infinite. Lévinas puts it this way:

> The face-to-face is a relation in which the *I* frees itself from being limited to itself...from its reclusion within itself, from an existence in which the adventures are but an odyssey, i.e. a return to the island. The exodus of that limitation of the *I* to itself, which is revealed in a whole series of reflections of contemporary philosophy on the meeting with the Other...is also worthy of the adjective infinite.[29]

Lévinas's philosophy is a response to the consequences of modernity, especially the processes of bureaucratization and rationalization that stood as an obstacle between the *I* and the Other through a long process of disciplinary actions and legislative morality. Here postmodern morality is offered as a way out of the universalistic ambitions that excludes the Other.

Fascinated with Lévinas's philosophy, Bauman believes that postmodern ethics can be based on the realization of the following ideas: (1) human beings are morally ambivalent; (2) the moral code is thoroughly personal; (3) moral phenomena are inherently non-rational because they are not regular, repetitive, and predictable; (4) morality is not universalizable since it is relative to time and place; (5) postmodern morality is neither relativistic nor nihilistic but it opposes the monopoly of ethical authority.[30] Postmodern ethics repudiates all attempts to impose a comprehensive ethical code that overlooks other temporalities and becomes nothing but an instrument of domination. Bauman maintains that humankind's moral unity is thinkable as the utopian horizon of deconstructing the claims of nation-states and nations-in-search-of-the-state.[31]

The presence of Lévinas in Bauman's thought becomes very obvious when he states that morality is a transcendence of being or the chance of such a transcendence through the choice of 'face to face' with the Other as if being had no voice, or if it had voice, that voice can be ignored.³² Though Bauman emphasizes that this vision does not imply the reign of subjectivity, relativism and nihilism, it is better to shed light on the criticism levelled against this notion of postmodern ethics.

Ross Abbinnett argues that western civilization in both its modern and postmodern versions, in almost all Bauman's writings, conceived of human beings as "technical utilities" with "functionally specific traits;" and therefore, it comes to denote "the instrumental, technical and materialistic relations" which Bauman views as "the determinants of cognitive, disciplinary space." Abbinnett maintains that a political structure is required to overcome the "functionalisation of both the cognitive and the aesthetic space." However, Bauman, according to Abbinnett, repeats a certain Rousseauist logic in which human nature, in its original and compassionate purity, is constantly set in a sharp contrast with the "corruptive" institutions of civilization.³³

Bauman's idealistic vision has been also repudiated by Shaun Best. The major problem of this perception of ethics, in Best's view, is that it attempts to give the impression that the "I am responsible for the Other," and "I am responsible for myself" come to mean the same thing.³⁴ The same critique has also been launched by Ruud Kaulingfreks who argues that Bauman comes very close to a "romantic and simplistic" view of organization being evil and man being essentially good as long as he stays in the proximity of the Other. It comes very close to a romanticism of emotions, impulses, spontaneity and passions versus the distance of reason and calculated behaviour.³⁵

5.3 FROM POSTMODERNITY TO LIQUID MODERNITY

In his late writings, Bauman comes to realize that the critical scene is abundant with confusing and conflicting interpretations of postmodernity. More importantly, the terms postmodernity and postmodernism have been "hopelessly confused" and used in many cases "synonymically." Bauman found himself "in the company of bedfellows" with whom he "would rather not share a bed," especially when the word "postmodernity" started to imply the "end of modernity."³⁶

Bauman, nevertheless, has rejected the alternative terms introduced by Anthony Giddens (late modernity); Ulrich Beck (second modernity); and George Balandier (*surmodernite*). He even decided to abandon the term postmodernity altogether, arguing that the postmodern age turned out to be, as Michael Hviid Jacobsen puts it, a "pandemonium instead of the promised paradise."37 Postmodernity, like modernity, has become an "anti-eschatological revolution."38 Bauman's realization of the loss of the aura of postmodernity became very obvious when he published *Postmodernity and its Discontents* (1997). Beilharz remarks:

> Around 1989 the idea of the postmodern still had the aura of a modernist mission, to save us from the stultifying past and high certainty that for Bauman characterizes modernity. Postmodernity seemed to offer so much; less than ten years later, a decade of living without an alternative, and the postmodern was beginning to look tawdry, having delivered little by way of new lives to either intellectuals or especially to vagabonds.39

"Liquid modernity" is the new metaphor Bauman introduces to map the transformation of western modernity. This metaphor echoes Karl Marx's metaphor "all that is solid melts into air," which he used in the Communist Manifesto in reference to the self-confident modern spirit and its ambitions to change the so-called stagnant traditions. The same metaphor was used in the early 1980s by Marshall Berman as the title of his well-known book *All That is Solid Melts into Air: The Experience of Modernity* (1982). Commenting on the cosmic scope and visionary grandeur of Marx's image, Berman argues that the affinities between Karl Marx and the modernists will be clearer if the entire image is quoted: "all that is solid melts into air, all that is holy is profaned, and men at last are forced to face with sober senses the real conditions of their lives and their relations with their fellow men." The significance of this metaphor lies in the fact that Marx's proclamation of the destruction of everything holy goes beyond the standard nineteenth-century materialist argument against the existence of God and highlights the absence of the very aura of holiness, affirming that it would be very difficult for us to understand ourselves in the present unless we confront what is absent.[40]

In the late twentieth-century and at the beginning of the 21st century, the melting of solids has acquired a new meaning or, to borrow Paul Ricoeur, a "surplus of meaning." According to Bauman, such Marxist concepts and terminology as "bourgeois society," "alien-ation," "reification" and even "liquefaction" had been used in a com-pletely different context and circumstances and for entirely different analytical purposes. In *Liquid Modernity* (2000), Bauman points out that modernity's call for melting all solids was feverishly sought "not in order to do away with the solids once and for all...but to clear the site for *new and improved solids*."[41]

In a conversation with Keith Tester, Bauman refers to Thomas Kuhn's notion of paradigm shift and stresses that new concepts are avidly sought when "the old concept tends to the aspects of realities which are no longer central and offers an axis around which the cur-rent experience no longer rotates."[42] In the present stage of the history of modernity, traditional metaphors have lost much of their "original cognitive capacity" because they no longer have a significant place in our contemporary experience.[43]

But why does Bauman choose this metaphor of liquidity in partic-ular? Among the crucial reasons behind Bauman admiration of the images of fluidity and liquidity as fitting metaphors to grasp the nature of this phase in the history of modernity is that liquids, unlike solids, "cannot easily hold their shape. Fluids...neither fix space nor bind time.... [They] do not keep to any shape for long and are constantly ready (and prone) to change."[44] In an interview with Milena Yakimova, Bauman points out the sensitivity of fluids, as opposed to solids, to time and change; they make salient the brittleness and break-ability of both inter-human bonds and identities. The liquidity metaphor has been dominating Bauman's recent publications: *Liquid Modernity* (2000), *Liquid Love* (2003), *Liquid Life* (2005), *Liquid Fear* (2006) and *Liquid Times* (2006).[45]

5.3.1 *From Gardeners to Hunters*

In *Liquid Life*, Bauman defines the present mode of being as "liquid life" dominated by a growing atmosphere of "uncertainty" and "fast-moving events," a "succession of new beginnings" or "the swift and painless endings."[46] This liquid mode of existence is compared to a risky and fearful game of musical chairs that threatens to exclude the powerless, the poor, and all those who cannot or do not want to cope with the fast-changing liquid life. Progress is no longer a metaphor of "sweet dreams and expectations," "radical optimism" and "promise of universally shared and lasting happiness" but a terrible nightmare and a sinister real "game of musical chairs" in which a second's inattention results in irreversible defeat and exclusion.[47]

Unlike solid modernity, liquid modernity can do without a strong emphasis on the ideas of patriotism and the modern hero who expresses his willingness to die for the nation. As Ulrich Im Hof suggests, patriotism did not refer only to loyalty to the king but also to a sense of identity with a fatherland, one that is different from other nations. This process required the creation of a glorified image of historical authenticity and patriotic virtue, thus implying a powerful state with a political will to achieve the ambitions of the Enlightenment.[48]

Bauman relates the dominance of national and heroic patriotism in solid modern times to secularization and the deification of the nation-state. The modern hero is enlisted by the modern nation-state not for the sake of moral salvation but for the sake of securing the secular and "material immortality of the nation;" the latter task is confirmed by the erection of memorials that could stand as an ample evidence of the material gains and benefits gained by death on the battlefield:

> [M]odernity also deified and enchanted the 'nation,' the new authority – and so by proxy the man-made institutions that claimed to speak and act in its name. 'The sacred' was not so much disavowed as made the target of an 'unfriendly takeover': moved under different management and put in the service of the emergent nation-state. The same happened to the martyr: he was enlisted by the nation-state under a new name of the hero.[49]

In liquid modernity, the utopian imagination of heroism, martyr-dom and sacrifice is severely ridiculed, stressing instead the primacy of the pleasure principle. Here it is very important to contrast Bauman's *Postmodernity and Its Discontents* with Sigmund Freud's *Civilization and Its Discontents*. Whereas Freud emphasized the reality principle and its connotations of repression, regulation, suppression and forced renun-ciation, Bauman underlines the reign of individual freedom combined with a growing sense of uncertainty and insecurity.[50]

Unlike solid modernity, liquid modernity is associated with "free reign of the pleasure principle in the realm of consumption" because reality is no longer the enemy of pleasure. On the contrary, "spending is a duty," since it gives "symbolic rivalry" and monopolizes the "definition of good life."[51] Here Bauman's thesis is set in a sharp contrast with Freud's old lamentations because the reality principle "has today to defend itself in the court of justice in which the pleasure principle is the presiding judge."[52]

According to Bauman, it is hardly surprising that the metaphors of the gamekeeper, the gardener, the martyr and the hero are thrown into the background in the modern liquid era. Bauman attributes the cele-bration of "the end of utopia" and the fading of utopian imagination to the transformation from solid modernity to liquid modernity i.e. the transformation from the gardener's intervention to the hunter's free-dom. In this sense, human beings are granted their freedom and are required to be independent and to play the role of the hunter. Bauman describes this stage as a fertile soil for the growing atmosphere of both individualization and deregulation.[53]

In the modern liquid era, the cognitive map of prospective con-sumers is manipulated by seductive commodity symbols: (1) the authority of celebrities (public personalities, great athletes, popular actors and singers) and (2) the authority of science (authority of scientific surveys, numbers and algebraic formulae). These authorities are "symbols of social approval," "rational and solid knowledge" and "well-informed choice."[54] Bauman suggests that liquid modernity can be seen as a "casino-like culture," in which life is turned into individual games of "self-enclosed, self-referential and self-centred episodes," a "series of new beginnings" or a "collection of short stories."[55] The saddest irony, according to Bauman, is that lavish consumption becomes the sign of success and fame. The possession and consumption of certain objects are seen as necessary conditions of happiness and perhaps even of human dignity.[56]

Liquid modern life is referred to as a "consuming life," since it transforms the whole world, including human beings and their lifestyles, into "objects of consumption" or, to borrow Elmessiri, "useful matter." When objects, humans and cultural traditions lose their "usefulness" or "instrumental value," they can be, and should be, easily disposed of. The saddest irony is that any attachment or expression of loyalty to old objects or traditions is conceived of as "a cause of shame, not pride."[57] When possession and consumption of objects become the central value of life, all human beings are thus haunted by "the spectre of exclusion."[58] The consumption race is merciless:

> The true task in the race is (temporary) rescue from being excluded into the ranks of the destroyed and avoiding being consigned to waste. And with the competition turning global, the running must now be done round a global track.[59]

5.3.2 *Sex and the Body: The Unwinnable Jihad*

In liquid consumerist societies, such lofty concepts as 'self' or 'identity' are thrown into the background and the metaphor of the body comes to the fore. The celebration of the body is no longer centred on the intensification of production and capital accumulation (the Weberian Protestant asceticism) in industrial plants or military service in the army. As Giddens suggests, the body, in the spheres of biological reproduction and medical interventions, has become a "phenomenon of choices and options."[60] This orientation is closely related to the dynamics of the market which has replaced both the factory floor and the battlefield. The consuming body "moves into the focus of life politics as its ultimate purpose, the body is caste in a unique position not comparable with the role assigned to any other entity in the *Lebenswelt*."[61]

Consumerism has created a "body-centred" and "body-fascinated" individual addicted to the struggle for pleasure and fitness. Bauman uses an originally Islamic concept as a metaphor to place emphasis on the significance of the struggle for fitness; the latter is compared to "the lifelong, unwinnable jihad."[62] The celebration of the body has become one of the most prominent characteristics of liquid "worldly transcendence" or, to be more precise, the neo-Gnostic immanence. In other words, it becomes the 'pattern' or 'supreme metaphor' for the effort to transcend individual immortality.[63] Bauman argues that

> the body itself turned into an object for technology; the owner of the body was now a manager, a supervisor and an operator rolled into one, and the medical profession supplied him or her with ever more complex technological products to perform these functions.[64]

The centrality of the body metaphor has transformed the denotations and connotations of the term 'individual.' At the beginning of the modern era, this term was usually associated with the notions of free choice and responsibility, and it referred to a complex social structure based on 'a combination of gravitation and repulsion' among the members of society. This meaning is no longer operative and the term 'individuality' comes to denote the collapse of the "dense social bonds that tightly wrapped the totality of life's activities."[65] Individuals in the liquid era are not just sensation seekers; they are obsessed with learning the art of enjoying and enhancing sensation. Here Bauman uses a sexual metaphor to explain the desire to enhance "sensual intensity" and the "overwhelming sensation":

> The purpose of such training is provided by the metaphor of multiple orgasm: a fit body, served by an equally well-trained mind, is a body capable of repeated, even continuous, intensity of sensations, a body forever 'on the high,' constantly open to all chances of experience which the world around may provide – a sort of well-tempered clavier always ready to emit tunes of sublime beauty.[66]

In the phase of solid modernity, sex was seen as one of the most outstanding areas where the panoptical modern power was exercised. Bauman puts it bluntly when he says, the role of the male master was "akin to that of the foreman in the factory or the sergeant in the army."[67] Bauman holds that sex was primarily functional and instrumental, but the rules of the game have changed or, to be more precise, have disappeared altogether.

Sex is no longer seen as an instrument of creating lasting social structures and it "serves as first and foremost the process of the ongoing atomization."[68] Liquid free-floating eroticism

> enters alliance with neither sexual reproduction nor love, claiming independence
> from both neighbours and flatly refusing all responsibility for the impact it may
> make on their fate; it proudly and boldly proclaims itself to be its own only, and
> sufficient, reason and purpose.[69]

As Bauman suggests in his thought-provoking paper "On Post-modern Uses of Sex," sexual activity in its postmodern rendition is "focused narrowly on its orgasmic effect.... Its paramount task is to supply ever stronger, infinitely variable, perfectly novel and unprecedented *Erlebnisse*."[70] The celebration of sex is accompanied not only with the liquefaction of the family as a basic social unit but also with the new danger of paternal love and intimacy:

> Children are now perceived mainly as sexual objects and as potential victims of
> their parents as sexual subjects; and since the parents are by nature stronger than
> their children and placed in the position of power, paternal sexuality may easily
> lead to the abuse of that power in the service of the parents' sexual instincts. The
> specter of sex, therefore, also haunts family homes.[71]

In liquid modernity, identities are no longer seen as 'meticulously designed,' 'carefully built' and 'rock-solid.' "Solidity," Bauman says, "is an anathema as is all permanence — now the sign of dangerous maladjustment to the rapidly and unpredictably changing world, to the surprise opportunities it holds and the speed with which it transforms yesterday's assets into today's liabilities."⁷² Commenting on Bauman's analysis and expressing his support for the postmodern turn, Steven Seidman remarks:

> [A]s a fellow traveller along the postmodern road, I am in broad sympathy with much of what Bauman says. I especially admire the moral vision that he articulates. My experience as a Jew, as gay, as a parent, as a left intellectual, as a feminist man, feels like it will more likely be validated within a postmodern discourse than within modernist orthodoxy, which seems uncomfortable with these heterogeneous identities.⁷³

This quotation uncovers the most remarkable ironies that Sigmund Freud himself failed to anticipate. Modern civilization has abandoned the notion of solidity; and therefore, a free liquid reign to the sexual constitution of human beings becomes a potential possibility, if not a constitutional right. Freud's old lamentations, or rather, unfulfilled aspirations have been realized.⁷⁴

The dominance of the pleasure principle has led Bauman to conclude that the whole world has been transformed into two classes: tourists and vagabonds. The latter are said to be the waste of the world which has dedicated itself to tourist services:

> The tourists stay or move at their hearts' desire. They abandon a site when new untried opportunities beckon elsewhere. The vagabonds know that they won't stay in a place for long, however strongly they wish to, since nowhere they stop are they likely to be welcome. The tourists move because they find the world within their (global) reach irresistibly *attractive* – the vagabonds move because they find the world within their (local) reach unbearably *inhospitable*. The tourists travel because *they want to*; the vagabonds because *they have no other bearable choice*.⁷⁵

Tourists and vagabonds are represented as the major 'metaphors of contemporary life' because we all are plotted on a continuum stretched between the poles of the "perfect tourist" and the "vagabond beyond remedy."⁷⁶ Bauman suggests that postmodern liquid life can be viewed as the transformation from the celebration of martyrs and heroes to the celebration of tourists and celebrities. The liquid post-modern era, however, cannot continue without the existence of vagabonds:

> The vagabonds, the victims of the world which made the tourists into its heroes, have their uses, after all; as the sociologists love to say – they are 'functional.' It is difficult to live in their neighbourhood, but it is unthinkable to live without them. It is their all-too-blatant hardships that reduce one's own worries to marginal inconveniences. It is their evident unhappiness that inspires the rest to thank God daily for having made them tourists.[77]

Liquid life, according to Bauman, can do without martyrs and heroes and it even fights the manifestations of any loyalty to martyr-dom or heroism and considers them useless and irrational. However, Bauman stresses that the contradictions of postmodernity, particularly ontological and existential insecurities, give rise to a new postmodern religion i.e. fundamentalism. He insists that if the Holocaust is a legitimate child of modernity, fundamentalism is a 'legitimate child of postmodernity.' Bauman declares that religious fundamentalism offers an "alternative rationality" that unloads the burden of responsibility proclaimed by omnipotent postmodern culture and promoted by omnipotent market publicity.[78] Postmodern liquidity is a fertile soil for the growth of the Manichean vision which consists of two separate worlds in which the 'other' half is ruled by Satan and 'our' half is the one where good and truth reign. Bauman stresses that this vision is by no means an 'invention of Islamic fundamentalism' and he invites the reader to reflect on this fact:

> Let's remember that Islam has no monopoly on this vision. If we look at Palestinian and Israeli radicals, they both, amazingly, use the same sort of vocabulary. Both the Palestinian and Israeli sides present the conflict as a final clash between Jehovah and Mohammed and not between Palestinians and Israeli settlers. We see a quite similar kind of vocabulary when we analyze the news coverage of the last American elections, although the gods being worshiped had different names. But one must admit that in this vast current of today's

Manichaeism, Islam has occupied a very important position, and this is for geo-political reasons.[79]

Karen Armstrong states that fundamentalism cannot be regarded as a purely Islamic phenomena; it is a global fact and has surfaced in very major faith in response to the problems of western modernity. Armstrong puts it this way:

> At first religious people try to reform their traditions and effect a marriage between them and modern culture, as we have seen the Muslim reformers do. But when these moderate measures are found to be of no avail, some people resort to extreme methods, and a fundamentalist movement is born.[80]

VI

Elmessiri and Postmodern Liquidity

THE solid phase of secular modernity, in Elmessiri's view, became impossible to hold by the end of the nineteenth century, and its inherent transformations reached their climax in the second half of the twentieth century. The major question of the period of solid modernity and the era of heroic materialism took the following formula: what was the centre of the universe, man or nature? More radical questions, however, emerged in the liquid era of modernity. Elmessiri formulates these questions in a way that is very close to Bauman's rhetorical questions in the opening pages of the previous chapter:

> How to believe in the existence of a meaningful, transcendent and permanent totality within the framework of materialist philosophy? How can there be a state of permanence within a materialist framework while matter is discovered to be constantly mobile? How to achieve transcendence while matter does not know transcendence? How can we find a meaning in the universe while matter is a meaningless and aimless movement? How to maintain the duality of man/nature in a materialistic and monistic world while matter knows only one law? How to escape from the grip of perpetual becoming in the framework of a materialist philosophy?[1]

Unlike Bauman who drew heavily on the philosophy of the French philosopher Emmanuel Lévinas to emphasize the potential of postmodernity for transcendence, Elmessiri devoted few pages in his

Mawsūᶜat to the analysis of Lévinas's philosophy as a way out from the crisis of modernity and its grave consequences. Elmessiri admits that Lévinas's philosophy is characterized by a feverish search for solid foundations that could resist the processes of liquefaction resulting from the modern and the postmodern worldview. However, Lévinas's philosophy, in Elmessiri's view, can be approached only within the framework of the death of God theology that attempts to establish relatively solid foundations.

Elmessiri repudiates Lévinas's idealistic philosophy though it attempts to replace the Hobbesian and Darwinian worldview with the metaphysical care for the Other. This repudiation can be attributed to two major reasons: (1) making the Other the eschatological hope and the infinite itself, and (2) stressing Judaism as the foundation of true humanity and the Jewish people as the best proponents of the care and responsibility for the Other. It is precisely for these reasons that Elmessiri conceives of Lévinas's attempt at transcendence as a form of immanentization. Judaism is represented as the ideal ideology that takes the form of a modern state and epitomizes the human ethical system. Above all, there exists, as Elmessiri suggests, not only one Other but two: acceptable Other and unacceptable Other. The very idea of the Care for the Other becomes problematic because the close Other (the Jewish Other) is preferred to the strange Other (the non-Jewish Other). The 'responsibility' for this perplexing Other can be promoted and protected by the State as the holy God and the Jews as the chosen people.[2] Elmessiri's critique of this philosophy is thus humanistic and convincing, since it repudiates the idea of the chosen community. This critique, however, does not include any reference citations that can prove the accusations levelled against Lévinas and his philosophy of the Other.

6.1 THE RHIZOME: ILLUSION OF TRANSCENDENCE

The early Bauman had great expectations of the postmodern turn, arguing that postmodernity is neither a mechanistic nor an organismic paradigm but an open system of pluralism and tolerance to difference.

Unlike Bauman, Elmessiri kept underlining the failure of modernity and its false consciousness:

> The humanist illusion of self-transcendence and of an ethics without metaphysics, or an ethics based on a metaphysics of immanence has been dealt an almost deadly blow by two world wars, environmental disasters, the increase of some negative social phenomena (crime, suicide, pornography, teenage pregnancy, etc.) and our increasing realization of the impossibility of ourselves or our environment.[3]

Elmessiri has never conceived of postmodernity as an open system, arguing instead that it is a completely closed system as it excludes all external manifestations of transcendence. The loss of all centres in the postmodern world does not necessarily entail that postmodernity is an open system, especially when the ideas of transcendence, identity, and permanence become outdated and old-fashioned. In other words, the destruction of reference cannot be equated with the liberation of man as it signals the reign of comprehensive liquidity and fragmentation. This perception of postmodernity helped Elmessiri develop his mapping of postmodernity without any sense of confusion and without a need for the long detour that Bauman took to introduce the metaphor of liquidity. Bauman, as a European Jew cannot easily abandon the civilizational adventure of Europe, but Elmessiri, who belongs to a completely different ideological background, can conceive of such a possibility.

Unlike Bauman, whose critique of modernity anticipated his early celebration of postmodernity, Elmessiri never saw postmodernity as a new horizon of emancipation, pluralism or tolerance of difference. On the contrary, he regarded it as a nihilistic and relativistic kind of philosophy with a highly sophisticated sense of pragmatism. It is precisely for this reason that Elmessiri's interpretation of postmodernity can be seen as a continuation of his critique of modernity in its new orientation, if there is any. In other words, the transition to a postmodern world of pluralism, multi-culturalism and alternative modernities is virtually absent, and it is merely a new phase that witnesses a radicalization or even a universalization of the consequences of modernity, one that has reached its climax, as Fredric Jameson suggests, in the "colonization and commercialization of the Unconscious" in the form of mass culture and the culture industry.[4]

One of the most outstanding features of Elmessiri's critique is a constant insistence that postmodernity and postmodernism are synonymous and negative terms usually associated with deconstruction, post-structuralism and the attempt to put an end to metaphysics and humanism. Unlike Bauman, who had great and lofty expectations from the postmodern turn, Elmessiri insists from the outset that postmodernity celebrates the world as nothing but a purely materialistic matter in perpetual flux without any origin or purpose. Unlike Bauman, who has remained faithful to the project of modernity and had great expectations to be realized through postmodernity, Elmessiri has never abandoned his basic assumption that postmodernity is almost synonymous with the failure of modernity and its bankruptcy.[5]

In his attempt to describe the new version of modernity, the early Bauman argued that postmodernity is best seen through the metaphor of the rhizome because it is constructed as an open map rather than a closed book or any other kind of rooted or structuring way of life.[6] Like Bauman, Elmessiri holds that the rhizome becomes the most dominant metaphor that effectively reflects the state of contemporary human condition. However, Elmessiri, unlike Bauman, never conceives of the rhizome as a possibility for openness and transcendence as it signals the absence of all notions of origins, centres and solid causality. Unlike Bauman, Elmessiri has elaborated on the significance of this metaphor, showing how it is intimately tied to the organismic paradigm and emphasizing that it provides us with a new interpretation that goes beyond the traditional and dominant nineteenth century organismic metaphors. The rhizome does not stand for the idea of an organic coherent and predictable whole based on solid causality. On the contrary, there is no distance between the root and the stem or the visible and invisible parts that grow endlessly in all directions. The rhizome signals the transformation from the predictable or monotonous organismic and mechanistic movement to the aimless and unpredictable movement of the postmodern world.[7]

6.2 NATURE AND THE BODY: NEW FUNCTIONAL GROUPS

Elmessiri defines postmodernity as the "epistemological framework underlying the new world order. It is an outlook that denies the centre and does away with referentiality. It refuses to give history or humanity any meaning or centrality. It discards ideology, history and humanity. The world is in a state of perpetual flux."[8] Postmodernity is seen as the transformation from solid modernity to liquid modernity because the project of modernity pronounced the "centrality of man and his ability to control Nature," but it has culminated with the declaration of the death of man in favour of such non-human categories as the machine, the state, the market and power, or in favour of such one-dimensional categories as the body, sex and pleasure.[9]

Elmessiri takes the beginning of the celebration of the body as the starting point of his critique of postmodernity. The celebration of the body, however, can be traced back, according to Jonathan Israel, to the radical Enlightenment erotic discourse or materialist *moralisme* that defended the erotic emancipation of men and women, repudiating the entire system of social pressures and promoting an erotic revolution or a whole new culture of desire and pleasure. What is at stake here is that this vision of nature as guaranteeing sexual utoptia or paradise on earth is an entirely anti-Hobbesian "state of nature."[10]

Here it is important to relate Elmessiri's critique of the celebration of the body to Marquis de Sade's (1740-1814) *La Philosophie Dans le Boudoir* [The Philosophy of the Bedroom] written in 1795. As William Connolly suggests, the Enlightenment viewed nature, particularly the Hobbesian and Rousseauian theories of nature as a state of war and a state of bliss, respectively, as the place where God's light is reflected. However, this transcendental view of nature was despised by Marquis de Sade in his notorious book *La Philosophie Dans le Boudoir* which attacked the very idea of nature as the ground of truth. Marquis de Sade attempted to convey the message that morality, compassion and modesty are all absurd notions that stand between man and pleasure as the sole aim of human existence. Thus nature is no longer conceived as a cohesive system of laws that can help man aspire for such lofty ideals as sacrifice and modesty; it is represented, on the contrary, as a mode of existence that allows everything and anything and thus blurs such established dualities of enlightened discourse as virtue and vice, reason and unreason, natural and unnatural, modesty and indecency. Unlike Hobbes and Rousseau who attempted to reincarnate God or reason in nature, Sade repudiated such attempts and emphasized that nature can no longer be associated with the revelation of God's light or truth but with the pursuit of seduction and the immediate satisfaction of desire.[11] In other words, following the "voice of Nature" cannot be seen as the pursuit of Enlightenment reason, the Rousseauian general will, the social contract, the Kantian transcendental subject or the Hegelian Spirit. Rather, it stands for the immediate gratification of desire and the spontaneous response to the human body and sexual desire, both of which have become the major metaphors in Bauman's and Elmessiri's critique of the epistemological and ontological foundations of postmodernity.

In the phase of liquid non-rational materialism, almost all human beings have been turned into functional groups or *Mamlūks*. We can say that the postmodern condition is the condition of, to borrow Ernest Gellner's phrase, *the universal Mamlūk*, or to borrow Elmessiri, *the functional group*. The latter is the code of the age of comprehensive secularism, and it includes, in Elmessiri's view, immigrants in both the West and the Gulf countries, workers in the pleasure industry (prostitutes, hostesses, movie stars, sports men and women, models and sex queens), tourists, military elites, cultural and political elites and even functional or client states.[12] Against the metaphor of the functional groups is set the metaphor of the tourist, who is ironically perceived as a functional being in the eyes of the hosting society. Tourists, according to Elmessiri, can be described metaphorically as "foreign and temporary contractual persons" who move to the "earthly paradise" for a few days or weeks and whose contractual relationships with the hosting society do not differ much form those of the "functional groups."[13] Elmessiri states:

It can be argued that the tourist is the paradigmatic secular figure. He/she is a mobile being separated from the world of fundamental and absolute values, combining the traits of both the *homo economicus* (who accumulates money) and the body-centred man/woman (who rushes to spend his/her money to gratify his/her desires). When moving to a country (transfer), the tourist becomes totally obsessed with consumption and fun (pleasure) without any human considerations. In the eyes of the hosting society, the tourist is a source of money (interest and utility); thus both the tourist and the hosting society desanctify each other.[14]

Elmessiri, like Bauman, holds that the tourist has become the major metaphor and the paradigmatic secular figure of postmodernity *par excellence*. The emergence of the tourist as the major metaphor of liquid non-rational materialism, in Elmessiri's view, necessarily entails a revision of the Weberian thesis of the "dis-enchantment of the world" because we are confronted again with "re-enchantment of the world" in its postmodern form. Here Elmessiri modifies Weber's image of rationalized society as a workshop, stressing that liquid non-rational materialism is a call for a one-dimensional earthly paradise based on the triangle: production, consumption and pleasure. Elmessiri concludes:

Natural men and women are bombarded with images that seduce them into the belief that life is made up of this highly reductive rhythm and that society is populated with one-dimensional men and women who move voluntarily and happily from a one-dimensional workshop to a one-dimensional supermarket to a one-dimensional tourist agency that promises them a one-dimensional earthly paradise.[15]

History, memory and the dream of full control disappear, and metaphors that affirm fluidity and extreme plurality come to the fore: the state as neither a god nor a dragon; the world as a machine (the video and the computer); the world as a plant (the rhizome) and human beings as celebrities. Human beings are forced to participate in a competitive system of "signs, indicators, symbols and signifiers" that reflect their status in society.[16] Elmessiri argues that postmodernity in its emphasis on liquidity is consistent with the so-called "culture of the disposable," which is nothing but an "imperialistic utilitarian culture that consumes, utilizes, and wastes everything: energy, raw materials, songs, the female body, and the ozone."[17] On the political level, the nation-state is marginalized, and faith in the notions of common good and just society is lost. This liquid phase, as Elmessiri suggests, celebrates the emergence of the "one-dimensional man."[18] Elmessiri sees this worldview as inconsistent with Islam as a value system and a universal humanistic ideology:

> From an Islamic perspective, we did not come to this world to buy or sell but to enjoin right conduct and forbid indecency. Honesty and dignity have their weight in the mind of Muslims and the Islamic worldview cannot reduce a Muslim to the two major realms of economy and sexuality, thus rejecting the reduction of these realms to nature/matter. A Muslim is not the natural man (the one-dimensional man) but a complex human being whom God made a viceroy in nature [the earth] so as to tend it for himself and the coming generations.[19]

6.3 SEX AND SIGNIFICATION

Like Bauman, Elmessiri draws on the heritage of the Frankfurt School to support his critique of modernity. This shows clearly in his admiration of Herbert Marcuse's notion of the "one-dimensional man"; one who is seduced by entertainment industries and manipulated by the media. As Elmessiri suggests, by the 1960s, in addition to the crucial contribution of the movement of the Neo-Left, western critical discourse had been crystallized and the works of the Frankfurt school were abundant, criticizing the ambitions of the Enlightenment, colonial exploitation and western crimes against the Asian and African peoples.[20] The mid-1960s and the 1970s, however, witnessed the eclipse of the very problems of modernity, self and history, celebrating instead the world of structuralism, a world that simply repudiates the notions of time and selfhood, or embracing a mystique of postmodernism, which emphasizes expressiveness, play, sexuality.[21]

With these facts in mind, Elmessiri argues that there is a transformation from partial secularism or "solid materialist immanentism" to
comprehensive secularism or "postmodern liquid materialist immanentism." "Partial secularism" or "the solid phase" of modernity started
form the mid-nineteenth century till 1965; it was not centred on
the natural law alone, and it allowed a space for human (and moral and
religious) law. The post-1965 phase, on the other hand, is the
starting point of "comprehensive secularism" or the "liquid period of
modernity."22

Elmessiri conceives of the celebration of sexuality as a radical turning point i.e. the point of the transformation of modernity from solidity
to liquidity. Sensual pleasure was no longer the monopoly of a particular
group or class and it became available to all in the name of the "democ-
ratization of hedonism."23 This orientation is described by Hannah
Arendt in the late 1950s as the avoidance of pain and celebration of
reality only in the form of bodily sensations.24 Though more dominant in western societies, the obsession with pleasure, according to
Elmessiri, has became a universal condition in the era of comprehensive secularism; pleasure industries "have infiltrated our dreams, have
shaped our images of ourselves, and have controlled the very direction
of our libidos."25 This point is also underlined by John Esposito when
he stresses that it is true that Christianity persisted in the consciousness
of western man and provided him with ethics necessary to manage his
personal and social life, but the culture industry and state security have
controlled man's dreams and even the "direction of his libido."26

Unlike Elmessiri, who does not refer to any western sources when
he approaches the significance of this historical moment, Heba Raouf
Ezzat, an Egyptian scholar of political sciences at Cairo University, has
attempted to show the significance of the 1960s by referring to three
major books published in 1993: David T. Evans' *Sexual Citizenship:
The Material Construction of Sexualities* (1993), Zygmunt Bauman's
Intimations of Postmodernity (1993) and Pat Caplan's *The Cultural
Construction of Sexuality* (1993). She refuses to approach this historical
moment as a single radical turning point and argues that it is, nevertheless, a key moment in the secularization/sexualization process because

the human body comes to be seen as the "sole tangible container, carrier and executor of all past, present and future identities."[27]

Like Bauman, who has traced the prominence of sex as one of the prime metaphors of postmodernity, Elmessiri holds that the increasing levels of rationalization, secularization and immanentization have led to the emergence and the development of new organismic metaphors: "the human body has been the fundamental metaphor in the era of modernization. Now sex becomes the major metaphor of the post-modern era *par excellence.*"[28] Elmessiri even argues that modern western philosophy gives sex "epistemological primacy over all things."[29] This primacy can be attributed to the endeavour to withdraw from the complex world of values, duties, obligations and responsibilities.[30] "Body and sex," according to Elmessiri, "have been given a moral and epistemological priority over everything. They have become the ultimate point of referentiality, and they, in the modern materialist system, play the role of God in the spiritual monotheistic worldviews."[31]

Though difficult to draw a clear cut distinction between the body metaphor and the sex metaphor, the former is said to be the major metaphor of the age of modernization whereas sex is argued to be the major metaphor of postmodern times. The emphasis on the centrality of the body, in Elmessiri's view, can be traced in the emphasis laid on "*élan vital* or vital impetus" (Bergson), "*l'instinct* or the instinct" (Rousseau), "the will to power" (Nietzsche), "survival" (Spinoza, Darwin and Nietzsche), "the creation of the human self in the process of creating economic life" (Marxism), "the unconscious realm and dreams in their relation to sex and the body" (Freud), the "ontology of the flesh" (Merleau-Ponty) and "the writing of the body" (Helene Cixous).[32]

The celebration of sex is also accompanied with the liquefaction of the family and the emergence of new liquid signifiers. With the celebration of casual sex, or what Elmessiri usually refer to as "instant sex," sex and value have been conspicuously separated and reduced to a temporary physical relationship that aims at immediate gratification. Not surprisingly, prostitution, for example, becomes a merely "economic activity" and the linguistic sign "prostitute" is transformed into "sex worker," a new sign with new signifier and signified, representing the prostitute as a labourer and an economic force in society.33

The same process of liquefaction, according to Elmessiri, can be seen in the change of other signifiers such as "illegitimate children" who have become "children of unwed mothers," "children of a single parent family," "children out of wedlock," "natural babies" and "love babies." In short, they are the children of nature. Elmessiri argues that liquid postmodern sex or, to be more precise, the secularization as well as the de-sanctification of sex, deconstructs man as a "complex human being" (father/mother, husband/wife, male/female). In an ironic, yet serious, tone, Elmessiri argues that the "natural evolution" of the liquefaction of sex shows in the indifference to incest taboo, homo-sexuality and celebration of zoophilia.34

The interest in 'philosophia' (the love of wisdom) is now replaced with an interest in pedophilia and zoophilia.35 The saddest irony is that sexual abnormality, which is an assault on human nature, is defended in the name of human rights. Human beings are reduced into mere flesh to be utilized and exploited as a source of sensual enjoyment.36

Postmodernists, according to Elmessiri, aspire to establish a world devoid of any reference to the notions of identity, memory, history, time, logos, origins, truth and sanctity, transcendence i.e. a world that celebrates the will to power, free play and desire. In his analysis of the postmodern celebration of the body, Elmessiri refers to Bauman's belief that the absence of a transcendental subject, divine or human, means the reign of absurdity and that the absence of religious absolutes have led, in Bauman's view, to the celebration of the body. When the body becomes the only, the ultimate point of reference, "the ideas of community, society and collective identity, all of which presuppose the transcendence of self/body, no longer exist."37

Elmessiri enumerates the examples that uncover the centrality of sex in the postmodern worldview: Derrida's description of decon-struction as "continuous orgasm," Barthes's "pleasure of the text" as an act of sexual gratification, the call for the celebration of invagination (a symbol of immanence) instead of imagination (as a symbol of tran-scendence) and the assimilation of logocentrism into phallogocentrism, aesthetics and hermeneutics into erotics, textuality into sexuality, discourse into intercourse, eschatology into scatology.[38]

Sex becomes the 'substitute of language' that defies interpretation as it becomes the actual, implicit, material point of reference that ridicules transcendence. As Elmessiri suggests, the postmodern era now relates aesthetics to erotics and intertextuality to sexuality. It is tempting to quote at length:

> A closed text, according to postmodernists, is a form of suppressing sexual desire or elevating or going beyond it through an independent form that has its boundaries and identity. Intertextuality, on the other hand, a galaxy of open texts…. There exist no limits to a text because texts are always dancing. Consequently, the idea of the text as a unified artistic work, as the fruit of complex human consciousness, disintegrates and aesthetics is thus equated with the denial of transcendence and total surrender to the seduction of the fleeting (feminine) structure that has no ultimate fullstop…. It is (exactly like the moment of the orgasm) a return to the womb and the loss of any sense of being or of history.[39]

In the post-modern phase, each text opens into further texts *ad infinitum*. There is always a surplus in meaning; one which is believed to be beyond man's control. As Andreas Huyssen suggests, both artists and critics share a sense of a fundamentally new situation because the claims of art and literature to truth and human value seem exhausted, and the belief in the constitutive power of the modern imagination seems to be nothing but an illusion. This strain freed art and literature from that "overload of responsibilities" to change life, society and the world. The focus is no longer on the "lofty horizons of high culture" or the "sensual experience of cultural artifacts" as defended by Susan Sontag.[40]

In this context Elmessiri refers to Susan Sontag's 1964 essay "Against Interpretation" as a foreshadowing of the liquefaction of all solids and the celebration of sensuality as the centre of interpretation.[41] Rejecting the role played by the "legislators" and the 'interpreters," to borrow Bauman's major metaphors, Sontag opted for a modest role or even no role for interpretation in the reception of art. Here Sontag

refers to the role of modern cinema in eliminating the need for interpretation of art, since the cinematic sensory experience is based on a
sophisticated level of transparence that helps us *see* more, *feel* more and
hear more. She puts it bluntly when she concludes her essay saying: "In
place of a hermeneutics we need an erotics of art."42

6.4 THE POSTMODERN, THE JEW AND ZIONISM

Elmessiri is very conscious of his subjectivity and ideology, and
therefore, he never confuses Judaism, Jewishness and Zionism. Over
and above, he repudiates the conspiracy theory that suggests that postmodernity or deconstruction is a Jewish trend aimed at the liquefaction of all solids. Elmessiri attributes this common, yet mistaken,
belief among western scholars to the Jewish historical experience of
the Jewish Diaspora (the pariah *Volk*) and the cognitive mapping of the
Jew as the resident/eternal wanderer who dreams of the land of
promise. The Jew is thus represented as a signifier separated from the
signified or a signifier with overloaded and infinite meanings.
Elmessiri's interest in the significance of the Jews in the interpretation
of postmodernity cannot be attributed only to his cultural bias but also
to a dominant paradigm that embraces the existential situation of the
Jews before and after the Second World War as an expression of the
consequences of both modernity and postmodernity. As Max Silverman suggests, post-Holocaust allegories of the Jew are very crucial to
approach much wider questions of modernity and postmodernity.43

Elmessiri, however, repudiates the assumption that the Jews can
be seen as promoters of the tenets of postmodernity (nihilism, deconstruction, fragmentation etc) in an attempt to take revenge from the
civilization that persecuted them since early Christianity. This common
belief according to Elmessiri expresses a racist ideology as it transforms
the Jews into one of the terrifying and evil forces of darkness.44

Elmessiri is not surprised at such demonization of the Jews, and he
affirms that it is consistent with the western arsenal of racist discourse.
Instead of viewing the Jew as an ordinary human being endowed with
both good and evil, the West represents all the Jews as a symbol of

either functionalism or nihilism. The writing of the history of Jewish communities is characterized, in Elmessiri's view, by an apparent dualism because it presents them as a totality i.e. as the "Jewry" or as the "Jewish chosen people," not as minorities belonging to different cultures and backgrounds. By and large, Jewish communities have been presented, paradoxically, as functional groups i.e. as traders, money lenders and human capital or, to borrow Elmessiri's term, as "human utilized matter" that can be transferred to serve the interests of others.45

With the transformation from solid materialism to liquid materialism, the cognitive mapping of the conceptual Jew has slightly changed, especially when the Jews are sanctified in post-Holocaust literature. Both demonization and sanctification of the Jews, however, throws them outside the contours of time and space. Elmessiri remarks:

> In its search for the sacred/satanic, the sacred of the era of liquid materialism, western civilization sanctified the Jew making him an icon of homelessness, absurdity, fragmentation and darkness [Bauman's images of the pariah and vagabond]. This sanctification provides the 'believers' [Bauman's image of the parvenu and the tourist] with a sense of bliss. Their 'faith,' however, does not necessarily entail an emphasis on morality and responsibility. On the contrary, it takes such theatrical forms as apologizing for the [crimes of the] Holocaust or the criminalization of those who [attempt to] violate its iconicity.46

This view has much in common with Max Silverman's suggestion that the Jew is employed as a "trope for alterity," including all real outsiders, strangers, Blacks, Arabs and real Jews. Postmodern philosophy adopts *Auschwitz* as an allegory of the "tragic decline of the West" and the "absurdity of the political process of assimilation," and the Jew as "the victim and witness to this tragedy."47 Elmessiri, however, sees this interpretation as an incomplete picture lacking in both details and explanations. It is precisely for this reason that Elmessiri attempted to relate postmodernity to Zionism.

Like Bauman, Elmessiri argues that the West conceived of the world as a "vacuum," an "instrumental matter for its own interest," a barbaric wasteland, an empty space, waiting for the civilizing mission. Unlike Bauman, however, Elmessiri always argues that Zionism is the legitimate offspring of European imperial legacy. Ruling out Arab and Islamic history, Zionists conceive of Palestine as "a land without people," a geographical space without history and an empty space inhabited by scattered and divided people. Elmessiri argues that what is common between postmodernity and Zionism is a feverish attempt to separate the signifier from the signified so that the identities of both Jews and Arabs can be easily deconstructed, reducing them to rootless objects that can be easily transferred to another place and endowed with a new identity. It comes as no surprise that the Jew becomes the Zionist settler; the Arab the Palestinian refugee; Palestine Israel; the West Bank (*al-Difa al-Gharbiyya*) Judea and Samaria and the Arab world the Middle East Market, consisting of "Turkish water," "Arab Gulf capital," "Egyptian labor" and "Israeli know-how."48

The concept of the region is very important as it is usually used to refer to the Middle East. It denotes a purely geographical reality without any reference to history, language and religion and thus pan-regionalism, as opposed to pan-Arabism or pan-Islamism, has been promoted by Europe and the United States. Within this vision, the whole Middle East, including Israel, could be integrated into the western globalized world. Like postmodernity, Zionism believes in absolute relativity and thus denies the notions of right and truth. It comes as no surprise then that violence becomes the ultimate pragmatic point of reference that decides the rules of the struggle game.49

Like postmodernity, Zionism celebrates only small narratives rather than meta-narratives of human emancipation. Elmessiri comments:

> Zionism is the ideology of small narratives which repudiate the belief in a human meta-narrative. A Zionist bases his vision of Jewish rights in Palestine on his eternal immemorable sense of Diaspora and longing for Zion; and therefore, he lives within the limits of his small narrative. And since the Palestinians' attachment and existence in Palestine lies outside this narrative, their narrative has no legitimacy or even existence.50

Like Bauman who approached the question of the end of history and geography as the major manifestation of solid modernity, Elmessiri conceives of both modernity and postmodernity as the celebration of the end of both history and geography. Postmodernity, in this sense, is a universalization or a radicalization of modernity. Elmessiri observes:

> Postmodernity – I believe – is the ideology of the New World Order, one that is closely associated with the ideologies of the end of history. What gives rise to these ideologies is the dualistic position of the Enlightenment era on the nature of history. The first is a Hegelian orientation that glorifies history and stresses that it has an ultimate goal and once it is achieved, we reach its end. The second is the anti-Hegelian position that embraces the notion that history has neither goal nor end.[51]

Elmessiri holds that liquid modernity extends beyond the end of history to embrace the end of geography. Unlike Bauman who saw genocide as one of the possibilities of modernity or as a test to modernity, to Elmessiri genocide is the product and the direct expression of western modernity which conceives of genocide as the final solution for its aggravating problems; and therefore, it is a recurrent motif in western paradigms that deny the right of the Other to existence. This is why the cognitive map of the West emphasizes the end of History as well as the end of Geography.[52]

Zionism is no exception from this imperial map because Zionist action is largely determined by the Zionist cognitive map which is based on power, myths, hopes, fears and divine promises rather than on a direct response to the complex reality and the contradictions surrounding it. Elmessiri always argues that Israel is not a Jewish state but a settler colonial depopulatory state that serves two major pragmatic and functional purposes: ridding Europe of its surplus Jews, and acting as a functional state to the interests of western imperialism.[53] Elmessiri uses the paradigm of "functional groups" to refer to Jewish communities and the term "functional state" to refer to Israel; the latter is nothing but a functional state serving the interests of the West in the Middle East. Bauman himself refers *en passant* to the role of the United

States in guaranteeing the "survival of countries from Israel to South Korea."[54]

In this context, Elmessiri defines postmodernity as the ideology of the pragmatic acceptance, the surrender and the adaptation of the weak to the status quo; it is the free and unbounded play with reality instead of seriously dealing with its contradictions and changing it.[55] Unlike Bauman's solid modernity or Elmessiri's solid rational materialism, postmodernity is a non-rational materialism that recognizes neither heroism nor tragedy, neither farce nor absurdist rebellion.[56]

CONCLUSION

WESTERN self-scrutiny discourse, as introduced by Zygmunt Bauman, had a great impact on Abdelwahab Elmessiri's deconstruction of the Enlightenment and modernity at large. Though belonging to different religions, ideologies and cultures, Elmessiri and Bauman mitigated the conceit of natural sciences, the deification of man and the perception of the world as a machine or as a self-sufficient organism. Both of them uncovered the other face of modernity, its tendencies and consequences. Modernity is represented as a Gnostic narrative, revolving around the human obsession with notions of perfection, salvation, purity and full clarity in the here-now rather than the Hereafter. This narrative of an Earthly Paradise has had grave consequences in the different phases of modernity.

The cognitive mapping of the secular modern as understood by Bauman and Elmessiri is based on the assumption that metaphors in modern western thought can never be treated as merely decorative or rhetorical figures of speech. Rather, they are indispensable hermeneutical tools of cognitive mapping, and they can provide us with a hermeneutical ontology or ontological hermeneutics that treats the text not of its own sense, but of some comprehensive theory of human existence. In cognitive mapping, metaphoricity stresses ontology, and thus it mitigates not only the previous structures of language but also the previous structures of the so-called reality. The major metaphors Bauman has used to map the ambitions and the consequences of modernity are 'solid modernity' and 'liquid modernity.' Elmessiri's mapping of western modernity is based on almost the same tropes: solid rational materialism and liquid non-rational materialism.

Aware of their existential experience and cultural bias, Elmessiri and Bauman have stressed the role of subjectivity and ideology, thus stressing the consequences of the secular modernity in relation to their existential experience and identity. However, they have transcended their ideological space and distanced themselves from it so as to represent a more humanistic critique that goes beyond ideology, ethnicity and existential experience.

Though belonging to a never-forsaken European identity, Bauman as a European Polish-born British Jew never hesitates to point out that the Enlightenment project was not a noble dream of bringing light to the ignorant and freedom to the oppressed. *Les philosophes* or the intellectuals of the Enlightenment, on the contrary, created a worldview that served the interests of the nation-state and its universalistic ambitions. Modern rulers and *les philosophes* were literally and metaphorically gardeners and legislators aspiring for the creation of a utopian and perfect world even if at the expense of demonizing, excluding or even exterminating other human beings. The discovery of the laws of Nature did not lead to man's mastery over and the spread of light, freedom and knowledge but to coercion, exclusion and even the advocation of endarkenment. With the advent of modernity, the entire world was perceived as no man's land and as a vacuum to be designed and perfected regardless of the human consequences.

In mapping modernity, Bauman takes the Holocaust as a possibility or a test of modernity, focussing on European Jews and their representation as strangers, weeds and parasites that threaten the garden of modernity. Bauman's focus on the conditions of Jewish communities, however, cannot be attributed only to his ideology or Jewishness. On the contrary, he goes beyond his ethnicity and introduces a humanistic mapping that defends all human beings or, to be more precise, all the victims of modernity who are socially excluded, unfairly colonized and ruthlessly driven out, not only from their lands but also from the universe of moral obligation itself.

Unlike Bauman, Elmessiri has not invented new sub-metaphors to map the solid phase of modernity or 'solid rational materialism,' but he has managed to trace and weave the major metaphors in modern western thought into a cohesive whole. The major metaphors that Elmessiri focused on to map western modernity are the organismic metaphor and the mechanistic metaphor. Both metaphors celebrate self-contained and closed systems that deny transcendence and pluralism and thus reduce human beings and human existence into the dynamics of 'nature' and 'matter.' Solid rational materialism, in Elmessiri's view, started with the deification of man and nature but ended tragically with man's alienation and ontological loss. Like Bauman, Elmessiri has always maintained that science and philosophy were used to legitimize immanent secular ideologies that promise the possibility of worldly transcendence, the establishment of an Earthly Paradise and the realization of the end of History.

While Bauman does not offer any alternative and sees the role of critical theory as a modest comment on the present and human experience, Elmessiri uncovers the dominance of immanence so as to contrast it with Islamic monotheism and transcendence. Elmessiri's mapping of the modern can be seen as a defence of man against materialism, monistic interpretation and all forms of totalitarianism. Elmessiri is aware of his cultural background as an Arab Egyptian Muslim living in a region dominated by a western imperial legacy and Israeli aggression against the neighbouring Arab countries. It is precisely for this reason that he has used his critical skills to highlight the consequences of Nazism and Zionism within the framework of western modernity, putting them in one and the same category of western gnostic modernity that celebrates the deification of man and conceives of him as the master of nature and the maker of history, though it leads ironically and in the final analysis to his alienation, exclusion and even extermination.

Western modernity as mapped by both Bauman and Elmessiri has given rise to a universal situation of strangers, vagabonds, *Mumlūks*, functional groups, *unwertes Leben*, *homo sacer*, *untermenschen* and *Muselmänner*.

Cognitive mapping is not a static process but an intellectual effort confronting a world dominated by a state of confusion, fluidity and ambivalence. This state of confusion does not exclude the cartographers themselves. However, this state is more obvious in Bauman's mapping of postmodernity. Bauman finds himself in a perplexing situation in which he hesitates to declare an explicit break with the foundations of modernity. However, he has lost hope in postmodernity as a promised paradise of transcendence, pluralism and tolerance. This moment of illumination is accompanied with the abandonment of the term postmodernity, celebrating instead the metaphor of liquid modernity. The state of liquefaction covers art, culture and human relations, giving rise to two major metaphors in mapping the contemporary human condition: sex and the body.

The use of these new metaphors in mapping the emergent human reality has signalled the liquefaction of all solids and the shift in emphasis from grand narratives to small stories and individualistic pleasures. The gardener and the legislator metaphors are no longer operative because the position of the intellectuals has been reduced to the modest role of interpreters and semiotic brokers. Though the intellectuals may remain loyal to their universal, elevated and lofty ideals of perfection, purity, full clarity, freedom and justice, they are confronted with the difficulty, if not the impossibility, of claiming the role of the legislators who defend the universalistic ambitions of modernity.

Unlike Bauman, Elmessiri has not taken this long detour to map the contemporary human condition as a process of liquefaction. From the outset, Elmessiri has equated postmodernity with "liquid non-rational materialism," arguing that it is not only an anti-metaphysical revolution but also a revolution against metaphysical materialism itself and its faith in humanism, worldly transcendence and the power of Reason to understand the world.

Elmessiri's existential experience and ideology, particularly his awareness of the decline of leftist movements and the rise of political Islam, have enabled him to envisage the possibility of a break with modernity and postmodernity. Islam represents a worldview that repudiates the materialist outlook and calls for a balance between man and the universe rather than the creation of paradise on Earth. Elmessiri has never seen postmodernity as a possibility of transcending the closed, mechanistic and organismic paradigm of modernity but as a worldview that denies history and does away with referentiality. The project of modernity has ended with the declaration of the death of man in favour of such non-human categories as the market and power or in favour of such one-dimensional categories as the body, sex and pleasure.

Due to Elmessiri's awareness of the other face of modernity in its both solid and liquid phases, he has been keen on establishing an intimate relationship between modernity and postmodernity on the one hand and Zionism on the other. *Auschwitz* is represented as an allegory of the tragic decline of the West and the absurdity of the political process of assimilation, and the Jew as the victim and witness to this tragedy. The aggressive nationalistic drive of modernity, its scientific racism and mechanistic rationalization led to the aggravation of the Jewish problem in Europe. As a non-national nation, European Jewish communities had only two solutions: socialism and Zionism. The latter was consistent with Nazism, since both aimed at ridding Europe of the Jews and transferring them to another place.

According to Bauman and Elmessiri, the Jews are not the only victims of modernity, since the whole world was seen as an instrumental matter and a barbaric wasteland in need of the civilizing mission. From this perspective, Zionism can be seen as a legitimate offspring of the European imperial legacy. Like western imperial powers, Zionists, who attempted to liberate the Jews from the nationalistic extremism in Europe, could conceive of Palestine as a land without people and a geographical space without history. The solution of the Jewish problem was thus achieved at the expense of another nation. Postmodernity and Zionism are united by an attempt to dissolve human identities, thus both Jews and Arabs can be reduced to rootless objects that can be easily transferred to another place for the sake of imagined chosen people armed with the most sophisticated weapons of value-free science and the most advanced products of neutral technology. Zionism, like postmodernity, is the ideology of small narratives which repudiate the belief in a human meta-narrative; it is the narrative of the Jewish chosen people in their pure and perfect nation/state.

This mapping of modernity and postmodernity underlines the fact that the deep structures of all utopian ideologies, including Nazism and Zionism, can be traced in the paradigm of comprehensive secularism and its inherent worldview. It is a paradigm that annuls human and cultural specificities, leading to the deconstruction and perhaps the destruction of all that is human, unique and authentic, throwing man away from complex history and civilization into the simple and monistic world of instrumental matter for the interests of imagined chosen communities.

APPENDIX

24 February 2006

Dear Professor Zygmunt Bauman,
I hope you are doing great and I really appreciate your kind permission to know your contact details. I am very interested in your work on culture, modernity and postmodernity. I was awarded the Excellent BA in English language and literature in May 1999 and the Excellent MA in semiology and literary theory in Nov. 2004. My MA thesis was on Paul Ricoeur and the challenge of semiology. In fact, my interest in your work grew at a rapid rate when I discovered that your thought has much sway on an Arab intellectual called Abdelwahab Elmessiri. I'm currently preparing a proposal for a PhD dissertation at Cairo University on The Cognitive Mapping of Modernity and Post-modernity. Kindly find attached a draft of this proposal. I look forward to reading your comments and critical remarks before I submit the proposal to the English Department at Cairo University.
Kind regards
Haggag Ali

25 February 2006

Dear Haggag Ali,
You put me to shame – it is only from you that I learned of Elmessiri's work (indeed, of his existence...)! I gather from what you wrote in your synopsis that he is an important, original thinker whose ideas should enter the mainstream of the 'Western self-scrutiny' discourse. Which of his works are available in English or French? I'll be obliged for any information.

Again from your synopsis I got the impression that there is a lot in common in Elmessiri's and mine 'cognitive maps' alongside quite a few important distinctions; an ideal situation for a fruitful critical comparison - from which a 'third' map can emerge (and the more of them, the better; I believe cognitive maps to be complementary rather than in competition – you can't have a 'theory of everything,' each theory being a stage light that draws some aspects of action out of dateness while casting other aspects in shade). I am looking forward to the results of your study.

One correction came to my mind when browsing the text: I embraced Claude Levi-Strauss' version of structuralism because he exploded the concept of culture as a self-enclosed and cohesive totality, as it was treated before, and replaced it with a vision of a matrix of possibilities and a potentially infinite string of permutations. In this sense I'd agree, not disagree with Elmessiri if he views structuralism as 'liquid modern' avant la lettre...

With best wishes
Zygmunt Bauman

28 March 2006
Dear Haggag Ali,
I am awfully sorry that, being pressed for time, I can't answer all your profound and demanding questions as they deserve. You will find attached my answer to the first question – but being as busy as I am for the moment answering of the other two would have to wait until long after you've (hopefully!) finished your dissertation! You can however find some oblique answers to those other questions in my little books on globalization and Europe.

With apology, and the best wishes of completion of your study
Zygmunt Bauman

1. In *The Rule of Metaphor,* Paul Ricoeur emphasizes the role of metaphor in our perception of the world and I have noticed that your writings are based on metaphors. To what extent do metaphors play a crucial role in your writing?

Were they still around and stooped to read my writings, ancient sages would be among those 'some' inclined to call my use of metaphors frivolous.... They (Plato most famously) held metaphors in rather low esteem, exiling them from the realm of pursuit of truth and relegating to the 'catch as you can' territory of rhetoric – even though they were anything but averse to lavishly availing themselves from the metaphors' cognitive capacity!

One uses metaphors, the ancients believed, as mere adornments of speech; as trinkets one could rather do without for the sake of clarity. Just as the Bauhaus people and other zealous modernists wished to cleanse buildings of all and any non-functional detail, they would cleanse the reasoning of metaphors. The sole purpose metaphors might serve, they insisted, was for the speaker to entreat and charm the listeners, to gain their applause, and obtain approval that is prompted by whipped up emotions instead of being solidly founded in alerted and watchful reason.

This is not however what metaphors do; or at least not the only task they may perform. In case of an unfamiliar experience in need of an adequate conceptual net to be caught and examined, metaphors render an enormously important service: they serve imagination and comprehension. They are the indispensable scaffoldings for imagination and perhaps the most effective tools of comprehension.

Let's recall for example that the core-concept of sociology, the concept of 'society,' was introduced into the emergent social-scientific discourse as a metaphor. Thus far almost synonymous with 'company,' evoking 'companionship,' 'fellowship,' 'association with one's fellow people in a friendly and intimate manner,' the term 'society' was applied to an abstract totality anything but 'intimate' and not necessarily 'friendly' – and all that in order to grasp and visualize the invisible and intangible roots of the new and unfamiliar, yet unnamed pressures/dependencies of, and to mentally map the lines of dependency too extended and too far reaching to be experienced 'at the first hand' and subjected to direct sensuous scrutiny. Through the metaphor of 'society,' it had been suggested that the unfamiliar condition could be absorbed into the familiar cognitive frame, that it was less alien or strange than otherwise would have been deemed, and that the already learned and tried forms of action could be still deployed to good effect. That operation was instrumental in making an aggregation inaccessible to senses, the abstract totality of population-within-a-nation-state, into an *imagined community.* It had as well the performative ('perlocutionary,' as Austin would say) function: it chimed well with the effort of the nascent modern state of the 'primitive accumulation of legitimacy' era to capitalize on the nostalgia its population displayed for the 'lost community.' The very fact that by now the metaphorical origins of 'society' have been largely forgotten and 'society' feels no longer as a metaphor when applied to the large, anonymous aggregate of state subject, testifies to the success of that operation.

Metaphorical juxtaposition has also another effect – largely unintended, though not necessarily for that reason cognitively useless, let alone harmful. On both sides of the juxtaposition, many a feature of juxtaposed objects is left out of sight: a similarity is suggested, not identity – and in the case of similarity differences are not denied, only bypassed and, so to speak, 'relegated to a lower league.' Metaphor takes, simultaneously, *pars pro toto* and *totus pro parte* – transforming the shapes of both invoked realms: noting and exposing existing similarities not as much as conjuring up a new 'third' object. Metaphorical juxtaposition is an act of selection and discrimination: some features are drawn into limelight, some others cast in shadow ('bracketed away'). While the traits of the first kind are assigned prime importance, the other traits are obliquely ascribed lesser relevance – and it is on the first that the attention is focused explicitly or tacitly. They are suggested to 'play the first fiddle,' to 'set the tune,' even to determine the rest of the object's traits. In all cases, metaphor 'prejudices' the perception of the object it tries to comprehend.

Each metaphor is for that reason 'reductionist' - partial or even partisan. This is however, I believe, a feature of all cognition. The metaphors' claim to distinction derives solely from rendering that universal feature *easier to spot*; it is an irony, or bad luck of the metaphors, that they tend to be reprimanded and denigrated for what could and should be counted among their great assets, not liabilities. Metaphors draw into light the sorry lack of an 'overlap,' indeed an ineradicable disparity between words and 'things,' knowledge and its object – as well as the inevitably 'construed' nature of objects: that limitation of all cognition that once spotted turn into most effective stimuli to further cognitive effort, but could otherwise stay undetected to the detriment, not the benefit of knowledge (remember, for instance, Thomas Kuhn's 'anomaly' triggering scientific revolutions...) For the cognitive efforts, for the intellectual assimilation and recycling of changing experience, for the articulation of the properly revised modes of life, the 'leftovers' of metaphorical juxtapositions are powerful fertilizers, while the hazy area surrounding the spotlighted bits is a most fertile ground for investigative action.

For the kind of sociology which I've chosen and try hard to practice, (a sociology addressed to the actors of life dramas rather than to their scriptwriters, directors, producers and stage managers, a sociology moved by the urge to participate in the on-going interpretation of their experience and of the strategies they construct and deploy in response, a sociology aimed at enhancing the scope of the actors' choices and to assist them in making the choices both reasonable and effective) such 'hazy areas' are natural habitat and so metaphors are among the principal tools: metaphors have the crucial advantage of opening new sights while simultaneously exposing their limitations, their incurable non-comprehensiveness and non-finality.

Georg Simmel (in *Bruchstücke aus einem Philosophie der Kunst*), having noted the profusion of vibrating, unclear contours and blurred borderlines in Rembrandt's paintings, praised those apparent violations of painting standards as manifestations of the painter's desire to grasp the true individuality of his (human!) objects which can never be reached through piling up crisply reproduced 'distinctive features' (which, unlike human individuality, are as a rule common to many human beings and so hardly ever unique). Descriptions of human experience fail (indeed, are chronically and incurably incapable) to meet the scientific standards of *Eindeutigkeit*. But then humans are not ideal objects for scientific treatment, which humans invented in order to tackle, overpower, conquer and master the non-human reality while preserving immunity of their own freedom from its bonds and so our, human, freedom to act....

Yet another of Simmel's precepts addressed to the arts (this time from *Der Fragmentcharakter des Lebens*) I believe to be applicable to sociology in equal measure. If it is true, says Simmel, that by their nature arts aim at composing a complete, exhaustive, all-embracing universe – it is also true that every historically given form of art is able to attain that purpose only in part: no historically finite set of artistic forms will ever embrace the totality of the world's contents (that is, let me add, to grasp, lock up and seal the infinity of possibilities which human worlds carry or bring into being). Metaphors are good for thinking because they lay bare this dialectics of intention and performance and are not frightened by what they expose while doing it....

To conclude: I believe that thinking with the help of metaphors is not an activity for which one should feel obliged to apologize – unless one needs to apologize for being human, alive, and living among humans.

The desperate efforts of many a scientist to cut off all metaphorical roots and hide all traces of kinship with 'ordinary' (read: non-scientific, inferior to scientific) perception and thought are (perhaps an inevitable and certainly expectable) part of a more general tendency of science, all too-evident since Plato commanded philosophers to venture out of the cave, to put a distance between itself and the 'common sense' of *hoi polloi* (Gaston Bachelard famously dated the birth of modern science by the appearance of first books that did not start from a reference to a common experience available to all).

Scientists were in this respect successful, though in part only. Some sciences, having fenced off for themselves or designed from scratch a realm of 'empirical data' inaccessible to non-insiders (that is, to the rest of humanity), may also design a language similarly free of all semantic bonds with ordinary life and ordinary experience, and composed instead of custom-made terms with no past and no lateral associations. In the case of such sciences the postulate of banishing metaphors is perhaps plausible and feasible; it is also pragmatically useful, as it offers an additional benefit of underscoring and reinforcing the exile of common sense and its common carriers. Let us note, however, that as the sciences' independence from common experience has acquired material, fleshy, technically armed, imperturbable and unassailable founda- tions that to be secure no longer need an active defense by a discursive superstructure – the crusade against the selective/reductionist and somewhat 'imprecise' metaphors have lost much of its vigour and is running fast out of steam. Voices that some decades ago would be condemned as heretical, are nowadays sounding ever louder.

One most recent example of such voices should suffice: S. Phineas Upham's article ('Is Economics Scientific? Is Science Scientific?' in the 2005 issue of the *Critical Review*). It develops Nancy Cartwright's description of nature as 'tending to a wild profusion' and follows her call to 'construct different (scientific) models for different (cognitive) purposes' (exactly what metaphors do!) as 'no single model serves all purposes best.' Rightly, Upham suggests that if in the case of 'natural sciences' (fortified, let me repeat, in a secure shelter of experience inaccessible and forever unfamiliar to the 'ordinary folks') such idea may be still viewed as a partisan, contentious standpoint, it is surely the sole and incontestable choice for the study of humans – as the behaviour of human beings is a domain that is too large, too complicated, and too unpredictable for any model to predict…. This is why *different models* have *different functions*, and why *no one model can perfectly correspond to all permutations of the reality of human behaviour*. (Italics added).

But this is precisely what the metaphors do – consciously and openly. This is why they obey more faithfully than their detractors the injunction to be 'better mindful of the provisional nature of models, and scorn any tendency to sanctify laws derived from even the most pleasing or useful models.'

I admit that using metaphors we set ourselves somewhat less ambitious, less pedantic or perfectionist goals than did modern sciences in their *Sturm und Drang* phase of independence wars (and the early social science when struggling to be admitted into their company). But I deny that this means that using metaphors is a sign of a lesser and inferior knowledge. Using metaphors derives from and signals our responsibility towards the prospective human objects/participants of activity known under the name of 'sociology' – activity that is the sole source of whatever authority we may claim and acquire. It signals refusal to act under false pretences, to bid for greater authority than realistically can be claimed, and above all to distort the subject-object communication (yes, communication, since both the subject and the object are human and both have tongue) in the subject's (that is, the sociologist's) favour. This is not only the matter of choosing a cognitive strategy; it is also (and yet more importantly) an *ethical* choice, a decision to assume responsibility for the voluntary or involuntary, subjective or objective responsibility of sociologists, and an act of assuming a moral stance towards the vocation and its prospective beneficiaries.

Siegfried Kracauer (in *History: The Last Things Before the Last*) points out that as the 'parochial security gave way to cosmopolitan confusion,' there is a 'widespread feeling of powerlessness and abandonment,' of 'being lost in uncharted and inimical expanses,' which – dangerously – 'stirs many, presumably the majority of people, to scramble for the shelter of a unifying and comforting belief.' He then proceeds to praise Erasmus for being 'possessed with fear of all that is definitely fixed,' since he believed that 'truth ceases to be true as soon as it becomes a dogma.' Knowing that 'none of the contending causes is the last word on the last issues at stake,' one needs, as Kracauer insists, to seek 'a way of thinking and living which, if we could only follow it, would permit us to burn through the causes and thus to dispose of them – a way which for the lack of a better word, or a word at all, may be called humane.'

Well, from such observations, much as their topicality must strike the 21st Century reader, the benefits of thinking with metaphors do not necessarily follow…. Or do they?

2. The garden metaphor prevails in most of your writings on solid European modernity and you have used it in connection with the attempt to fight ambivalence but the application of this metaphor excludes the attempts of European imperialism to turn the rest of the world into a useful substance/matter that can help Europe establish its modern garden or earthly paradise. Would you please elaborate on this point?

3. You have used the hunter metaphor in connection with liquid modernity to place a great emphasis on the fragmentation of identity in what you refer to as the modern liquid era. Don't you think that this metaphor can be used in connection with solid modernity and the European attempts to perform hunting practices in the rest of the world to achieve its utopian dreams?

I am looking forward to your answers and elaborate discussion.

CONVERSATION WITH ABDELWAHAB ELMESSIRI

This conversation was conducted over almost 18 months, starting from January 2006 to early June 2007. I had been working with Prof. Abdelwahab Elmessiri during that period and had the chance to raise all questions, which he kindly answered. In June 2007, I travelled to Germany on a short-term doctoral scholarship and I kept editing the conversation. Then I travelled to Turkey and my studies helped me raise new questions in relation to modernity and secularism. In both Germany and Turkey, I devoted much time to the study of the thought of Eric Voegelin and I told Elmessiri about the amazing similarity in their methodology, assumptions and conclusions. Therefore, I referred to the influence of Eric Voegelin on Elmessiri in a few pages in my PhD dissertation. During my stay in Turkey, Elmessiri sent me some articles that could help me see the convergence of his thought with and its divergence from that of Voegelin. Elmessiri asked me to send him the conversation on his thought and that of Bauman so that he could edit it before including it in my PhD dissertation.

Wednesday, May 14, 2008 at 12:30 pm

Dear Haggag,
Assalamu Alaykum wa Rahmatuh Allah wa Barakatuh
Kindly find attached the articles that might be useful in the comparison between me and Eric Voegelin. There are some articles, only in Arabic; we will translate them and send them to you once translated.

Please send me the conversation that compares my thought to that of Bauman so as to edit it and send it back to you.

By the way, I have read your PhD dissertation [first draft] and I find it really an outstanding work. May Allah bless you and Peace be upon you.
Kind regards,
Dr. Abdelwahab Elmessiri

Saturday, May 17, 2008 at 7:29

Dear Haggag,
Kindly find attached the edited conversation. I believe now that you know my ideas more than I; you can edit the conversation as you like.
Kind Regards,
Dr. Abdelwahab Elmessiri

Tuesday, June 3, 2008 at 2:02 am

Dearest Prof. Messiri,
Thanks a lot for your concern and the details of the coming conference on Abdul Aziz Hamouda. I still have two requests:
First, I do appreciate if you edit the last question in the interview that will be included in the thesis.
Second, I appreciate if you recommend some names of other Arab or Islamic intellectuals who touch on the idea of gnosticism or secularism in a similar way to yours and Voegelin's. This is very crucial to the postdoctoral project.
With warmest greetings,
Haggag

Elmessiri did not answer this email; he was then very busy and exhausted and passed away one month later, 3rd July 2008.

The Conversation:

1. In a correspondence with Zygmunt Bauman in February 2006, he commented on my PhD proposal stating that he felt that you are an original thinker whose ideas are worth incorporating into the mainstream discourse on 'Western self-scrutiny.' He even went so far as to request whether your works are available in English or French. He also asked why a prominent Arab intellectual,

meaning yourself, had decided to use his critical skills as a professor of English
literature to map the modern and the post-modern worldviews?

Though I believe in neither determinism nor fatalism, I do believe
that we are part of our historical and cultural context, one that has been
shaped for the last 200 years by western modernity and its imperialistic
ambitions to put an end to both history and geography. In my early
writings that go back to the 1970s, especially *The End of History*
(1973) and *The Earthly Paradise* (1979), I represented modernity as a
worldview that promotes the dream of perfection and the establishment of an earthly paradise, a dream shared also by both Nazism and
Zionism. Of course, the Arab-Israeli conflict has played a crucial role
in my decision to represent a new critique of modernity, one which is
more comprehensive and includes all Gnostic movements that search
for final solutions to establish a perfect society. At that time, however, I
was very surprised that before the late 1980s, western scholarship
rarely approached Nazism and Zionism within the critical discourse
on modernity. After getting my doctoral degree in poetry from
Rutgers University in 1969, I was introduced to Mohamed Hassanein
Heikal who was then the editor-in-chief of the Egyptian daily newspaper *Al-Ahram*. When he discovered that I was extremely interested
in Zionism as a worldview that has much in common with western
modernity, he advised me to devote myself to the study of Zionism.

In mapping modernity, I was much influenced by humanist
Marxism. At the beginning I embraced historical materialism and the
materialist interpretation of human existence. However, I was attracted
much to Marxism because it had strong theoretical foundations and
offered me at the time a humanist critique of man's alienation in the
modern world. However, with the decline of leftist movements and the
rise of political Islam, I came to abandon the materialist interpretation
of history, embracing instead an Islamic paradigm which I developed,
a paradigm that places a distance between the creator and the created,
the creator and nature, and finally between man and nature. I came to
realize that Islam represents a worldview that rejects the materialist
Promethean and Faustian outlook. It calls for balance between man
and the universe rather than establishing paradise on earth or putting

an end to history or harnessing man and nature in the service of the powerful. In other words, I discovered the humanism of Islam.

The expression 'End of History' has of late been widely used. It means that history, with all its complexity and simplicity, would at some point reach its end, becoming completely fixed, devoid of conflicts, dualities and specificities. Man will then entirely dominate his environment and himself, and he will find final scientific solutions to all his problems and sufferings. Scientific knowledge, according to this view, is the knowledge that will make us control the law of necessity and will give us the capacity to found a scientific Zion, that is, a technocratic, technological utopia. We note that those who proclaim the end of history base their ideas on a narrow scientific view and operate within the framework of a concept of a rigid causality. They imagine that science will lead to a comprehensive, complete and certain knowledge. It is ironical to note that these hypotheses have lost their credibility in scientific circles which have become increasingly aware of the indeterminacy of natural phenomena and the physical uncertainty of the sciences. Nevertheless the attempt to reach a high level, if not complete, certainty still prevails among many scholars in the field of the human sciences.

The problem of the end of History is latent in many philosophic systems, but it has become a basic theme in Western civilization after the Renaissance as the nature-centred outlook gained ground. We may say that the utopias of the Renaissance in the West are a manifestation of this theme. Most of them are technological, technocratic utopias standing outside the course of human history, because they are allegedly managed in an entirely rational manner, on the basis of an awareness of natural and scientific law that is not related to social historic or man-made laws. The laws of reason were supposed to be identical with the laws of nature, and therefore the 'rational' came to be synonymous with the 'natural' or 'materialistic' or as I prefer to say 'naturalist-materialist.'

The rejection of history manifests itself in a more complex fashion in the age of the Enlightenment. The Enlightenment view of history manifested itself in both Hegelian and anti-Hegelian philosophies.

While anti-Hegelian philosophies have an explicitly anti-historical stance, the case is slightly different when it comes to Hegelian philosophies, which often refer to historical laws, historical epochs and inevitabilities. However, I argue that, Hegelian philosophies are no less antagonistic to history than the anti-Hegelian ones, for Hegelianism presupposes the existence of an Idea which has no material or relative existence, which propels history, society, mankind and nature. This Idea has many names: Absolute Idea, Absolute Mind, the Infinite Spirit, etc. This non-divine Absolute, however, is not motionless, for it can never know itself, nor can it realize itself fully outside nature, time and history. This is achieved through a dialectical process in the context of which opposites interact and interpenetrate and are eventually reconciled and synthesized. The idea of humanity as an independent unique phenomenon within the system of nature is thereby eradicated. It was therefore rightly said that Hegelianism has no place for duality nor does it separate the material from the ideal, the natural from the human, or the sacred from the temporal, for everything will eventually be reduced to one element, material in fact, spiritual only in name. Hegelian thought only considers reality in relation to the idea of the end of history, when the Absolute Mind will be embodied, and even incarnated, in nature and the general law is realized in history, a time which will mark the end of dialectics and of human suffering, when man will find final solutions to all his problems and fully control all things. However, one of the ironies of this situation is that the moment of total control is itself the moment that will mark the victory of simplism over complexity, of one-dimensionality over multi dimensionality, and of the natural over the human.

2. *In mapping the Enlightenment as a major narrative category of modernity, Zygmunt Bauman referred to it as a Gnostic narrative that attempted to achieve transcendence but this attempt was transformed into a form of transgression against transcendence, whether materialistic or metaphysical. To what extent do you agree with this vision?*

The philosophical discourse on modernity relies on code words, which convey an integrated worldview. These code words, nevertheless, can stand as an obstacle between ourselves and knowledge. As employed in Arab analytical discourse, the term 'Enlightenment' is inextricably tied to the concept of modernity, especially the faith in the ability of the human mind to acquire the knowledge it needs to illuminate most, if not all, phenomena and things, depending on an understanding of material reality. It is precisely for this reason that we can call the Enlightenment 'solid rational materialism,' one that attempts to give centrality to man and to establish universal ethical systems without reference to the existing religious traditions. The Enlightenment, in this sense, gave centrality to the human subject and expected him to transcend both the world of nature and his own natural self. This worldview gives man enormous self-confidence and optimism in regards to his present and future.

But this idealistic vision was accompanied, paradoxically, with the perception of man as a child of nature. The dream of the human self that can apprehend reality and dominate and reshape it was replaced by a self that had been deconstructed and reduced to material elements. Man becomes an indivisible part of a material becoming with no fixity, unity, transcendence or meaning. The philosophers of the Enlightenment proved to be nothing but promoters of 'dark Enlightenment,' a hermeneutics of doubt, which denies the reality of subject and object and reveals that materialist rationalism leads, in the final analysis, to materialist irrationalism.

The discourse of the Frankfurt School revolves around the 'tragedy of the Enlightenment' and the 'cold night of the Enlightenment.' It shows how the Enlightenment invited man to regard nature as usable matter. The Enlightenment project was an attempt to liberate man from his fear of natural forces. However, the progress in controlling nature is accompanied with an erosion of man's inner emotional life and feelings. As nature is ever more efficiently broken down to facilitate its exploitation, man is deconstructed and the human whole gradually disappears. This is the Enlightenment dialectic: progress in dominating nature is matched by the fragmentation of man. Western literature was conscious of the dark aspects of the Enlightenment. Romantic literature for example was a protest against man's increasing isolation from the world, as well as against the natural sciences, which converted man into dead matter. Modernist literature dealt with man from a dark Enlightenment perspective. Themes such as isolation, suicide, worry, a sense of the absurdity of existence and the meaningless of nature, man's inability to transcend his reality and his absorption into vast entities that crush him and direct his existence, all sprung from the modernist novelist's awareness of, and protest against, the dark Enlightenment.

3. *In his mapping of the role of les philosophes, Bauman refers to them metaphorically as gardeners and legislators who were obsessed with establishing perfection and an earthly paradise. How do you perceive them and other leading western philosophers?*

In almost all of my writings, I prefer to refer explicitly to *les philosophes* and other western philosophers as materialists who promoted monistic and simplistic interpretation of the complex reality of our existence. Thomas Hobbes was perhaps the first to identify the dark theses immanent in materialist rationalism when he stated that the state of nature was a state of war of all against all and that man was a wolf to his brother man. The social contract between men was not a product of their intrinsic goodness but their excessive fear of one another and desire for survival. They establish a state to rule over them for their own peace of mind. Machiavelli agrees with Hobbes on this point. Spinoza and Newton, however, described a completely mechanical world: the self dissolves in the mechanical motion of the universe. John Locke described the mind as a *tabula rasa* on which sense impressions are accumulated as knowledge. Bentham states that's man's morals are tied to his motivations and instincts alone. The Marquis de Sade, Darwin and Freud all argued that man has a wolf lurking within him and that his civilized self is but a frail shell concealing this inner darkness. Jung believed that there is no individual self but rather a collective self freighted with original paradigms. Nietzsche crystallized the foundations of the dark Enlightenment when he described the self as a trick used by the weak to smother the innocence and spontaneity of the powerful. It imposes illusory ideals of a fixed existence on the world of becoming. However one chooses to describe it, as a mask, a myth, a fairytale, an ideology or a linguistic coinage i.e. the self is not real. Marx, in his non-humanist materialist moments, adopted a largely similar position. He, too, believed that the independent human self was an illusion and that behind the independent individualist façade lay an ongoing class struggle and the means of production.

4. But how can we put Niccolò Machiavelli (1469-1527), Thomas Hobbes (1588-1679), John Locke (1632-1704), Baruch de Spinoza (1632-1677), Isaac Newton (1643-1727), Jan Jacque Rousseau (1712-1778), Marquis de Sade (1740-1814), Charles Darwin (1809-1882), Karl Marx (1818-1883), Friedrich Nietzsche (1844-1900), Sigmund Freud (1856-1939) and many others in one and the same category, though they belong to different historical periods and intellectual trends?

This is a very important question and its answer is the key to my intellectual output. In approaching western modernity, we are expected to transcend historiography, embracing instead the notion of paradigm. The explanatory power of paradigms lies in the fact that they go beyond differences and minute details to establish similarities among seemingly different theories and philosophers. These similarities can provide us with a dominant motif and a common worldview. Hobbes claimed that 'man is a wolf to man' and that reality was no more than an arena where a 'war of all against all' raged incessantly. Machiavelli was a materialist utilitarian who advocated the instrumentalization of all things, including man. Copernicus and Newton refuted the centricity of Earth and replaced it with a heliocentric vision of the universe. A number of other materialist philosophers, such as Spinoza, mounted a comprehensive deconstruction of the human self and developed a mechanistic materialist vision of man and the universe. The same motif can be traced in Locke's concept of the human mind as a *tabula rasa*, one that records, mechanically and automatically, an accumulation of sensory perceptions from which it forms thoughts and then complex ideas. Behaviourist psychology is no exception as it promoted this materialist and mechanical conception of man and the mind.

*5. But does the notion of paradigm in this sense justify the reduction of the
entire output of a specific philosopher to an oft-quoted phrase?*

As a professor of English literature, I was much influenced by the
New Critics who came into prominence in the 1950s. I was very
much attracted to the idea of 'close reading,' one which enables the
critic to trace key phrases and metaphors that can help a literary critic to
reach the specific meaning of the text, without claiming it to be the
final and the only valid interpretation. It is hardly surprising that I have
used metaphors as the best method to trace the dominant paradigms in
western thought. I came to discover that the paradigms can be defined
as the result of the ability to weave comprehensive and dominant
metaphors into a consistent whole. The paradigms I have formulated
did not come into existence overnight but they are the product of an
intensive and extensive reading of western philosophy. I come to the
conclusion that western thought can be understood through two
major metaphors or paradigms: the mechanical and the organic. The
latter compares human beings or the entire human existence to a plant
or an animal while the former compares human society to a self-
sufficient machine. However, both metaphors belong to a materialistic
paradigm that is believed to be self-operative and self-generating.
During the 19th century the mechanical metaphor, promoted by
Newton and mechanistic philosophy, was replaced by an organic
metaphor, but the materialist paradigm remained the same. Darwin
explained that man had arisen as a single link in the chain of evolution,
descended not from the divine but from a lineage of apes in accordance
with the laws of biological evolution. He was followed by Marx and
Adam Smith, who both asserted that society was essentially a conflict
governed by economic materialistic determinants. Next came Freud,
declaring that the conscious and the unconscious were governed by
the laws of mechanical and biological movement, and that it is primarily
our unconscious that drives us, which is itself governed by dark forces,
like sex. Not only are we descendants of apes, the ape lurks in our depths
and dominates all we do. Freud also argued that we never become aware
of the truth within ourselves, but rather what appears to be the truth.

6. You attempt to uncover the significance of the dominant paradigms in west-
ern thought in relation to modernity and the Holocaust, how is the Holocaust
different from, for example, the Spanish inquisition or the Crusades?

The Holocaust can be regarded as a paradigmatic moment of
western modernity, a moment that uncovers an immanent possibility
of the modern urge towards perfection and efficiency. Zygmunt
Bauman argues in *Modernity and the Holocaust* that the Nazis after
Kristallnacht discovered that they could not achieve their objectives
through a series of well-orchestrated popular pogroms, for it would
have taken too many years to exterminate the Jews. Moreover, pogroms
require popular agitation and involve emotions, emotions of hatred it
is true, but emotions nevertheless. The Nazis were iron-fisted secular
modernizers who developed an extremely rational purist model of fast
mo- dernization. Therefore, they could not tolerate emotions or any
other elements that would slow them down or that would hinder their
full and rational utilization of the natural and human resources at the
fastest possible rate. Therefore any human being deemed parasitical
and useless, from the standpoint of the rational Nazi state and from
the standpoint of the equally rational Nazi science, had to be dealt
with. The category of 'the useless' – also referred to as 'useless eaters,'
'disposable' and 'transferable' – included gypsies, homosexuals, Slavs,
intellectuals with the wrong kind of ideas, handicapped children, old
people, and Jews. Neither the Spanish inquisition nor the Crusades
embraced an ideology that would exterminate a whole race to establish
paradise on earth.

7. Is this the reason behind your mapping of Gnostic totalitarianism as one of
the major consequences of modernity, one that has given rise to Übermenschen
and Untermenschen?

Your use of the German words here is very crucial because, as I said
before, the Nazi Holocaust is a paradigmatic moment and the use of
these German words has thus a more explanatory power. Modern
man, despite all talk about equality, sees humankind from the same
dualistic vision. On the one hand, there is the *Übermensch* (superman),

Nietzsche's man, the peak of natural development that has its own law. There is also the member of the ruling technocrat elite, the possessor of the gnosis who will solve all problems. On the other hand, there are the masses, the common people, and the bureaucrats, who receive orders and blindly obey them, then execute them without any questioning; they represent the *Untermensch* (sub-man), who moves in the space previously chosen for him.

The modern Western man implemented the same strict dualistic vision on the population of the globe, therefore, there is the Western man, the possessor of the gnosis who has all the rights on the one hand, and on the other, there is the rest of humankind who has no rights, yet exists to be matter that is functionalized and no more than a means. In Gnostic thought, a spiritual man has no relation to our time or place. He found himself in this world by mistake and therefore he always remembers his divine origin and feels alienated from his surroundings. As a consequence, he refuses the world, his human state, the dialectic, the dualistic vision, death and the unity of body and soul, i.e. he refuses his finality and he longs for the state of pleroma, when dialectic and dualism will be purged.

As for modern Gnostic man, he is an alienated man, without a homeland and in a state of continuous conflict with nature. He found himself in a world not of his own making, and he always dreams of a scientific technocratic utopia where the complete scientific domination over nature will be realized and all dualisms will be purged after the accumulation of scientific knowledge. However, for both the spiritual man and the modern man, the concept of return is a basic one in Gnosticism. The spiritual man returns to the state of pleroma and merges with it. His true human essence, which is the divine essence, appears, as there is no difference between god and man, because the part merges with the whole and the whole is the pleroma.

Modern ideologies are ideologies that return to the absolute and merge with it; the romantic poet returns to nature and merges with it, the populist returns to the people and merges with them, the Zionist returns to the land and merges with it, the revolutionary intellectual returns to the working class and merges with it in order to establish the communist society, which is the state of pleroma. All secularist societies, despite all obstacles and difficulties, are in a state of infinite continuous progress that ends in utopia. After the process of merging, the true essence of man appears – the Jew for example, can only become a true Jew in the Promised Land – and man can only discover his essence and conquer his alienation after this process of merging.

Gnosis is the radical solution to all problems of the universe, a solution that has no disparities and explains everything: evil, the creation, the return, the beginning and the end. Therefore, it is characterized by solid and absolute interpretation that covers all possibilities, enables the spiritual man to decode all codes and realize complete freedom and merge with the pleroma. It must be noted that gnosis is always linked to numbers and mathematical patterns. Revolutionary, scientific, and secular ideologies are a continuous search for an interpretation of everything through science and for a utopian technocratic solution. The dream remains a dream with quantitative mathematical scientific formulas without any disparities, covering all possibilities. The aim of revolutionary scientific gnosis is knowledge of the law of necessity, dominance over the universe and total control. The moment of total control is technocratic utopia or the technocratic Zion; comprehensive society, everything has been brought under control, the parts have merged with the whole and are subjugated to it, and no man suffers any problems or struggle, history ends and paradise on earth appears – and the return to the myth is noted again in the modernist thought and literature and in modernism's anti-historical tendency.

We can say that the system underlying all comprehensive secular ideologies, including Nazism, Marxism, Liberalism, Zionism, is what might be termed 'unilinear evolution,' that is, the belief that there is a single scientific and natural evolutionary law to which all societies and human phenomena conform. Progress in reality is nothing but a cumulative process of materialistic rationalization, namely a reformulation of human reality after the model of nature-matter, so that all the qualitative, complex, ambiguous and mysterious elements are eliminated. Reality is thereby turned into mere matter that can be utilized, and into a one-dimensional being that can be instrumentalized.

It would then be possible to utilize both man and nature very efficiently. After taking this step, the process of rationalization, including
standardization and levelling, gradually escalates until the dream of
technological utopias is fulfilled. Everything is programmed and man
himself is controlled from within and without. Total rationalization is
achieved through progressive stages which all human societies undergo.
Hence the Western passion for dividing history into neatly separate
stages).

The escalation of rationalization and its application on a world-
wide scale is globalization, whereby the whole world is brought under
control and turned into mere matter that can be utilized and instrumentalized. Max Weber predicted that rationalising processes would
lead society to the condition of the workshop and drive it into an iron
cage. The image of the iron cage is quite appropriate but stands some
revisions, for the modern world is actually run in accordance with a
triadic rhythmic sequence: the workshop (where man produces), the
market (where he goes shopping), and places of recreation (where he
rids himself of his surplus energy, tensions, complexes and dimensions).
It is a rhythmic sequence that would absorb economic and libidinal
men, and would satisfy all their simple, natural, one-dimensional
desires, that are totally unrelated to any human complexity.

*8. Post-modernity was seen as the way out from the consequences of modernity.
But you never conceived of it as a mode of transcendence. On the contrary, you
always maintain that it is a radicalization of modernity and the notion of the
one-dimensional man. Why have you taken such a negative attitude towards
postmodernity?*

I always argue that post-modernity is the philosophical outlook that
affirms the absence of any principles that could serve as a final point
of reference, the erosion of both the subject and object and their
boundaries, and the hegemony of moral and epistemological relativism. Post-modernity is the ultimate revolt against Hegelianism and
it is the crystallization of what came to be termed the 'anti-philosophical
trends' within Western philosophy. This means in fact the disappearance of reason, the faculty which allows man to accumulate meaning

and achievements. This represents what someone called 'the memory of crossword puzzles,' that is, scattered information without any link. The feeling arises that we are in an eternal present, constant change without past or future, repeated experiments without depth or meaning. History is transformed into mere rigid moments, a flat time without depth, coiled around itself without features or significance. The present is identical with the past and the future, and simultaneous with them, just as the self is identical with the object and man with things. Hence, the post-modernist talk about substituting small narratives for the grand narrative. Man is incapable of reaching a comprehensive over-all historical outlook shared by all mankind. He is only capable of going through partial experiences which he can narrate with varying degrees of success and failure, but in no way does his narrative reach the level of a general history of mankind because it has no legitimacy outside the limits of his own experience.

Post-modernity may not produce evolutionary linear paradigms or final solutions. It may not proclaim the arrival of an earthly paradise or a technological technocratic utopia, but it too in its own way is proclamation of the end of history and the end of man as a complex social entity capable of free moral choice. He is replaced by uni-dimensional man, either revolving around a point of reference immanent in the phenomena surrounding him, or surviving with no point of reference whatsoever. He is centred either around his self-referential natural self that has nothing to do with anything external to it, or around abstract non-human wholes unrelated to man as we know him. Such man has no memory and lives in the moment only, within his small narrative. Someone summed up post-modernity as an active forgetfulness of historical memory. It is an inflated blown up way of proclaiming the end of history. We can say that if Fukuyama has 'discovered' and proclaimed the end of History, then post-modernity has 'murdered' it.

9. Zygmunt Bauman argues that post-modernity promotes seduction rather than repression. Also Fredric Jameson places a great emphasis on post-modernity as representing the cultural logic of late capitalism. Where do you stand in relation to these views?

In the post-modern world, the West decided to resort to seduction rather than coercion. I often describe post-modernity as a 'liquid non-rational materialism' because it represents the epistemological framework underlying the New World Order. It is an outlook that denies the centre and does away with referentiality. It refuses to give history any *telos* or to give man any meaning or centrality. It discards all ideologies, it denies history, and it denies man. It is a world in a state of flux. As Frederic Jameson, the Marxist American critic maintains, the post-modernist spirit is an expression of the capitalist spirit. Here, capital has cancelled all specificities as well as the coherent self within which history and personal depth are unified. General exchange value has replaced the original value of things.

Though Jameson's analysis of post-modernity is very original, I prefer to substitute the term 'capitalism' with 'comprehensive secularism.' The reference to general exchange value which cancels specificities is not a reference to capital as an economic affair but rather to capital as an epistemological mechanism that deconstructs and demolishes anything that is unique, specific, profound, sacred or charged with mystery. It is therefore a mechanism hostile to man because it is hostile to history and civilization. Capital here is the mechanism which drives man out of the complex world of civilization and history into a simple unidimensional world of nature. It is the mechanism leading to the dominance of the monist material natural law. It is the most important instrument to desacralize man, though it is not the only one, for in the age of post-modernism there are other mechanisms, the most important of which are pornography and the pleasure industry.

10. Critics hardly attempt to establish any relationship between post-modernity and Zionism. Why are you keen on foregrounding the similarities between them? Is it only a matter of ideology and prejudice?

Contrary to the anti-Semitic tract that was conjured in the critics' minds, my encyclopaedia on the Jews, Judaism and Zionism was no campaign of denunciation or vilification; nor did it cater to a propagandistic agenda for 'rallying forces in defence of Arab rights.' Rather, it was an attempt to comprehend and explain Judaism and Zionism through the processes of deconstruction and reconstruction and the development of new paradigms capable of encompassing the various aspects of these phenomena in their totality and specificity. Indeed, in Zionist literature there is an acute awareness of this convergence between anti-Semitism and Zionism. Herzl himself spoke of 'our friends the anti-Semites,' and Balfour was perfectly conscious that his Zionist bias was rooted in his own anti-Semitism and the desire to rid Europe of the Jews as the solution to the 'Jewish question.' It was only a small step from Balfour to Hitler. Both wanted to achieve the same end – to rid Europe of the Jews – but whereas Balfour's solution was to pack them off to the British colonies, Hitler's was the concentration camps and the gas chambers. Then again, Hitler did not have the luxury of foreign colonies, Germany having been stripped of its colonial possessions following World War I (although in fact Hitler had contemplated a Balfour-like solution in Mozambique).

Some critics believe that to 'humanise' the Jews is to acquit Zionism and to sympathise with its advocates. Nothing could be more erroneous. Our conflict with the Zionists is not a trial and we are not bringing suit against them. What we are, or should be, trying to do is to understand them and their behaviour so as to be able to deal with them better in war or in peace. 'Humanise,' moreover, is by no means equivalent to 'sympathise.' I am reminded in this context of Mark Twain's famous remark that "Jews are members of the human race, worse than that I cannot say of them." Colonialism is a human phenomenon, as are racism, exploitation and other evils; and as part of the very core of human existence we can observe and attempt to explain most of their aspects. To attempt to explain and understand is a far cry from condoning these ills, and we must make the effort to comprehend if we are to grasp reality and therefore change it. Conversely, without this effort, all we have are hollow slogans, and the struggle to counter these ills becomes suicidal, because it entails hurling ourselves blind and unprepared into an obscure and raging storm.

11. Al-Ahram Weekly published in its issue 30 March–7 April your article 'Pattern on the Sand' next to Zygmunt Bauman's 'Many Cultures, One Humanity.' Do you see any common grounds between your mapping of modernity and post-modernity and Bauman's in this article?

As I pointed out in the article, our cognitive map of modernity can be best introduced through two major anecdotes. The first one is related to an Algerian "shaikh" who was once told that the French forces had come to his country to spread modern Western civilization. The answer came, brief and revealing: "Why then, did they bring all of this ammunition with them?" The shaikh perceived, at the very onset, the relationship between Western imperialist modernity, and the framework of conflict from which such modernity emanates. This revelation has been perceived by many others since then. The second anecdote is related to the protagonist of that marvellous novel *The Season of Emigrating to the North* written by Sudanese writer El-Tayyib Saleh. The protagonist underlined the dominant pattern of Darwinian modernity when he said: "I hear... the sound of the Romans' swords in Carthage, and the clash of spurs of Allenby's horses stampeding the earth of Jerusalem. The boats glided across the Nile waters, for the first time carrying guns not bread. Railways were built to carry soldiers, and schools founded to teach us to say yes in their language."

Reading Bauman's article, I come to realize that his mapping of modernity and post-modernity is still endowed with a humanistic touch and a comprehensive interpretative paradigm that marked his book *Modernity and the Holocaust*. What is unique about this article is that it condemns all Manichean visions of the world, all of which call for a holy war against satanic forces, reducing economic, political and social conflicts to an apocalyptic vision of the last, life and death confrontation between good and evil. As Bauman suggests these tendencies recognize no differences between civilizations or faith systems and we can easily find them in the 'West' as often as in the 'East,' and among the Muslims as easily as among Christians and Jews. As Bauman points out globalization is only confined to capital, finance, trade, criminal mafias or terrorists. We are really in need of positive globalization to really share the same humanistic ambitions.

NOTES

I

COGNITIVE MAPPING AND METAPHORICITY

1   Hodgson, *Rethinking World History*. Edmund Burke (ed.) (Cambridge: Cambridge University Press, 1993), p.29.

2   Golledge, *Wayfinding Behavior* (Baltimore: Johns Hopkins University Press, 1999), p.ix.

3   Huyssen, *After the Great Divide* (Bloomington & Indianapolis: Indiana University Press, 1986), p.184.

4   Berman, *All That Is Solid Melts into Air* (New York: Penguin, 1982), p.17.

5   Blackshaw, *Zygmunt Bauman* (London and New York: Routledge, 2005), p.6.

6   Anderson, *The Origins of Postmodernity* (London: Verso, 1998), pp.25-32.

7   Pawling, "The American Lukács? Fredric Jameson and Dialectical Thought" in *Fredric Jameson: A Critical Reader*, Douglas Kellner and Sean Homer (ed.) (New York: Palgrave Macmillan), 2004, pp.31-32.

8   Jameson, *Postmodernism, Or, the Cultural Logic of Late Capitalism* (London: Verso, 1991), p.418.

9   Buchanan, *Fredric Jameson: Live Theory* (New York: Continuum, 2006), pp.106-108.

10   Roberts, *Fredric Jameson* (New York: Routledge, 2000), pp.141-142.

11   Elmessiri, "Features of the New Islamic Discourse." Azzam Tamimi (trans.). A paper delivered at the conference on "The West and Islam: Clashpoints and Dialogues," held in Cairo on 15-23 February 1997, organized by 21st Century Trust. www.muslimphilosophy.com

12   Elmessiri, *Al-ʿAlmāniyyah al-Juzʿiyyah wa al-ʿAlmāniyyah al-Shāmilah* [Partial Secularism and Comprehensive Secularism] (Cairo: Dār al-Shurūq, 2002), vol. 2, p.219.

13   Elmessiri, *Riḥlaty al-Fikriyyah* [My Intellectual Journey – The Seeds, The
     Roots, and The Harvest] (Cairo: Dār al-Shurūq, 2005), p.137.

14   Ibid., p.137.

15   Ibid., pp.131-136.

16   Ibid., p.164.

17   Ibid., p.116.

18   Ibid., p.122.

19   Elmessiri, *Riḥlaty al-Fikriyyah*, p.376.

20   Tipps, "Modernization Theory and Comparative Study of Societies: A Critical
     Perspective," *Comparative Studies in Society and History*, vol. 15, no .2, 1973,
     p.208.

21   Zubaida, "Trajectories of Political Islam," *Political Quarterly*, 2000, Supplement 1,
     vol. 71, p.61.

22   Elmessiri, *Riḥlaty al-Fikriyyah*, p.542.

23   Ibid., p.380.

24   Elmessiri, *Al-Ṣuhyūniyyah wa al-Nāziyyah wa Nihāyat al-Tārīkh* [Zionism,
     Nazism and the End of History] (Cairo: Dār al-Shurūq, 3rd edn. 2001), p.17.

25   Ali, Haggag, "Conversation with Abdelwahab Elmessiri," in *The Cognitive
     Mapping of Modernity and Postmodernity* (Cairo University, PhD dissertation,
     2008), pp.193-194.

26   Elmessiri, *Dirāsāt Maʿrifiyyah* [Epistemological Studies in Western Modernity]
     (Cairo: Dār al-Shurūq International, 2006), pp.69-70.

27   Elmessiri, *Al-ʿAlmāniyyah al-Juzʿiyyah*, vol. 1, pp.101-126.

28   Elmessiri, *Dirāsāt Maʿrifiyyah*, p.34.

29   Elmessiri, "Secularism, Immanence and Deconstruction," in *Islam and Secularism
     in the Middle East*. John Esposito and Azzam Tamimi (eds.)(London: Hurst &
     Co, 2000a), p.68.

30   Elmessiri, *Dirāsāt Maʿrifiyyah*, pp.101-102.

31   Elmessiri, "Secularism, Immanence and Deconstruction," p.55.

32   Elmessiri, *Al-Ṣuhyūniyyah wa al-Nāziyyah*, p.299.

33   Elmessiri, *Riḥlaty al-Fikriyyah*, p.318.

34   Elmessiri, *Al-ʿAlmāniyyah al-Juzʿiyyah*, vol. 1, pp.59-63.

35   Ibid., pp.97-99.

36   Ibid., p.50.

37   Elmessiri, "Secularism, Immanence and Deconstruction," p.53.

NOTES

38 Elmessiri, *Al-ʿAlmāniyyah al-Juzʿiyyah*, vol. 1, pp.101-108.

39 Bauman, *Intimations of Postmodernity* (London; New York: Routledge, 1992), pp.166-167.

40 Elmessiri, *Al-ʿAlmāniyyah al-Juzʿiyyah*, vol. 1, p.51.

41 Elmessiri, *Riḥlaty al-Fikriyyah*, p.543.

42 Achcar, *The Arabs and the Holocaust*. G.M. Goshgarian (trans.) (London: Saqi, 2011), p.20.

43 Bunting, "Passion and Pessimism," London: *Guardian*, 5 April, 2003, p.20.

44 Bauman and Vecchi, *Identity* (Cambridge: Polity Press, 2004), p.11.

45 Bauman, *Intimations of Postmodernity*, p.28.

46 Bauman, *Postmodernity and its Discontents* (New York: New York University Press, 1997), p.97.

47 Shapira, "Life in a Liquid World," *Haaretz Daily Newspaper*, 16 November 2007.

48 Bauman, *Intimations of Postmodernity*, pp.226-227.

49 Bauman, *Modernity and Ambivalence* (Ithaca, N.Y.: Cornell University Press, 1991), pp.129-140.

50 Bauman, "Assimilation into Exile," *Poetics Today*, vol. 17, no. 4, 1996, pp.571-581.

51 Bauman, *Modernity and Ambivalence*, pp.129-140.

52 Ibid., p.148.

53 Elmessiri, *Riḥlaty al-Fikriyyah*, pp.451-452.

54 Elmessiri, *Epistemological Bias in the Physical and Social Sciences* (London - Washington: International Institute for Islamic Thought), 2006, pp.1-76.

55 Bauman, *Hermeneutics and Social Sciences* (New York: Columbia University Press), 1978, p.16; and *Towards a Critical Sociology* (London; Boston: Routledge, 1976), pp.70-75.

56 Bauman, *Legislators and Interpreters* (Cambridge, UK: Polity Press, 1987), p.125.

57 Bauman, *Culture as Praxis* (London: Routledge and Kegan Paul Ltd., 1973), p.165; and *Towards a Critical Sociology*, p.42.

58 Bauman, *Towards a Critical Sociology*, p.41.

59 Bauman, *Hermeneutics and the Social Sciences*, pp.17-48.

60 Bauman, "Critical Theory," in *The Bauman Reader*. Peter Beilharz (ed.) (Oxford: Blackwell, 2001), pp.140-143.

61   Ibid., pp.147-148.

62   Voegelin, *The New Science of Politics* (Chicago: University of Chicago Press, 1952), p.4.

63   Voegelin, *Science, Politics and Gnosticism*. Ellis Sandoz (ed.) (Washington, DC: Regnery Publishing, 1997), p.14.

64   Voegelin, *From Enlightenment to Revolution*. John H. Hallowell (ed.) (Durham, North Carolina: Duke University Press, 1975), p.101.

65   Kearney, *Modern Movements in European Philosophy* (Manchester: Manchester University Press, 1986), p.21.

66   Kuhn, *The Structure of Scientific Revolution* (Chicago, IL: University of Chicago Press, 1962), p.93.

67   Maasen, S. & Peter Weingart, *Metaphor and the Dynamics of Knowledge* (London: Routledge, 2000), p.89.

68   Kinloch, *Sociological Theory* (New York: McGraw-Hill, 1977), pp.31-32.

69   Bauman, 2004, "Liquid Modernity." Lecture on ANSE-Conference.

70   Bauman, *Intimations of Postmodernity*, p.90.

71   Bauman, *Legislators and Interpreters*, p.115.

72   Bauman, *Socialism: The Active Utopia* (New York: Holmes & Meier, 1976), p.39.

73   Bauman, *Postmodernity and its Discontents*, p.10.

74   Ibid., p.12.

75   Bauman, *Intimations of Postmodernity*, p.31.

76   Ibid., p.12.

77   Jameson, *A Singular Modernity* (London: Verso, 2002), pp.34-36.

78   Ali, "Correspondence with Zygmunt Bauman," in *The Cognitive Mapping of Modernity and Postmodernity*, pp.186-192.

79   Murdoch, *Metaphysics as a Guide to Morals* (London: Vintage, 2003), p.329.

80   Ibid., p.327.

81   Jacobsen and Sophia Marshman, "Metaphorically Speaking," *Polish Sociological Review*, 3 (155), 2006, p.108.

82   Bauman, *Freedom* (Minneapolis: University of Minnesota Press, 1988), p.5.

83   Bauman, *Postmodernity and its Discontents*, p.132.

84   Maasen and Peter Weingart, *Metaphor and the Dynamics of Knowledge* (London: Routledge, 2000), pp.21-37.

85   Bauman, *Modernity and Ambivalence*, p.28.

86 Elmessiri, *Al-Lughah wa al-Majāz: Bayna al-Tawḥīd wa Wiḥdat al-Wujūd* [Language and Metaphor: between Monotheism and Pantheism] (Cairo: Dār al-Shurūq, 2002), p.13.

87 Ibid., pp.28-46.

88 Elmessiri, *Al-Ḥadāthah wa mā Baʿda al-Ḥadāthah* [Modernity and Postmodernity] (Damascus: Dār al-Fikr, 2003), p.15.

89 Elmessiri, *Mawsūʿat al-Yahūd wa al-Yahūdiyyah wa al-Ṣuhyūniyyah* [Encyclopedia of the Jews, Judaism and Zionism] (Cairo: CD. Bayt al-ʿArab li al-Tawthīq al-ʿAṣrī wa al-Naẓm, 2001), vol. 1.

90 Elmessiri, *Riḥlaty al-Fikriyyah*, p.360.

91 Ibid., p.9.

92 Elmessiri, "The Cognitive Map," *Al-Ahram Weekly*, no.878, 2008.

93 Elmessiri, *Difāʿ ʿan al-Insān* [Defense of Man: Theoretical and Applied Studies in Complex Paradigms] (Cairo: Dār al-Shurūq, 2003), pp.304-305.

94 Honderich, *Oxford Companion to Philosophy* (Oxford: Oxford University Press, 2005), p.260; pp.590-592.

95 Davutoğlu, *Alternative Paradigms* (Lanham: University Press America, 1994), p.153.

96 Rosen, "Theory and Interpretation," in *Hermeneutics as Politics* (Oxford: Oxford University Press, 1987), p.168.

97 Ricoeur, "The Function of Fiction in Shaping Reality," in *A Ricoeur Reader: Reflection and Imagination*. Mario Valdes (ed.) (Toronto: University of Toronto Press, 1991), p.129.

98 Ricoeur, "Word, Polysemy, and Metaphor," in *A Ricoeur Reader: Reflection and Imagination*. Mario Valdes (ed) (Toronto: University of Toronto Press, 1991), p.85.

99 Ricoeur, "Metaphor and the Main Problem of Hermeneutics," in *A Ricoeur Reader: Reflection and Imagination*. Mario Valdes (ed.) (Toronto: University of Toronto Press, 1991), p.312.

100 Elmessiri, *Al-Lughah wa al-Majāz*, p.18.

101 Ricoeur, "Metaphor and the Main Problem of Hermeneutics," p.316.

102 Elmessiri, *Riḥlaty al-Fikriyyah*, p.9.

103 Elmessiri, *Mawsūʿat*, vol. 1.

104 Bernstein, *Beyond Objectivism and Relativism* (Philadelphia: University of Pennsylvania Press, 1983), pp.12-13.

105 Elmessiri, *Al-ʿAlmāniyyah al-Juzʿiyyah*, vol. 1, pp.44-45.

106 Lukács, "The Ideology of Modernism," in *20th Century Literary Criticism: A Reader*. David Lodge (ed.) (London and New York: Longman, 1972), p.476.

107 Elmessiri, *Difāʿ ʿan al-Insān*, p.302.

108 Elmessiri, *Al-Lughah wa al-Majāz*, p.37.

109 Elmessiri, *Al-ʿĀlam min Manẓūr Gharbī* [The World from a Western Perspective] (Cairo: Dār al-Hilāl, 2001), p.210

110 Elmessiri, *Epistemological Bias in the Physical and Social Sciences*, p.xiii.

111 Elmessiri, *Riḥlaty al-Fikriyyah*, p.123.

112 Ibid., p.21.

113 Elmessiri, *Epistemological Bias in the Physical and Social Sciences*, p.5.

114 Maasen and Weingart, *Metaphors and the Dynamics of Knowledge*, p.4.

115 Harrington, "Metaphoric Connections," *Social Research*, 1995, vol. 62, no. 2, pp.359-60.

116 Lakoff and Mark, *Metaphors We Live By* (Chicago: The University of Chicago Press, 1979), p.145.

117 Harrington, "Metaphoric Connections," p.363.

118 Maasen and Weingart, *Metaphors and the Dynamics of Knowledge*, p.42.

119 Ibid., p.41.

II
RADICAL ENLIGHTENMENT

1 Hof, Ulrich, *The Enlightenment*. William E. Yuill (trans.) (Oxford and Cambridge: Blackwell, 1994), pp.4-6.

2 Beck, *Kant Selections* (New York: Macmillan, 1998), p.462.

3 Edwards, *Encyclopedia of Philosophy*, 8 volumes (New York: Macmillan, 1967), vol. 2, pp.519-571.

4 Bauman, "Biology and the Modern Project," Humburger Institut für Sozialforschung: Diskussionspapier, 2-93. 1993, pp.189-191.

5 Harvey, *The Condition of Postmodernity* (Cambridge MA and Oxford UK: Blackwell, 1990), p.249.

6 Bauman, *Modernity and Ambivalence*, pp.7-11.

7 Dupré, *The Enlightenment* (New Haven and London: Yale University Press, 2004), p.204.

NOTES

8   Bauman, *Modernity and the Holocaust* (Cambridge: Polity Press, 1989), p.92.

9   Bauman, *Postmodernity and its Discontents*, p.174.

10 Bauman, "Living in Utopia," LSE Public Lecture, 27 October, 2005.

11 Tester, *The Two Sovereigns* (London: Routledge, 1992), p.54.

12 Hofstadter, *Social Darwinism in American Thought* (Boston: Beacon Press, 1955), p.95.

13 Gellner, Ernest, *Nations and Nationalisms* (Ithaca, New York: Cornell University Press, 1983), p.50.

14 Bauman, *Modernity and Ambivalence*, p.15.

15 Bauman, *Intimations of Postmodernity*, p.xv.

16 Bauman, *Modernity and Ambivalence*, p.7.

17 Ibid., p.24.

18 Bauman, *Legislators and Interpreters*, p.28.

19 Bauman, *Modernity and Ambivalence*, p.24.

20 Bauman, *Socialism*, p.24.

21 Bauman, *Intimations of Postmodernity*, p.86.

22 Arendt, "Philosophy and Politics," *Social Research*, vol. 57, no. 1, 1990, pp.75-102.

23 Bauman, *Legislators and Interpreters*, p.58.

24 Kilminster & Ian Varcoe, "Addendum: Culture and Power in the Writings of Zygmunt Bauman," in *Culture, Modernity and Revolution: Essays in Honour of Zygmunt Bauman* (London: Routledge, 1996), p.217.

25 Bauman, *Towards a Critical Sociology*, pp.70-74.

26 Bauman, *Modernity and Ambivalence*, p.71.

27 Bauman, *Legislators and Interpreters*, p.13.

28 Hof, *The Enlightenment*, p.270.

29 Bauman, *Legislators and Interpreters*, p.80.

30 Ibid., p.94.

31 Torevell, "The Terrorism of Reason in the Thought of Zygmunt Bauman," (The Dominican Council/Blackwell Publishing Ltd), (New Blackfriars, 1995), vol. 76, issue 891, p.145.

32 Elmessiri, *Al-ʿAlmāniyyah al-Juzʿiyyah*, vol. 1, p.289.

33 Elmessiri, "Towards a More Comprehensive and Explanatory Paradigm of Secularism," *Encounters: Journal of Inter-cultural Perspectives*, vol. 2. no. 2, 1996, p.143.

34 Elmessiri, *Al-ʿAlmāniyyah al-Juzʿiyyah*, vol. 1, p.290.

35 Ibid., vol. 1, pp.289-290.

36 Ibid., vol. 1, pp.294-297.

37 Elmessiri, "Of Darwinian Mice and Pavlovian Dogs: a Critique of Western Modernity," 1997, *Al-Ahram Weekly*, no.319.

38 Ibid.

39 Israel, *Enlightenment Contested* (Oxford and New York: Oxford University Press, 2006), p.12.

40 Wellman, *La Mettrie* (Durham, NC.: Duke University Press, 1992), p.264.

41 Bernstein, *The New Constellation* (Cambridge: Polity Press, 1991), p.40.

42 Dupré, *Passage to Modernity* (New Haven and London: Yale University Press, 1993), pp.50-54.

43 Elmessiri, *Mawsūʿat*, vol. 1.

44 Edwards, *The Encyclopedia of Philosophy*, vol. 1, pp.122-124.

45 Ibid., p.89.

46 Elmessiri, *Dirāsāt Maʿrifiyyah*, p.30.

47 Ibid., p.21.

48 Dupré, *The Enlightenment*, p.8.

49 Elmessiri, *Al-Lughah wa al-Majāz*, p.43.

50 Ali, "Conversation with Abdelwahab Elmessiri," pp.195-196.

51 Bauman, *Towards a Critical Sociology*, p.2.

52 Ibid., p.4.

53 Ibid., p.5.

54 Bauman, *Legislators and Interpreters*, p.69.

55 Bauman, *Modernity and Ambivalence*, pp.104-107.

56 Bauman, *Legislators and Interpreters*, p.74.

57 Bauman, *Modernity and the Holocaust*, p.68.

58 Bauman, *Towards a Critical Sociology*, p.7-17.

59 Elmessiri, *Al-ʿAlmāniyyah al-Juzʿiyyah*, vol. 1, pp.264-273.

60 Ibid., vol. 1, p.278.

61 Ibid., vol. 1, p.281.

62 Elmessiri, *Riḥlaty al-Fikriyyah*, p.399.

63 Ibid., p.354.

64 Ibid., p.364.

65 Ibid., p.470.

66 Connolly, *Political Theory and Modernity* (Ithca and London: Cornell University Press, 1993), p.2.

67 Elmessiri, *Al-ʿAlmāniyyah al-Juzʿiyyah*, vol. 2, p.452.

68 Dupré, *The Enlightenment*, 2004, p.20.

69 Arendt, *The Human Condition* (Chicago: The University of Chicago Press, 1958), p.312.

70 Elmessiri, *Al-Lughah wa al-Majāz*, p.6.

71 Ibid., p.36.

72 Ibid., pp.36-37.

73 Elmessiri, *Mawsūʿat*, vol. 1.

74 Bauman, *Modernity and Ambivalence*, p.11; pp.262-265.

75 Bauman, *Legislators and Interpreters*, pp.110-111.

76 Voegelin, *Science, Politics and Gnosticism*, pp.61-63.

77 Elmessiri, *Al-ʿAlmāniyyah al-Juzʿiyyah*, vol. 1, pp.101-102.

III
MODERNITY AS A GNOSTIC NARRATIVE

1 Jameson, *A Singular Modernity*, p.94.

2 Arendt, *The Human Condition*, p.292.

3 Edwards, *Encyclopedia of Philosophy*, vol. 1, pp.85-86; vol. 5, p.303.

4 Bertens, *The Idea of the Postmodern* (London and New York: Routledge, 1995), p.44.

5 Siedel, *Knowledge as a Sexual Metaphor* (Selinsgrove: Susquehanna University Press, 2000), pp.168-175.

6 Sandoz, (ed.), "Introduction," in *Science, Politics and Gnosticism* (Washington, DC: Regnery Publishing, 1997), p.xii.

7 Voegelin, "Renaissance and Reformation," in *The Collected Works of Eric Voegelin*, vol. 22. D. Morse & W.M. Thompson (eds.) (Columbia & London: University of Missouri Press, 1998), pp.178-179.

8 Voegelin, *Science, Politics and Gnosticism*, pp.57-69

9 Delanty, *Modernity and Postmodernity* (London: Sage Publications, 2000), p.65.

10 Bauman and Vecchi, *Identity*, p.73.

11 Bauman and Keith Tester, *Conversations with Zygmunt Bauman* (Cambridge: Polity, 2001), pp.134-135.

12   Bauman, *Postmodernity and its Discontents*, p.201.

13   Jacobsen, "From Solid Modern Utopia to Liquid Modern Anti-Utopia?" *Utopian Studies*, vol. 15, no.1, 2004, p.66.

14   Bauman, "Biology and the Modern Project," pp.7-8.

15   Giddens, *Modernity and Self-Identity* (Stanford: Stanford University Press, 1991), pp.2-48.

16   Bauman, "Living in Utopia," LSE Public Lecture.

17   Arendt, *The Human Condition*, pp.15-139.

18   Izetbegovic, *Islam Between East and West* (Indiana: The American Trust Publications, 1999), 3rd edn., pp.8-15.

19   Elmessiri, *Dirāsāt Maʿrifiyyah*, pp.17-24.

20   Elmessiri, *Al-Ḥadāthah wa mā Baʿda al-Ḥadāthah*, p.16.

21   Badawi, *Mawsūʿat al-Falsafah* [Encyclopedia of Philosophy] (Beirut: al-Muʿassasah al-ʿArabiyyah li al-Dirāsāt wa al-Nashr, 1984), p.86.

22   Elmessiri, "Secularism, Immanence and Deconstruction," p.58.

23   Ibid., p.59.

24   Elmessiri, *Mawsūʿat*, vols. 5-6.

25   Ibid., vol. 6.

26   Delanty, *Modernity and Postmodernity*, p.65.

27   Bauman, *Life in Fragments* (Oxford UK and Cambridge USA: Blackwell, 1995), pp.15-16.

28   Bauman, *Postmodernity and its Discontents*, p.201.

29   Elmessiri, "Secularism, Immanence and Deconstruction," p.75.

30   Elmessiri, *Al-Lughah wa al-Majāz*, p.56.

31   Voegelin, *Science, Politics and Gnosticism*, pp.68-69.

32   Voegelin, "Race and State," in *The Collected Works of Eric Voegelin*. K. Vondung, (ed.) (Baton Rouge: University of Missouri Press, 1997), vol. 2, p.139.

33   Voegelin, *"Religion and the rise of modernity,"* in *The Collected Works of Eric Voegelin*. J.Wiser, (ed.) (Columbia & London: University of Missouri Press, 1998), vol. 23, p.140.

34   Voegelin, *The New Science of Politics*, p.118.

35   Ibid., pp.118-125.

36   Voegelin, *Race and State*, p.138.

37   Voegelin, *Religion and the Rise of Modernity*, p.142.

38 Voegelin, *Race and State*, p.148.

39 Elmessiri, "Secularism, Immanence and Deconstruction," p.62.

40 Elmessiri, *Al-ʿAlmāniyyah al-Juzʿiyyah*, vol. 1, p.149.

41 Elmessiri, *Al-Lughah wa al-Majāz*, pp.40-48.

42 Bauman, *Intimations of Postmodernity*, p.179.

43 Elmessiri, *Al-ʿAlmāniyyah al-Juzʿiyyah*, vol. 2, pp.83-142.

44 Elmessiri, *Al-Ṣuhyūniyyah wa al-Nāziyyah*, p.48.

45 Bauman, "The Fate of Humanity in the Post-Trinitarian World," 2002, pp.283-303.

46 Elmessiri, *Al-ʿAlmāniyyah al-Juzʿiyyah*, vol. 2, pp.53-83.

47 Bauman, *Modernity and the Holocaust*, p.43.

48 Elmessiri, *The Land of Promise* (New Brunswick, N. J: North American, 1977), pp.44-45.

49 Elmessiri, *Al-Ṣuhyūniyyah wa al-Nāziyyah*, p.61.

50 Bauman, *Modernity and the Holocaust*, p.70.

51 Bauman, "The Fate of Humanity in a Post-Trinitarian World," pp.283-303.

52 Bauman, *Modernity and the Holocaust*, pp.67-68.

53 Ibid., p.7.

54 Bauman, Janina, "Demons of Other People's Fear: The Plight of the Gypsies," *Thesis Eleven*, 1998, vol. 54, no. 1, pp.51-56.

IV

MAPPING THE CONSEQUENCES OF MODERNITY

1 Bauman, "Critical Theory," p.151.

2 Bauman, "The Fate of Humanity in a Post-Trinitarian World," pp.283-303.

3 Bauman, *Legislators and Interpreters*, pp.110-111.

4 Bauman, "The Fate of Humanity in a Post-Trinitarian World," pp.283-303.

5 Bauman, *Legislators and Interpreters*, pp.115-116.

6 Bauman, *Modernity and the Holocaust*, p.96.

7 Bauman, *Legislators and Interpreters*, p.111.

8 Giddens, *Modernity and Self-Identity*, p.15.

9 Bauman, *Legislators and Interpreters*, p.125.

10 Bauman, *Modernity and Ambivalence*, p.64.

11 Bauman, *Legislators and Interpreters*, pp.49-50.

12 Bauman, *Modernity and Ambivalence*, p.20.

13 Ibid., p.29.

14 Bauman, *Europe: An Unfinished Adventure* (Cambridge: Polity, 2004), pp.10-77.

15 Bauman, "The Fate of Humanity in a Post-Trinitarian World," pp.283-303.

16 Bauman, *Modernity and the Holocaust*, pp.42-43.

17 Ibid., pp.50-68.

18 Stone, Dan, *Theoretical Interpretations of the Holocaust* (Amsterdam – Atlanta: Rodopi, 2001), pp.5-6.

19 Bauman, *Modernity and Ambivalence*, pp.107-110.

20 Bauman, *Modernity and the Holocaust*, pp.1-2.

21 Ibid., p.31.

22 Ibid., p.66.

23 Ibid., p.13.

24 Ibid., pp.14-18.

25 Ibid., p.26.

26 Ibid., pp.71-72.

27 Ibid., p.126.

28 Ibid., p.108.

29 Harrington, "Metaphoric Connections," p.365.

30 Bauman, *Modernity and Ambivalence*, p.29.

31 Ibid.

32 Ibid., pp.33-36.

33 Maasen and Weingart, *Metaphors and the Dynamics of Knowledge*, p.42.

34 Varcoe, "Identity and the Limits of Comparison," *Theory, Culture and Society* (London, Thousand Oaks, CA., and New Delhi: Sage, 1998), vol. 15 (1), p.58.

35 Joas, Hans, "Bauman in Germany," *Theory, Culture & Society* (London, Thousand Oaks, CA., and New Delhi: Sage, 1998), vol. 15 (1), p.94.

36 Bauman, "Sociology after the Holocaust," *British Journal of Sociology*, vol. 39, no. 4, 1988, pp.478-481.

37 Ibid., p.475.

38 Bauman, *Modernity and the Holocaust*, p.68.

39 Bauman, *Modernity and Ambivalence*, pp.46-48.

40 Ibid., pp.104-107.

41 Ibid., p.17.

42 Bauman, *Legislators and Interpreters*, pp.41-42.

43 Bauman, *Postmodernity and its Discontents*, p.6.

44 Bauman, *Legislators and Interpreters*, p.33.

45 Ibid., pp.43-44.

46 Bauman, *Postmodernity and its Discontents*, pp.18-19.

47 Bauman, *Modernity and Ambivalence*, p.65.

48 Ibid., p.56.

49 Bauman, "The Fate of Humanity in a Post-Trinitarian World," pp.283-303.

50 Bauman, *Modernity and Ambivalence*, p.56.

51 Wolff, Kurt H, (ed.), *The Sociology of Georg Simmel* (New York: Free Press, 1950), pp.402-407.

52 Bauman, *Modernity and the Holocaust*, p.53.

53 Bauman, *Modernity and Ambivalence*, p.61.

54 Ibid., pp.71-82.

55 Ibid., pp.117-128.

56 Ibid., pp.111-112.

57 Ibid., p.13.

58 Ibid., pp.161-162.

59 Bauman, *Postmodernity and its Discontents*, p.78.

60 Bauman, "The Fate of Humanity in a Post-Trinitarian World," pp.283-303.

61 Bauman, *Intimations of Postmodernity*, p.228.

62 Clarke, Simon, "On Strangers: Phantasy, Terror and the Human Imagination," *Journal of the Human Rights*, 2002, vol. 1 (3), pp.345-355.

63 Nietzsche, *The Birth of Tragedy and the Genealogy of Morals*. Francis Golffing (trans.) (New York: Doubleday & Company, INC.), pp.168-181.

64 Bauman, *Postmodern Ethics* (Oxford, UK; Cambridge, Mass.: Blackwell, 1993), p.228.

65 Elmessiri, *Dirāsāt Maʿrifiyyah*, pp.100-125.

66 Ibid., pp.101-102.

67 Lukács, "The Ideology of Modernism," in *20th Century Literary Criticism: A Reader*. David Lodge (ed.) (London and New York: Longman, 1972), p.483.

68 Tipps, "Modernization Theory and Comparative Study of Societies," p.207.

69 Elmessiri, "Towards a More Comprehensive and Explanatory Paradigm of Secularism," p.137.

70 Elmessiri, *Difāʿ an al-Insān*, pp.180-181.

71   Elmessiri, "The Imperialist Epistemological Vision," *The American Journal of Islamic Social Sciences* (Washington, DC, Kuala Lumpur, Malaysia, 1994), vol. 11, no. 3, pp.406-407.

72   Elmessiri, *Al-Lughah wa al-Majāz*, pp.40-48.

73   Ali, "Conversation with Abdelwahab Elmessiri," p.195.

74   Elmessiri, *Dirāsāt Maʿrifiyyah*, pp.109-111.

75   Elmessiri, *Al-ʿAlmāniyyah al-Juzʿiyyah*, vol. 2, pp.77-83.

76   Elmessiri, *Riḥlaty al-Fikriyyah*, p.590.

77   Elmessiri, *Mawsūʿat*, vols. 1-2.

78   Gellner, *Nations and Nationalism*, pp.36-37.

79   Dobbelaere, *Secularization: An Analysis at Three Levels* (Brussels: Peter Lang, 2002), p.38.

80   Bauman, *Modernity and the Holocaust*, p.43.

81   Elmessiri, *Mawsūʿat*, vol. 2.

82   Bauman, *Modernity and the Holocaust*, p.50.

83   Elmessiri, *Mawsūʿat*, vol. 2.

84   Bauman, *Modernity and the Holocaust*, p.61.

85   Elmessiri, *The Land of Promise*, pp.44-45.

86   Elmessiri, "Understanding the Holocaust," 2000b, *Al-Ahram Weekly*, no.507.

87   Elmessiri, *Dirāsāt Maʿrifiyyah*, p.279.

88   Ibid., p.280.

89   Elmessiri, *Al-Ṣuhyūniyyah wa al-Nāziyyah*, p.27.

90   Elmessiri, *Dirāsāt Maʿrifiyyah*, p.197.

91   Elmessiri, *Al-Ṣuhyūniyyah wa al-Nāziyyah*, pp.36-38, p.59.

92   Ibid., p.79.

93   Elmessiri, *Al-Ṣuhyūniyyah wa al-Ḥadārah al-Gharbiyyah al-Ḥadīthah* [Zionism and Modern Western Civilization] (Cairo: Dār al-Hilāl, 2003), pp.156-159.

V

BAUMAN AND THE POSTMODERN SECULAR DILEMMA

1   Bauman, 2004, "Liquid Modernity." Lecture on ANSE-Conference.

2   Armstrong, *Islam: a Short History* (Phoenix Press: London, 2001), p.134.

3   Bauman, 'Living in Utopia.' LSE Public Lecture.

4   Bauman, *Intimations of Postmodernity*, p.187.

5   Bauman, *Legislators and Interpreters*, p.124.

6   Bauman, *Intimations of Postmodernity*, p.104.

7   Ibid, p.42.

8   Bauman, *Postmodernity and its Discontents*, p.31.

9   Bauman, *Intimations of Postmodernity*, p.viii.

10   Bauman, *Legislators and Interpreters*, p.118.

11   Huyssen, *After the Great Divide*, p.10.

12   Bauman, *Legislators and Interpreters*, p.131.

13   Harding, Luke, "Ruthlessly Exposed," *Guardian*, 8 April, 2005.

14   Bauman, *Intimations of Postmodernity*, p.vii.

15   Beilharz, *Zygmunt Bauman: Dialectic of Modernity* (London: Sage Publications, 2000), p.51.

16   Bauman, *Intimations of Postmodernity*, pp.188-189.

17   Beilharz, *Zygmunt Bauman: Dialectic of Modernity*, p.76.

18   Vanicek, "Zygmunt Bauman: Thoughts on the Age of Postmodernity," *Perspectives: Central European Review of International Affairs* (Prague Institute of International Relations, 2005), vol. 23, p.77.

19   Bauman, *Intimations of Postmodernity*, p.26.

20   Ibid., p.188.

21   Ibid., pp.187-188.

22   Bauman, *Modernity and Ambivalence*, pp.101-252.

23   Bauman, *Intimations of Postmodernity*, p.xxiv.

24   Bernstein, *The New Constellation*, p.7.

25   Bauman, *Postmodern Ethics*, p.219.

26   Tester, "Paths in the Social Thought of Zygmunt Bauman," *Thesis Eleven*, vol. 70, no.1, 2002, p.68.

27   Abbinnett, Ross, *Culture and Identity: Critical Theories* (London: Sage Publications, 2003), p.16.

28   Lévinas, *Alterity and Transcendence*. Michael B. Smith (trans.) (New York: Columbia University Press, 1999), pp.23-29.

29   Ibid., pp.56-57.

30   Bauman, *Postmodern Ethics*, pp.10-13.

31   Ibid., p.14.

32   Ibid., p.72.

33   Abbinnett, "Postmodernity and the Ethics of Care: Situating Bauman's Social Theory," *Cultural Values*, vol. 2, no. 1, 1998, pp.103-112.

34   Best, Shaun, "Zygmunt Bauman: Personal Reflections within the Mainstream of Modernity," *British Journal of Sociology*, vol. 49, issue no. 2, 1998, p.317.

35   Kaulingfreks, "Are We All Good? Zygmunt Bauman's Response to Hobbes," *The Sociological Review*, vol. 53 (1), 2005, p.40.

36   Bauman and Tester, *Conversations with Zygmunt Bauman*, p.97.

37   Jacobsen, "From Solid Modern Utopia to Liquid Modern Anti-Utopia?" p.66.

38   Bauman, *Postmodernity and its Discontents*, p.173.

39   Beilharz, *Zygmunt Bauman: Dialectic of Modernity*, p.131.

40   Berman, *All That Is Solid Melts into Air*, 1982, p.89.

41   Bauman, *Liquid Modernity* (Cambridge: Polity Press, 2000), p.3.

42   Bauman and Tester, *Conversations with Zygmunt Bauman*, p.71.

43   Bauman, *Postmodernity and its Discontents*, p.132.

44   Bauman, *Liquid Modernity*, p.2.

45   Yakimova and Bauman, "A Postmodern Grid of the Worldmap?" *Euronize*, 11 August, 2002.

46   Bauman, *Liquid Life* (Cambridge; Malden, MA: Polity, 2005), p.2.

47   Ibid., p.68.

48   Hof, *The Enlightenment*, pp.283-287.

49   Bauman, *Liquid Life*, p.44.

50   Freud, *Civilization and Its Discontents*. Strachey, James (trans.) (New York & London: Norton & Company, 1989), 2nd edn., p.26.

51   Bauman, *Intimations of Postmodernity*, p.50.

52   Bauman, *Postmodernity and its Discontents*, p.2.

53   Bauman, "Living in Utopia." LSE Public Lecture.

54   Bauman, *Freedom*, p.65.

55   Bauman, "As Seen on TV," *Ethical Perspectives*, vol. 7 (2), 2000a, pp.107-121.

56   Bauman, *Postmodernity and its Discontents*, p.40.

57   Bauman, *Liquid Life*, p.9.

58   Bauman and Vecchi, *Identity*, p.47.

59   Bauman, *Liquid Life*, p.3.

60   Giddens, *Modernity and Self-Identity*, p.8.

61   Bauman, *Liquid Life*, p.91.

62 Ibid., p.94.

63 Ibid., p.25.

64 Bauman, "Biology and the Modern Project," 1993, p.13.

65 Bauman, *Liquid Life*, pp.19-20.

66 Bauman, *Intimations of Postmodernity*, p.181.

67 Ibid., p.6.

68 Ibid., p.146.

69 Bauman, "On Postmodern Uses of Sex," *Theory, Culture & Society* (London: Sage, 1998), vol. 15 (3-4), p.21.

70 Ibid., p.24.

71 Bauman, *Postmodernity and its Discontents*, p.149.

72 Ibid., p.27.

73 Seidman, "Modernity and Ambivalence," *Contemporary Sociology*, vol. 21, no. 2, 1998, pp.284-285.

74 Freud, *Civilization and its Discontents*, p.60.

75 Bauman, *Globalization: the Human Consequences* (New York: Columbia University Press, 1998), pp.92-93.

76 Bauman, *Postmodernity and its Discontents*, p.93.

77 Ibid., p.49.

78 Ibid., pp.184-185.

79 Galecki, Lukasz interview with Bauman, "The Unwinnable War," *Eurozine*, 1 Dec. 2005.

80 Armstrong, *Islam: A Short History*, p.140.

VI

ELMESSIRI AND POSTMODERN LIQUIDITY

1 Elmessiri, *Al-ʿAlmāniyyah al-Juzʿiyyah*, vol. 1, 2002, p.282.

2 Elmessiri, *Mawsūʿat*, vol. 5.

3 Elmessiri, "Secularism, Immanence and Deconstruction," p.57.

4 Jameson, *A Singular Modernity*, p.12.

5 Elmessiri, *Al-Ḥadāthah wa mā Baʿda al-Ḥadāthah*, pp.83-86.

6 Blackshaw, *Zygmunt Bauman*, p.93.

7 Elmessiri, *Al-Lughah wa al-Majāz*, p.46.

NOTES

8   Elmessiri, "The Tools of Seduction," *Al-Ahram Weekly*, no.388, 1998.

9   Elmessiri, *Al-Ḥadāthah wa mā Baʿda al-Ḥadāthah*, p.15.

10   Israel, *Enlightenment Contested*, pp.586-588.

11   Connolly, *Political Theory and Modernity*, pp.69-88.

12   Elmessiri, *Al-ʿAlmāniyyah al-Juzʿiyyah wa al-ʿAlmāniyyah al-Shāmilah*, vol. 2, pp.286-293.

13   Ibid., p.173.

14   Elmessiri, *Dirāsāt Maʿrifiyyah*, p.284.

15   Elmessiri, "Of Darwinian Mice and Pavlovian Dogs: a Critique of Western Modernity," *Al-Ahram Weekly*, no.319, 1997.

16   Elmessiri, *Dirāsāt Maʿrifiyyah*, p.106.

17   Elmessiri, "The Imperialist Epistemological Vision," p.411.

18   Elmessiri, *Dirāsāt Maʿrifiyyah*, pp.109-111.

19   Elmessiri, *Al-ʿAlmāniyyah al-Juzʿiyyah*, vol. 2, p.228.

20   Elmessiri, "Secularism, Immanence and Deconstruction," p.53.

21   Berman, *All That Is Solid Melts into Air*, p.33.

22   Elmessiri, *Riḥlaty al-Fikriyyah*, pp.389-396.

23   Ibid., p.233.

24   Arendt, *The Human Condition*, pp.308-312.

25   Elmessiri, "Towards a More Comprehensive and Explanatory Paradigm of Secularism," p.138.

26   Esposito, "Islam and Secularism in the Twentieth-first Century," in *Islam and Secularism in the Middle East*. Azzam Tamimi & John L. Esposito (eds.) (London: Hurst & Company, 2000), pp.53-57.

27   Ezzat, Heba, "Secularism, the State and the Social Bond," in *Islam and Secularism in the Middle East*. Azzam Tamimi & John L. Esposito (eds.) (London: Hurst & Company, 2000), p.127.

28   Elmessiri, *Al-Lughah wa al-Majāz*, p.73.

29   Elmessiri, *Riḥlaty al-Fikriyyah*, p.248.

30   Elmessiri, *Al-Lughah wa al-Majāz*, p.47.

31   Ibid., p.50.

32   Ibid., pp.52-56.

33   Elmessiri, *Dirāsāt Maʿrifiyyah*, pp.256-260.

34   Elmessiri, *Al-ʿAlmāniyyah al-Juzʿiyyah*, vol. 2, pp.160-168.

35 Elmessiri, *Riḥlaty al-Fikriyyah*, p.246.

36 Elmessiri, "The Imperialist Epistemological Vision," p.413.

37 Elmessiri, *Al-ʿAlmāniyyah al-Juzʿiyyah*, vol. I, p.108.

38 Elmessiri, *Al-Lughah wa al-Majāz*, pp.74-88.

39 Elmessiri, *Riḥlaty al-Fikriyyah*, p.249.

40 Huyssen, *After the Great Divide*, pp.189-211.

41 Elmessiri, *Al-Ḥadāthah wa mā Baʿda al-Ḥadāthah*, p.13.

42 Sontag, Susan, "Against Interpretation," in *20th Century Literary Criticism: A Reader.* David Lodge, (ed.) (London and New York: Longman, 1972), p.660.

43 Silverman, *Facing Postmodernity* (London and New York: Routledge, 1999), p.23.

44 Elmessiri, *Al-Ḥadāthah wa mā Baʿda al-Ḥadāthah*, pp.140-143.

45 Elmessiri, "Understanding the Holocaust," *Al-Ahram Weekly*, no.507, 2000b.

46 Elmessiri, *Al-Ḥadāthah wa mā Baʿda al-Ḥadāthah*, p.152.

47 Silverman, *Facing Postmodernity*, p.24.

48 Elmessiri, "The Imperialist Epistemological Vision," p.415.

49 Elmessiri, *Al-Ḥadāthah wa mā Baʿda al-Ḥadāthah*, p.155.

50 Ibid., p.156.

51 Ibid., p.159.

52 Elmessiri, *Al-Ṣuhyūniyyah wa al-Ḥadārah al-Gharbiyyah al-Ḥadīthah*, p.229.

53 Elmessiri, "The Cognitive Map," *Al-Ahram Weekly*, no.878, 2008.

54 Bauman, *Europe: An Unfinished Adventure* (Cambridge: Polity, 2004), p.48.

55 Elmessiri, *Al-Ḥadāthah wa mā Baʿda al-Ḥadāthah*, p.93.

56 Elmessiri, *Mawsūʿat*, vol. I.

GLOSSARY OF TERMS

Apocalyptic Vision: An assumption that the universe runs according to a divine plan based on the struggle between good and evil; God will destroy the world, and only the believers will be saved and transferred into the perfect divine order.

Assimilation: A theory of Anglo conformity to the effect that an American is expected to embrace what is known as WASP values, that is, white, Anglo-Saxon, and Protestant characteristics. Accordingly, Catholics, Jews, and Turks were seen as inferior believers lacking the attitudes and characteristics of a truly American culture. In Europe, the failure of the dominant cultures to establish a melting pot or cultural pluralism resulted in the attempt to clean Europe from the Jews and finally exporting the Jewish question to the Middle East.

Behaviorism: An approach in psychology that aspires for scientific legitimacy by focusing on outward reactions to a stimulus rather than the content of the mind. Russian physiologist Ivan Pavlov (1849-1936) chose the dog as his experimental animal, yet his results were believed to be applicable to human beings. In the United States, John Watson (1878-1958) rejected the very concept of the mind, and dealt with imagery, thought and language in terms of behavior. Watson conducted his experiments on children and trained them to give specific responses and reactions.

Causality: A notion that presupposes a necessary link between the cause and the effect. In metaphysical and religious systems, God is sometimes seen as the only proper efficient cause or the "ultimate unmoved mover". In mechanical philosophy, there is no obsession with final causes, goals or purposes but with efficient and concrete sources of motions. Deterministic causality is based on a solid and closed network of causes and effects, seeing every sequence as a consequence. Open causality, on the other hand, sees the phenomena of human reality as neither necessarily materialistic nor necessarily bound to the closed network of clear causes and effects.

Cognitive Paradigm: A seemingly harmonious conceptual structure generated from a wide range of selected details, facts and/or events. It is a pattern or an organizing principle generated by human skill and creativity; it is not attained by learning rules or acquiring a body of knowledge. Emotions, imagination, and subjectivity – including moral attitudes, social dispositions, and political views – are also important in the construction of paradigms. Cognitive paradigms uncover the ultimate end of human existence in relation to God, Nature and Man.

Comprehensive Secularism: A worldview that does not aim merely at the separation of church and religion or the independence of science and technology from human subjectivity, but at the separation of all values not only from the state but also from public and private life, and from the world at large. It sees the centre of the universe as entirely immanent and non-transcendent i.e. self-operating, self-generating and self-explanatory. The entire world is primarily composed of one matter, one which is in a permanent and purposeless motion, remaining indifferent to human and/or divine specificities, uniqueness, and absolutes. Thus comprehensive secularism can be referred to as 'naturalist/materialist secularism' or 'nihilistic secularism.'

Determinism: A theory that assumes that events are settled in advance; they had to happen and could not have been otherwise. Thus human choices, decisions and actions are just effects. In this sense, deciding to move one's finger, to go for a walk, to buy something, to make love, to kill someone, or to get divorced is just an effect.

Embryonic/Fetal Tendency: A phrase that describes a human tendency to reject all bounds, boundaries and limits. This tendency uncovers a desire to get rid of the complexity of human existence and the burden of responsibility, specificity and consciousness. It is an attempt to escape human reality and its potentials for good and evil, success and failure, freedom and unfreedom. It is the life of an embryo, a fetus or a baby living in a vicious organic circle and monistic existence.

Empiricism: A technical and philosophical doctrine that assumes that all knowledge about nature and human behavior is based primarily on experience. Thus Empiricists tend to emphasize concrete experience rather than the real essences of things. John Locke believed that all simple ideas come from experience, and that there are no innate ideas. In short, the mind is a *tabula rasa*, i.e., a blank slate at birth, and knowledge cannot go beyond the limits of experience.

End of History: A phrase that describes an expected moment dominated by materialist monism, where all dualities vanish and only one principle governs the direction of history. Time and struggle on earth are expected to cease to exist, and man as a complex human being will vanish and become a materialist/natural object. Materialist monism dominates modern times and it reflects an obsession with a technocratic utopia, an earthly paradise and the notion of a return to Zion.

Enlightenment: A social philosophy and a historical period extending from the late seventeenth to the late eighteenth or early nineteenth century. It advocates individual and collective emancipation along with the search for laws that govern nature and society. It led, however, to exclusion, domination and the mastery of nature over man. It is highly ironic that the proponents of the Enlightenment were convinced that man is also an organic part of organic nature and thus controlled by the same materialistic laws governing physical phenomena.

Epistemology: A process of systematic understanding of a body of truths rather than the mere awareness of isolated facts or opinions. Modern epistemology is rationalist and empiricist, underlining the necessity of determining the nature and limits of human knowledge. In other words, the intellect and sense experience are the foundations of all modern human knowledge.

Eschatology: A genre of religious treatises about the last days and things: death, resurrection, the last judgment and immortality in the Beyond.

Eugenics: A twentieth century movement that aspired for the improvement of the human race by applying the scientific principles of heredity which were believed to determine physical, physiological and mental traits. This racist ideology led to the belief in the inferiority of some races and the superiority of others. It also advocated sterilization as a solution to crime, violence, prostitution, mental disease and alcoholism. The movement was not restricted to Germany, and it appeared in Britain in 1907, in the United States in 1908-1910, and later in Western Europe, Russia, Latin America, Canada, and Japan.

Euro-centricism: A tendency to interpret the histories and cultures of non-European societies from a European, progressive, perspective, constructing different cultures as inferior, barbaric, poor, backward, underdeveloped, despotic, servile, superstitious, inflexible and ultimately unchangeable. This ideology justifies colonization and imperialism in the name of civilizing non-European or non-Western societies.

Fascism: A term applied to dictatorial regimes that emerged in interwar Europe. The fascist epoch designates the triumph of Francisco Franco in the Spanish Civil War and the success of Adolf Hitler's lightening war in France, Scandinavia and Poland. Such regimes developed organic conceptions of the nation as well as cultural, biological and political racism.

Functional Groups: People recruited from within society or from outside it. They are defined in terms of their definite, limited and abstract function rather than their complex humanity. They are also referred to as intermediate groups or servant groups. Their major characteristics include isolation, powerlessness, mobility, neutrality, rationality and double standards. Modern bureaucracy has transformed modern man into a purely functional civil servant whose honour and success derive from his blind obedience to orders.

Genocide: A term coined by Raphael Lemkin to designate the Nazi policies of mass extermination, deportations and slave labor. Genocide is perceived as a designed plan aiming at the destruction of essential foundations of the life of ethnic groups or cultural identities. The term, however, is not confined to the designation of the Nazi atrocities against the Jews, and it can refer to all attempts to exterminate every member of a targeted group.

Globalization: A theory closely connected with modernization, the necessity of rapid change and the intensification of political, economic and cultural interconnectedness. This aspiration for global hegemony takes the form of privatization, liberalization of trade and capital mobility rather than imperialism and direct colonization. This hegemony is ironically accompanied with the globalization of crime, violence and poverty.

Gnosis: In the realm of religion, gnosis is seen as a spiritual pursuit that promises the liberation of individuals and humanity at large. Revealed knowledge is conceived as the only means of salvation and the return to one's divine origin. In the realm of natural philosophy and science, gnosis refers to the possibility of reaching the scientific laws of perfection, truth, beauty and goodness.

Gnosticism: A term that designates a family of trends and schools that believe in the power of revealed knowledge to fulfill salvation. Gnosticism – whether in Christianity, Hinduism, Buddhism, Hebrew Kabbalah or Islamic esoteric traditions – is based on sophisticated mythologies of fall and salvation which attempt to explain the existence of evil in the world and the ways to overcome it. The term has been applied to all modern ideologies that advocate the salvation of man in the here-now rather in the Hereafter.

Hegelianism: A term that refers to the overall influence of Hegel's philosophy on Western philosophers and sociologists, particularly its emphasis on the historical nature of reason. Rationality is tied to history, and the development of the capacities of reason is revealed in various social and historical epochs.

Holocaust: A term used in the late 1950s to displace such terms as catastrophe, disaster and even genocide. The meaning of the Holocaust, however, differs from one writer to another. Since the 1960s, the term Holocaust has become the most widely used name to refer to the genocide of six million Jews during the Nazi era, though twenty million people were killed at Hitler's behest, including Gypsies, communists, political opponents, homosexuals and the mentally retarded. Sadly, these victims of the Holocaust have been thrown into oblivion for lack of means to publicize their cause. Unlike the Jews, they did not have many professors, writers and journalists to represent their suffering and advocate their rights.

Humanism: A tendency to stress the capacities of human beings. The humanism of Greek antiquity, Islam, medieval and Renaissance Europe was driven by spiritual, moral and cultural ideals. European humanism since the eighteenth century has embraced a more materialistic position and a secular naturalism that promises human perfectibility. It places emphasis on human life and human action in the here now and underlines the role of punishment and redemption, only in the here now.

Idealism: A philosophy that gives priority to mental or spiritual ideas in the foundation of human reality, knowledge, and morality. Life is assumed to originate from a supernatural process of creation by a non-material being. Thus non-ideal entities such as material things are believed to be secondary and even illusory. Though idealists do not deny the material reality of living organisms, they see the special essence of living beings as existing only in the mind of the Creator; and therefore, never to be understood!

Immanentism: A strong belief in necessary materialization, especially that of God in man and/or nature, including the revelation of Jesus as the Son of God. Since the advent of modernity, God has incarnated in such non-personal categories as Reason, Nature, Progress, the laws of History, the invisible hand, Historical Inevitability and the nation/state.

Imperialism: Western imperialism from the seventeenth century aimed at political hegemony or territorial acquisition, seeking new resources and markets. It was accompanied with an intellectual, linguistic and cultural imperialism that constructs other cultures as exotic worlds in need of a civilizing mission.

Instrumentalization: A philosophical term that underlines instrumental knowledge which uses an object – human or non-human – to achieve certain goals. This knowledge serves the effectiveness of technique, expanding power and control but with no guarantee that the ends are good. Human beings, animals and inanimate objects can be thus instrumentalized in the service of value-free control and expansion.

Kabbalah: A Jewish mystical tradition concerned with theophilosophy, magic and ecstasy to fulfil a direct communication and union with God. Kabbalists believe in linguistic immanence, i.e., in a profound affinity between a name and the entity it designates. Thus Jerusalem is not just a conventional name for a geographical entity or an earthly city, but also the divine city.

Materialism: A family of theories that conceives of matter as the only one principle of reality. Living organisms are material beings without any unique status, and therefore, they submit to the same laws of physical systems. Mechanistic materialism treats living organisms as types of machines that conform to the laws of physics. This philosophy promotes secular politics, ethics, and reason rather than supernatural or divine intervention. With deterministic materialism, man becomes a machine devoid of free will, religion an untrue myth, and the ethics of hedonism the only proper path to happiness.

Modernism: A movement that represented a seemingly radical break with the dominant nineteenth century literary and artistic norms. It explored such negative states as violence, irrationality, aggressiveness, eroticism and nihilism. Modernism witnessed the emergence of an oppositional culture that protests against the dominance of realism, the mechanized social world and materialist philosophy.

Modernity: A condition characterized in its radical western form by a strong rejection of traditional and religious authorities, underlining instead the authority of science, the narratives of progress and the possibility of individual and collective emancipation. Modernity, however, has its inherent ironies and contradictions as shown in the history of colonialism, the injustices of the nation/state, class conflict, and the mastery of materialism over individuals.

Modernization Theory: A product of American social science that came into prominence in the 1960s. It places emphasis on industrialization, technology, social change and market-based economies. The theory has its intellectual roots in the Enlightenment narrative of progress and nineteenth century evolutionary theories of social change.

Monism: A family of doctrines that advocate only one principle of reality. Religious monism shows in atheism and pantheism, both of which deny the existence of a transcendent deity. Cosmic and materialist monism assumes that God, Man and

Nature are one organic whole. The laws of nature govern human reality, whereas human and divine ends are excluded since the natural world is the only foundation of ethical and epistemological systems. Ethics are thus attributed to purely materialist considerations, be they political, social or economic.

Nature/Matter: In materialist philosophy, nature is a non-teleological system, i.e., it is a closed, self-sufficient, aimless and purposeless system. Nature is prior to man, thus reducing him to its laws, determinism and flux.

Objectivity: Knowledge based on facts, aspiration for truth without the intrusion of opinions, viewpoints, perspectives, beliefs or value-judgments. It is often argued, however, that there are no simple objective facts of reality, since it is shaped by socio-economic, political and/or scientific interest. This view mitigates the diametrical opposition of objectivity and subjectivity.

Organicism: A doctrine which upholds the view that a living creature is an integrated whole or an organic unity in which the whole is prior to the parts. The concept refers to the unity of Being in metaphysics; the beautiful totality or inner form of a work of art in aesthetics; and the unity and purity of a human community in political and social thought. The latter gave rise to modern racist and nationalistic ideologies, culminating in Nazism and Zionism.

Pantheism: Whether materialist or spiritual, this philosophy assumes that the centre of the universe is within the world, i.e. immanent or non-transcendent. Spiritual pantheism posits a deity that is immanent to the world and on which the world completely depends. God becomes immanent in his creatures and dissolves into them; only His name remains, though He is in fact nothing but nature/matter. Hegel's Absolute Spirit (Geist) or the Spirit of History seems to be spiritual and idealistic whereas in fact it is materialist. In explicitly materialist pantheism, spiritual and idealist language is entirely abandoned, designating the only foundation of reality as the laws of nature, scientific laws, physical laws and/or laws of motion.

Partial Secularism: A worldview that advocates the necessity of separating religion from the world of politics and perhaps economy, yet it does not necessarily deny the existence of moral and human and perhaps religious totalities or the existence of metaphysics. It is the solid phase of western modernity which secularized Christian and non-Christian values and metaphysical notions of the Hereafter, Resurrection and the Day of Judgment. God was replaced with different secular absolutes, including Reason, Progress, the nation/state, society and the proletariat.

Positivism: A family of theories that sees empirical science as the only foundation of objective and reliable knowledge about nature and society. Emphasis is placed on the value-free methods of the natural sciences, which are believed applicable to the humanities.

Postmodernism: An umbrella term that covers intellectual and aesthetic currents in art and literature since the 1960s. Among the characteristics of postmodern art and literature are the tendencies towards fragmentation, discontinuity, the erosion of the boundaries between high and low art, and the celebration of small narratives rather than grand narratives, particularly the histories of women, children, the working classes and minorities.

Postmodernity: A culture that emerged since the late 1960s to go beyond the con-tradictions of western modernity and to act as a better platform for democracy and justice for previously oppressed or marginalized groups. Global capitalism, however, has determined the experience of postmodernity, its dynamics and consequences, leading to new contradictions and injustices.

Rationalism: A belief in the capacity of pure intellect alone as the foundation of knowledge of truths about the universe and the nature of reality. This belief encour-aged the advocates of the Enlightenment to trust in human abilities without reliance on divine illumination.

Rationalization: A major concept in Max Weber's perception of modernization. Within monotheism, the prophet becomes the man of rational spirit that stands for the final victory of the process of monotheistic rationalization over magical elements. In modern times, such traditional value-oriented rationalization is marginalized in favour of a value-free rationalization which always takes place within the laws of nature/matter. This process transforms society into mathematical equations to be solved in a factory environment that renders society as efficient as a machine, thus enhancing effectiveness, yet threatening individual freedom and leading society to the iron cage of materialism in both capitalist and socialist systems alike.

Transcendence: Latin *Transcendentia*, German *Transcendenz*, a deep-rooted word in philosophy, coined during the Middle Ages. Yet the experience of transcendence was very crucial to human consciousness before the birth of philosophy itself. Theologi-cally, divine transcendence refers to the idea that God is absolutely outside of and beyond the material world. Transcendence can simply mean going beyond the limits of the mind, rationality and sense perception for the sake of a superior spirituality by means of insight, imagination, intuition and the perception of another universe. This understanding includes the transcendence of nature/matter, the unity of good, truth, beauty, and the delight in art.

Zion: A place name used as a synonym for Jerusalem and/or a specific mountain near Jerusalem, i.e. Mount Zion. This term provides a wonderful example of linguistic immanence as it refers now to the World to come, the age to come or heaven on earth, all of which are eschatological phrases reflecting the dissatisfaction with the current world and the aspiration for a better world or paradise in the future. Thus the term can designate the aspirations of modern ideologies and their aspirations for the end of struggle on earth and the establishment of a utopia and an earthly paradise.

Zionism: A nationalistic movement that emerged in the nineteenth century and defined itself in definite secular terms rather than religious language of reviving Jewish tradition and bringing about the age of the messiah. A national Jewish home was seen as the best solution to the problem of persecution and the failure of Jewish assimilation in Europe. The Jewish question has been transferred to the Middle East; the Balfour Declaration of 1917 affirmed British colonial support to Zionists and their desire to establish a Jewish homeland in Palestine, though the Jews constituted only 12% of the population in 1920.

BIBLIOGRAPHY

Abbinnett, R., "Postmodernity and the Ethics of Care," *Cultural Values*, vol. 2, no.1, 1998.

_____, *Culture and Identity: Critical Theories* (London: Sage Publications, 2003).

Achcar, G., *The Arabs and the Holocaust*. G.M. Goshgarian (trans.) (London: Saqi, 2011).

Ali, H., "Correspondence with Zygmunt Bauman," & "Conversation with Abdel-wahab Elmessiri," in *The Cognitive Mapping of Modernity and Postmodernity*. PhD dissertation (Cairo University, 2008).

Anderson, P., *The Origins of Postmodernity* (Verso: London, 1998).

Arendt, H., *The Human Condition* (Chicago: The University of Chicago Press, 1958).

_____, "Philosophy and Politics," *Social Research*, vol. 57, no.1, 1990.

Armstrong, K., *Islam: A Short History* (London: Phoenix Press, 2001).

Badawi, A., *Mawsūʿat al-Falsafah* [Encyclopedia of Philosophy] (Beirut: al-Muʿassasah al-ʿArabiyyah li al-Dirāsāt wa al-Nashr, 1984).

Bauman, J., "Demons of Other Peoples' Fear: The Plight of the Gypsies," *Thesis Eleven*, vol. 54, no.1, 1998.

Bauman, Z., *Culture as Praxis* (London: Routledge and Kegan Paul Ltd, 1973).

_____, *Socialism: The Active Utopia* (New York: Holmes & Meier, 1976).

_____, *Towards a Critical Sociology* (London; Boston: Routledge, 1976).

_____, *Hermeneutics and Social Sciences* (New York: Columbia University Press, 1978).

_____, *Legislators and Interpreters* (Cambridge, UK: Polity Press, 1987).

_____, *Freedom* (Minneapolis: University of Minnesota Press, 1988).

_____, "Sociology after the Holocaust," *British Journal of Sociology*, vol. 39, no.4, 1988.

_____, *Modernity and the Holocaust* (Cambridge: Polity Press, 1989).

_____, *Modernity and Ambivalence* (Ithaca, N.Y.: Cornell University Press, 1991).

_____, *Intimations of Postmodernity* (London; New York: Routledge, 1992).

_____, "Biology and the Modern Project," *Diskussionspapier* 2-92 (Humburger Institut für Sozialforschung, 1993).

_____, *Postmodern Ethics* (Oxford, UK; Cambridge, Mass.: Blackwell, 1993).

_____, *Life in Fragments: Essays in Postmodern Morality* (Oxford and Cambridge: Blackwell, 1995).

____, "Assimilation into Exile: The Jew as a Polish Writer," *Poetics Today*, 1996, vol. 17, no.4.

____, *Postmodernity and its Discontents* (New York: New York University Press, 1997).

____, *Globalization: The Human Consequences* (New York: Columbia University Press, 1998).

____, "On Postmodern Uses of Sex," *Theory, Culture & Society* (London: Sage, 1998), vol. 15 (3-4).

____, "As seen on TV," *Ethical Perspectives*, 7 (2), 2000.

____, *Liquid Modernity* (Cambridge: Polity Press, 2000).

____, "Critical Theory," in *The Bauman Reader*. Peter Beilharz (ed.) (Oxford: Blackwell, 2001).

____, & Keith Tester, *Conversations with Zygmunt Bauman* (Cambridge: Polity, 2001).

____, "The Fate of Humanity in a Post-Trinitarian World," *Journal of Human Rights*, 2002, vol.1 (3).

____, & Vecchi, *Identity: Conversations with Benedetto Vecchi* (Cambridge: Polity Press, 2004).

____, "Liquid Modernity." Lecture on ANSE-Conference, 2004.

____, *Europe: An Unfinished Adventure* (Cambridge: Polity, 2004).

____, "Living in Utopia," LSE Public Lecture, 27 October, 2005.

____, *Liquid Life* (Cambridge; Malden, MA: Polity, 2005).

Beck, L., (trans. & ed.), *Kant Selections* (New York: Macmillan, 1998).

Beilharz, P,. *Zygmunt Bauman: Dialectic of Modernity* (London: Sage Publications, 2000).

Berman, M., *All That is Solid Melts into Air: The Experience of Modernity* (New York: Penguin, 1982).

Bernstein, R., *Beyond Objectivism and Relativism* (Philadelphia: University of Pennsylvania Press, 1983).

____, *The New Constellation* (Polity Press: Cambridge, 1991).

Bertens, H., *The Idea of the Postmodern: A History* (London and New York: Routledge, 1995).

Best, S., "Zygmunt Bauman," *British Journal of Sociology*, vol. 49, no.2, 1998.

Blackshaw, T., *Zygmunt Bauman* (London/New York: Routledge, 2005).

Buchanan, I., *Fredric Jameson: Live Theory* (New York: Continuum, 2006).

Bunting, M., "Passion and Pessimism," *Guardian* (London, 5 April, 2003).

Clarke, S., "On Strangers," *Journal of the Human Rights*, vol. 1 (3), 2002.

Connolly, W., *Political Theory and Modernity* (Ithca and London: Cornell University Press, 1993).

✳ Davutoğlu, A., *Alternative Paradigms* (Lanham: University Press America, 1994).

Turkish society

____, "Philosophical and Institutional Dimensions of Secularization," in *Islam, Secularism and the Middle East*. Azzam Tamimi & John L. Esposito (eds.) (London: Hurst & Company, 2000).

Delanty, G., *Modernity and Postmodernity* (London: Sage Publications, 2000).

Dobbelaere, K., *Secularization: An Analysis at Three Levels* (Brussels: Peter Lang, 2002).

Dupré, L., *Passage to Modernity* (New Haven and London: Yale University Press, 1993).

____, *The Enlightenment and the Intellectual Foundations of Modern Culture* (London: Yale University Press, 2004).

Edwards, P., (ed.), *The Encyclopedia of Philosophy*. 8 vols (New York: Macmillan, 1967).

Elmessiri, A., *The Land of Promise* (New Brunswick, N. J: North American, 1977).

____, "The Imperialist Epistemological Vision," *The American Journal of Islamic Social Sciences* (Washington, DC and Kuala Lumpur, Malaysia, 1994), vol. 11., no.3.

____, "Towards a More Comprehensive and Explanatory Paradigm of Secularism," *Encounters: Journal of Inter-cultural Perspectives*, 1996, vol. 2, no.2.

____, "Of Darwinian Mice and Pavlovian Dogs: A Critique of Western Modernity," *Al-Ahram Weekly*, no.319, 1997.

____, "Features of the New Islamic Discourse," Azzam Tamimi (trans.), a paper delivered at the conference on "The West and Islam: Clashpoints and Dialogues," held in Cairo on 15-23 February 1997, organized by 21st Century Trust.

____, "The Tools of Seduction," *Al-Ahram Weekly*, no.388, 1998.

____, "Secularism, Immanence and Deconstruction," in *Islam and Secularism in the Middle East*. John L. Esposito and Azzam Tamimi (eds.) (London: Hurst & Co, 2000a).

____, "Understanding the Holocaust," *Al-Ahram Weekly*, no.507, 2000b.

____, *Al-Ṣuhyūniyyah wa al-Nāziyyah wa Nihāyat al-Tārīkh* [Zionism, Nazism and the End of History], 3rd edn (Cairo: Dār al-Shurūq, 2001).

____, *Mawsūʿat al-Yahūd wa al-Yahūdiyyah wa al-Ṣuhyūniyyah* [Encyclopedia of the Jews, Judaism and Zionism] (Cairo: CD. Bayt al-ʿArab li al-Tawthīq al-ʿAṣrī wa al-Naẓm, 2001).

____, *Al-ʿĀlam min Manẓūr Gharbī* [The World from a Western Perspective] (Cairo: Dār al-Hilāl, 2001)

____, *Al-Lughah wa al-Majāz* [Language and Metaphor: between Monotheism and Pantheism] (Cairo: Dār al-Shurūq, 2002).

____, *Al-ʿAlmāniyyah al-Juzʾiyyah wa al-ʿAlmāniyyah al-Shāmilah* [Partial Secularism and Comprehensive Secularism]. Two vols (Cairo: Dār al-Shurūq, 2002).

_____, *Difāᶜ ᶜan al-Insān: Dirāsāt Naẓariyyah wa Taṭbīqiyyah fī al-Namādhij al-Murakkabah* [Defense of Man: Theoretical and Applied Studies in Complex Paradigms] (Cairo: Dār al-Shurūq, 2003).

_____, *Al-Ḥadāthah wa mā Baᶜda al-Ḥadāthah* [Modernity and Postmodernity] (Damascus: Dār al-Fikr, 2003).

_____, *Al-Ṣuhyūniyyah wa al-Ḥadārah al-Gharbiyyah al-Ḥadīthah* [Zionism and Modern Western Civilization] (Cairo: Dār Al-Hilāl, 2003).

_____, *Riḥlaty al-Fikriyyah* [My Intellectual Journey – The Seeds, The Roots, and The Harvest] (Cairo: Dār al-Shurūq, 2005).

_____, *Dirāsāt Maᶜrifiyyah* [Epistemological Studies in Western Modernity] (Cairo: Dār al-Shurūq International, 2006).

_____, *Epistemological Bias in the Physical and Social Sciences* (London – Washington: The International Institute of Islamic Thought (IIIT), 2006).

_____, "The Cognitive Map," *Al-Ahram Weekly*, no.878, 2008.

Esposito, J., "Islam and Secularism in the Twentieth-first Century," in *Islam and Secularism in the Middle East.* John L. Esposito and Azzam Tamimi (eds.) (London: Hurst & Company, 2000).

Ezzat, H., "Secularism, the State and the Social Bond: The Withering Away of the Family," in *Islam and Secularism in the Middle East.* John L. Esposito and Azzam Tamimi (eds.) (London: Hurst & Company, 2000).

Freud, S., *Civilization and its Discontents*, James Strachey (trans.), 2nd edn. (New York & London: Norton & Company, 1989).

Galecki, L. interview with Zygmunt Bauman, "The Unwinnable War," *Eurozine*, 1 Dec., 2005. http://www.eurozine.com/articles/2006-12-13-bauman-en.html.

Gellner, E., *Nations and Nationalism* (Ithaca, New York: Cornell University Press, 1983).

Giddens, A., *The Consequences of Modernity* (Cambridge UK: Polity Press, 1990).

_____, *Modernity and Self-Identity* (Stanford: Stanford University Press, 1991).

Golledge, R., *Wayfinding Behavior: Cognitive Mapping and Other Spatial Processes* (Baltimore: Johns Hopkins University Press, 1999).

Harding, L., "Ruthlessly Exposed," *Guardian*, 8 April, 2005.

Harrington, A., "Metaphoric Connections: Holistic Science in the Shadow of the Third Reich," *Social Research*, vol. 62, no.2, 1995.

Harvey, D., *The Condition of Postmodernity* (Cambridge MA and Oxford UK: Blackwell, 1990).

Hodgson, M., *Rethinking World History*. Edmund Burke (ed.) (Cambridge: Cambridge University Press, 1993).

Hof, I., *The Enlightenment*. William E. Yuill (trans.) (Oxford UK and Cambridge USA: Blackwell, 1994).

Hofstadter, R., *Social Darwinism in American Thought* (Boston: Beacon Press, 1955).

Honderich, T., *The Oxford Companion to Philosophy* (Oxford: Oxford University Press, 2005).

Huyssen, A., *After the Great Divide* (Bloomington & Indianapolis: Indiana University Press, 1986).

Izetbegovic, A., *Islam Between East and West*. 3rd edn. (Indiana: The American Trust Publications, 1999).

Jacobsen, M., "From Solid Modern Utopia to Liquid Modern Anti-Utopia?" *Utopian Studies*, 2004, vol. 15, no.1.

_____, & Sophia Marshman, "Metaphorically Speaking: Metaphors as a Methodological and Moral Signifier of the Sociology of Zygmunt Bauman," *Polish Sociological Review*, 2006, 3 (155).

Jameson, F., *Postmodernism, or, the Cultural Logic of Late Capitalism* (London: Verso, 1991).

_____, *A Singular Modernity: Essay on the Ontology of the Present* (London: Verso, 2002).

Joas, H., "Bauman in Germany: Modern Violence and the Problems of German Self-Understanding," *Theory, Culture & Society* (Sage, London, Thousand Oaks & New Delhi), 1998, vol. 15 (1).

Israel, J., *Enlightenment Contested* (Oxford and New York: Oxford University Press, 2006).

Kant, I., "What is Enlightenment?" in *Kant Selections*. Lewis Beck (trans. & ed.) (New York: Macmillan, 1988).

Kaulingfreks, R., "Are we all good?" *The Sociological Review*, 2005, vol. 53 (1).

Kearney, R., *Modern Movements in European Philosophy* (Manchester: Manchester University Press, 1986).

Kilminster, R. & Ian Varcoe, "Addendum: Culture and Power in the Writings of Zygmunt Bauman," in *Culture, Modernity and Revolution: Essays in Honour of Zygmunt Bauman* (London: Routledge, 1996).

Kinloch, G., *Sociological Theory: its Development and Major Paradigms* (New York: McGraw-Hill, 1977).

Kuhn, T., *The Structure of Scientific Revolutions* (Chicago, IL: University of Chicago Press, 1962).

Kurt H. Wolff., (trans. & ed.), *The Sociology of Georg Simmel* (New York: Free Press, 1950).

Lakoff, G. & Mark Johnson, *Metaphors We Live By* (Chicago: The University of Chicago Press, 1979).

Lévinas, E., *Alterity and Transcendence*. Michael B. Smith (trans.) (New York: Columbia University Press, 1999).

Lukács, G., "The Ideology of Modernism," in *20th Century Literary Criticism: A Reader*. David Lodge (ed.) (London and New York: Longman, 1972).

BIBLIOGRAPHY

Maasen, S. & Peter Weingart, *Metaphors and the Dynamics of Knowledge* (London: Routledge, 2000).

McGowan, J., *Postmodernism and its Critics* (Ithaca and London: Cornell University Press, 1991).

Murdoch, I., *Metaphysics as a Guide to Morals* (London: Vintage, 2003).

Nietzsche, F., *The Birth of Tragedy and the Genealogy of Morals*. Francis Golffing (trans.,) (New York: Doubleday & Company, INC, 1956).

Pawling, C., "The American Lukas? Fredric Jameson and Dialectical Thought," in *Fredric Jameson: A Critical Reader*. Douglas Kellner and Sean Homer (eds.) (New York: Palgrave Macmillan, 2004).

Ricoeur, P., "Science and Ideology," in *Hermeneutics and the Human Sciences*. John B. Thompson, (ed. and trans.) (Cambridge: Cambridge University Press, 1981).

_____, "Metaphor and the Main Problem of Hermeneutics," in *A Ricoeur Reader: Reflection and Imagination*. Mario Valdes (ed.) (Toronto: University of Toronto Press, 1991).

_____, "The Function of Fiction in Shaping Reality," in *A Ricoeur Reader: Reflection and Imagination*. Mario Valdes (ed.) (Toronto: University of Toronto Press, 1991).

_____, "Word, Polysemy, Metaphor" in *A Ricoeur Reader: Reflection and Imagination*. Mario Valdes (ed.) (Toronto: University of Toronto Press, 1991).

Roberts, A., *Fredric Jameson* (New York: Routledge, 2000).

Rosen, S., "Theory and Interpretation," in *Hermeneutics as Politics* (Oxford: Oxford University Press, 1987).

Sandoz, E., "Introduction," in *Science, Politics and Gnosticism* (Washington, DC: Regnery Publishing, 1997).

Seidman, S., "Modernity and Ambivalence," *Contemporary Sociology*, vol. 21, no.2, 1992.

Shapira, Avner, "Life in a Liquid World," *Haaretz Daily Newspaper*. 16 November, 2007.

Siedel, G., *Knowledge as a Sexual Metaphor* (Selinsgrove, PA: Susquehanna University Press, 2000).

Silverman, M., *Facing Postmodernity* (London and New York: Routledge, 1999).

Simmel, G., "The Stranger" in *The Sociology of Georg Simmel*. Kurt H. Wolff, (trans. & ed.) (New York: Free Press, 1950).

Sontag, S., "Against Interpretation" in *20th Century Literary Criticism: A Reader*. David Lodge (ed.) (London and New York: Longman, 1972).

Stone, D., *Theoretical Interpretations of the Holocaust* (Amsterdam – Atlanta: Rodopi, 2001).

Tester, K., *The Two Sovereign: the Social Contradictions of European Modernity* (London: Routledge, 1992).

_____, "Paths in the Social Thought of Zygmunt Bauman," *Thesis Eleven*, vol. 70, no.1, 2002.

Tipps, D., "Modernization Theory and Comparative Study of Societies: a Critical Perspective," *Comparative Studies in Society and History*, vol. 15, no.2, 1973.

Torevell, D., "The Terrorism of Reason in the Thought of Zygmunt Bauman," *New Blackfriars* (The Dominican Council/Blackwell Publishing Ltd, 1995), vol. 76, no.891.

Vanicek, V., "Zygmunt Bauman: Thoughts on the Age of Postmodernity," *Perspectives: Central European Review of International Affairs* (Prague Institute of International Relations, 2005), vol. 23.

Varcoe, I., "Identity and the Limits of Comparison: Bauman's Reception in Germany," *Theory, Culture and Society* (Sage, London, Thousand Oaks and New Delhi, 1998), vol. 15 (1).

Voegelin, E., *The New Science of Politics: An Introduction* (Chicago: University of Chicago Press, 1952).

_____, *From Enlightenment to Revolution*. John H. Hallowell (ed.) (Durham, North Carolina: Duke University Press, 1975).

_____, *Science, Politics and Gnosticism*. Ellis Sandoz (ed.) (Washington, DC: Regnery Publishing, 1997).

_____, "Race and State," in *The Collected Works of Eric Voegelin*. K. Vondung (ed.) (Baton Rouge: University of Missouri Press, 1997), vol. 2.

_____, "Renaissance and Reformation," in *The Collected Works of Eric Voegelin*. D. Morse & W.M. Thompson (eds.) (Columbia & London: University of Missouri Press, 1998), vol. 22.

_____, "Religion and the Rise of Modernity," in *The Collected Works of Eric Voegelin*. J. Wiser (ed.) (Columbia & London: University of Missouri Press, 1998), vol. 23.

Wellman, K., *La Mettrie: Medicine, Philosophy, and Enlightenment* (Durham, NC.: Duke University Press, 1992).

Yakimova, M. and Zygmunt Bauman, "A Postmodern Grid of the Worldmap?" *Euronize*, 11 August, 2002.

Zubaida, S., "Trajectories of Political Islam: Egypt, Iran and Turkey," *Political Quarterly*, Supplement 1, vol. 71, 2000.